Alfred Schmidt

The Concept of Nature in Marx

First published as
Der Begriff der Natur in der Lehre von Marx
by Europäische Verlagsanstalt, 1962
© Europäische Verlagsanstalt, 1962
Appendix first published in
Existentialismus und Marxismus, 1965
© Suhrkamp Verlag, 1965

This edition first published 1971
Translated from the German by Ben Fowkes
© NLB, 1971

Reprinted 1973

NLB, 7 Carlisle Street, London W1

Designed by Gerald Cinamon
Typeset in Monotype Ehrhardt
and printed by
Western Printing Services Ltd, Bristol

SBN 902308 41 6

At the same pace that mankind masters nature, man seems to become enslaved to other men or to his own infamy. Even the pure light of science seems unable to shine but on a dark background of ignorance. All our invention and progress seem to result in endowing material forces with intellectual life, and in stultifying human life into a material force.*

* Karl Marx, 'Speech at the Anniversary of the *People's Paper*', April 1856. Quoted in D. Ryazanov (ed.), *Karl Marx. Man, Thinker, and Revolutionist* (London, 1927), p. 74.

Preface to the English Edition

This book was written between 1957 and 1960 under Horkheimer and Adorno as a doctoral dissertation in philosophy and was published for the first time in 1962. Every page is impregnated with the influence of 'critical theory' as developed by the Frankfurt School since the early 1930s. 'Critical theory' was of course a specific interpretation of Marx, formulated under unique conditions, and was eventually itself bound to become the object of critical and many-sided debates. In the course of these debates I too found it necessary to clarify my position on a number of issues, and there is no doubt that today I should adopt a somewhat different approach to my subject. However, other urgent commitments make it impossible at present to revise or extend the book as much as I would like to, and I shall therefore simply indicate, however briefly, a few points to which only a future revised edition and further study can do proper justice.

It will help the English reader to understand this book if from the outset he bears in mind its polemical aspect. It was one of the first attempts to draw on the politico-economic writings of middle-period and mature Marx, in particular *Capital* and the so-called 'Rohentwurf' of the years 1857–59 (later published as *Grundrisse der Kritik der politischen Ökonomie*), for a 'philosophical' interpretation of Marx's life-work. In doing this, the book opposed the widespread Western European, often neo-Existentialist, tendency of the 1950s to reduce Marx's thought to an unhistorical 'anthropology' centred on the alienation problematic of the early writings (in particular the Paris Manuscripts of 1844) and sought to point out the philosophical content (or at least the philosophically relevant content) of Marx's post-1850 work. The intention was to introduce into the discussion a number of texts which had so far been insufficiently considered, or even entirely disregarded. Hence, the philological nature of my approach.

Today I should take in many respects a different view of the relation between Marxism and philosophy, discussed so often since the days of Lukács and Korsch, Merleau-Ponty and Sartre. In Chapter One my aim was to make a detailed analysis of the real connection between Marxist materialism and philosophical materialism in general. Now however I have definitely adopted the opinion (only implicit in the book) that Marxist materialism emerged only in a secondary sense from the 'inner-philosophical' opposition to idealism; that it represents, first and foremost, the negation of all philosophy, although this negation is itself burdened with philosophy, i.e. 'determined' by it. Accordingly, the characterization given in Chapter One of Feuerbach's role in Marx's development would now be more positive. In a study of Feuerbach,* I have endeavoured to show that the very concept of 'mediating practice' which Marx and Engels polemically turned against Feuerbach owes in fact a great deal to him. Feuerbach's anthropocentro-genetic method, his sensualism and his realism, oriented as they are towards the epistemological problematic of the everyday world, not only anticipate dialectical materialism's doctrine of historical practice as the general horizon of all human and extra-human reality, but are capable of enriching dialectical materialism in important respects, a fact which Marx and Engels overlooked, but which Plekhanov and Lenin showed some sign of grasping.

When understood critically, Marxist materialism does not attempt to assert anything of the material world in abstraction from the practico-intellectual forms of its 'appropriation' by a given society, without however disputing the objectivity of our knowledge in the spirit of historicism, scepticism, or agnosticism. Objections from the

* 'Für eine neue Lektüre Feuerbachs', in *Anthropologischer Materialismus* Vol. I (Frankfurt and Vienna, 1967).

orthodox camp* have not succeeded in convincing me that my criticism of Engels's fragmentary outlines for a 'dialectic of nature', in section B of Chapter One, is wrong. It appears to be impossible to derive the idea of a revolutionary humanism from the self-movement of 'matter' conceived through the eyes of particular natural sciences. The critical epistemological objections to this view have, it is hoped, been unfolded more concretely still in the essay entitled 'On the Relation between History and Nature in Dialectical Materialism', printed as an appendix to this edition.

I have included this essay also because it was an attempt to define the Marxist concept of the 'metabolism of man and nature' more closely than in the corresponding section of the book (Chapter Two, section B). In the essay, my intention was to show the 'natural' limits of all historical dialectics: the fact that it is the 'concrete', not the 'abstract' form of human work which cannot be superseded. Here, I would like historically to delimit the 'elemental', peculiarly unhistorical dialectic of the process of metabolism, namely to confine it to pre-bourgeois social formations. This is in full awareness of the contradiction between emphasizing the 'non-ontological' character of Marxist materialism and then introducing the term 'negative ontology': this is a contradiction within the facts, not an error to be eliminated by changing a word, or the result of a logical inconsistency.

As far as Chapter Three is concerned, it is particularly unfortunate that it cannot at present be brought up to date, since its specific epistemological considerations were what primarily interested me. It is only possible here to refer to a number of the more substantial essays I have published since 1962 on the theory of history as a theory of knowledge.†

* cf. the 'Marxist–Leninist' collection of essays entitled *Die 'Frankfurter Schule' im Lichte des Marxismus* (Frankfurt, 1970), on pp. 134–40 of which I have sketched the outlines of a critique of my critics.

† These include: (1) 'Henri Lefèbvre und die gegenwärtige Marx-Interpretation' (appendix to a translation of Henri Lefèbvre's *Le Materialisme dialectique: Der dialektische Materialismus*, Frankfurt, 1966); (2) 'Über Geschichte und Geschichtsschreibung in der materialistischen Dialektik', in *Folgen einer Theorie. Essays über 'Das Kapital' von Karl Marx*, Frankfurt, 1967; (3) 'Zum Erkenntnisbegriff der Kritik der politischen Ökonomie', in *Kritik der politischen Ökonomie heute. 100 Jahre 'Kapital'*, ed. by Walter

For the rest, I can only say that I am at present in the process of extending section C of Chapter Three into a systematic reconstruction of Marx's epistemology. My aim is to determine more exactly the position of Marx between Kant and Hegel, only crudely sketched in the book. Marx's intermediate position was a consequence of the fact that, like Hegel, he refused to make epistemological reflections *before* the investigation of the concrete content of knowledge, but that at the same time, as a materialist, he could not accept the conclusion Hegel drew from his rejection of epistemology, namely the speculative identity of Subject and Object. Kant's problem of the 'constituents' of the objects of knowledge was thus (objectively) restored for Marx, not in the sense of a simple return to transcendental philosophy, but on the basis definitively attained by Hegel in his critique of Kant.

In Marx, what 'constitutes' the 'normal' world of everyday experience, and what establishes intersubjectivity, is not an aggregate of purely intellectual ordering functions possessed by a supra-individual 'consciousness in general', but collective, 'objective activity', i.e. practice. This forms in each case an historical totality of relations of production, to be distinguished both from individual technological, natural-scientific, and political practices within an already constituted world, and from the 'transforming practice' of the *Theses on Feuerbach*, which is directed towards the establishment of a qualitatively new world.

These distinctions are not always made sharply enough in the existing version of the book. In relation to the conception of utopia exposed in Chapter Four, this has led to the technocratic and scientistic misinterpretation that Marx was solely concerned to secure a quantitative increase in the existing forms of mastery over nature. On the contrary, Marx wanted to achieve something qualitatively new:

Euchner and Alfred Schmidt, Frankfurt and Vienna, 1968; (4) 'Der strukturalistische Angriff auf der Geschichte', in *Beiträge zur marxistischen Erkenntnistheorie*, edited and with an introduction by Alfred Schmidt, Frankfurt, 1969; (5) *Die 'Zeitschrift für Sozialforschung'. Geschichte und gegenwärtige Bedeutung*, Munich, 1970; (6) 'Geschichte und Soziologie im Denken des jungen Lenin' (introductory essay to the volume edited by Alfred Schmidt: Lenin, *Über historischen Materialismus*, Munich, 1970).

mastery by the whole of society of society's mastery over nature. This mastery would certainly still depend on the functions of instrumental reason. But since it would 'finalize' these functions, and subject them to truly human aims, the mastery of society would undertake its own self-correction; society's mastery over nature would thereby be freed from the curse of being simultaneously a mastery over men, and of thus perpetuating the reign of blind natural history.

The book has been revised stylistically and, as far as possible, in its content. I submit it to the critical examination of the English reader in the hope that it will prove of some value in its present form.

ALFRED SCHMIDT
Frankfurt, November 1970

Introduction

This book is a contribution to the philosophical interpretation of Marx. It concerns the concept of nature, which appears at first sight to have a purely peripheral significance in Marx's theory. The fact that Marx rarely referred in his writings to nature 'in itself' does not mean that nature has little importance for his theory of society but is the result of his particular approach.

The theory of society, as a critique of political economy, presents the process of the production of material goods as a 'labour-process and, at the same time, a process of creating value'.[1] In this theory, attention is mainly focused on the exchange-value of the commodity. The commodity as the embodiment of abstract human labour, expressed in units of socially necessary labour-time, is independent of any determination by nature.

The natural form of the commodity, called by Marx its use-value, only appears in the analysis of the process of creating value in so far as it is 'the material substratum, the depositary of exchange-value'.[2] Here, on the contrary, we are concerned primarily with the philosophical elements of Marxist theory, and the process of production will be considered above all in its historical movement, as a labour-process bringing forth use-values.

It is the socio-historical character of Marx's concept of nature which distinguishes it from the outset. Marx considered nature to be 'the primary source of all instruments and objects of labour',[3] i.e. he saw nature from the beginning in relation to human activity. All other statements about nature, whether of a speculative, epistemological, or scientific kind, already presuppose social practice, the ensemble of man's technologico-economic modes of appropriation.

Natural phenomena and all consciousness of nature have been reduced in the course of history more and more to functions of objective social processes. Marx showed, however, that society itself was a natural environment. This was meant not only in the immediately critical sense that men are still not in control of their own productive forces *vis-à-vis* nature, that these forces confront them as the organized, rigid form of an opaque society, as a 'second nature' which sets its own essence against its creators, but also in the 'metaphysical' sense that Marx's theory is a theory of the world as a whole.

The human life-process, even when understood and controlled, remains in a natural environment. Under all forms of production, human labour-power is 'only the manifestation of a force of nature'.[4] In his work, man 'opposes himself to nature as one of her own forces'.[5] 'By acting on the external world and changing it, he at the same time changes his own nature.'[6] The dialectic of Subject and Object is for Marx a dialectic of the constituent elements of nature.

The work here presented to the reader can be described as an attempt to present in its main aspects the mutual interpenetration of nature and society as it takes place within nature, conceived in its widest sense as the total reality comprising both moments. Its basic sources are the whole of Marx's available works. The writings of Engels have been drawn on for the elucidation of Marx's position, except where they are open to criticisms arising out of that position, as is the case in particular with Engels's conception of the dialectics of nature.

Where the early writings of Marx have been used, the author's intention has been more to present their genetic connection with specific themes in middle-period and mature Marx than, fashionably and mistakenly, to reduce the strictly *philosophical* thought of Marx to what is written in those texts, namely to the anthropology of the Paris Manuscripts of 1844.

In the conviction that Marx was by no means at his most philosophical when he made use of the traditional, scholastic language of the philosophers, his middle and later, politico-economic writings will be consulted much more than is customary in interpretations of Marxist philosophy. Particular attention has been paid to the *Grundrisse der Kritik der politischen Ökonomie* (*Rohentwurf*), the preliminary draft of *Capital*, which is of the utmost importance for understanding the relation between Hegel and Marx, and which has so far hardly been used.

Apart from the sheer extent of the literature to be taken into account, considerable difficulties are involved in the attempt to delineate the concept of nature in dialectical materialism. There is no systematic Marxist theory of nature of such a kind as to be conscious of its own speculative implications. It was therefore necessary to develop our theme by bringing together often widely disparate motifs from the main phases of development of Marxist thought. In view of the extraordinary entanglement of these motifs, it was not possible wholly to avoid occasional repetitions, overlaps, and cross-references, so that the subjects dealt with in the individual chapters or sections do not always coincide precisely with what is announced in the headings.

Chapter One

Karl Marx
and Philosophical Materialism

A. THE NON-ONTOLOGICAL CHARACTER
OF MARXIST MATERIALISM

The question of Marx's concept of nature necesssarily extends outwards to the question of the relationship between the materialist conception of history and philosophical materialism in general. This has been dealt with by past interpreters of Marx only occasionally and then hardly in a satisfactory manner.[1] There can be no disputing the fact that Engels was a materialist in the general philosophical sense. *Ludwig Feuerbach and the End of Classical German Philosophy*, *Anti-Dühring*, and the *Dialectics of Nature* all point clearly in this direction. With Marx the situation is somewhat different. The kernel of philosophical materialism contained in his theory of history and society and implicitly presupposed by it does not come so plainly into view and is difficult to establish. Most of the existing literature, while it correctly brings out the qualitative distinction between Marx's materialism as a theory oriented primarily towards history and society, and all the forms of materialism which had arisen in the history of philosophy, fails to take into account sufficiently those aspects of Marx's thought which link him to the materialists of antiquity. Here the question of the connection between the materialist conception of history and philosophical materialism is of by no means secondary or purely terminological interest. Marx himself was aware that the term 'materialist' as applied to his thought was more than a mere figure of speech intended *pour épater le bourgeois* and lacking in philosophical implications. He considered that his thought belonged to the history of materialist philosophy in a quite precise sense. Thus, in the 1857 Introduction to *A Contribution to the Critique of Political Economy*, Marx not only made it a necessary part of his programme of work to defend the view that the forms taken by the state and by consciousness depend on the existing relations of production and distribution against 'objections to the materialistic character of this view',[2] but also referred to its 'relation to naturalistic materialism',[3] although this was something he never explicitly discussed.

How far is philosophical materialism presupposed by a theory according to which the manner of the production and reproduction of man's immediate life is the moment which in the last resort determines the historical movement of society? In order to settle this question properly, it is necessary to bring to light a number of hitherto ignored aspects of Marx's theoretical development. In the *Holy Family* we meet with Marx's judgment on the French thinkers of the Enlightenment, and the currents of thought within utopian socialism which arose out of the Enlightenment. Materialism is described here without qualification as 'the teaching of real humanism and the logical basis of communism'.[4] Marx expressed a high estimation of Helvetius, because of the latter's tendency to carry over the sensualist epistemology of Locke into a materialist theory of society:

If man draws all his knowledge, sensation, etc., from the world of the senses and the experience gained in it, the empirical world must be arranged so that man experiences and gets used to what is really human and that he becomes aware of himself as man. . . . If man is shaped by his surroundings, his surroundings must be made human. . . . If man is social by nature, he will develop his true nature only in society, and the power of his nature must be measured not by the power of separate individuals but by the power of society.[5]

Alongside such ideas of the Enlightenment, in which socialist theory is directly anticipated, an important part was played in the development of the young Marx by the contemporary criticism of Hegel's system, including that of Schelling. In the *Critique of Hegel's Philosophy of Right*, Marx described the family and civil society as 'the dark natural background from which the light of the state blazes forth'.[6] This expression is reminiscent of Schelling, when he first came under the influence of Böhme. Later on, of course, Feuerbach's terminology predominates. In the Feuerbachian and still inconsistent original formulations of historical materialism in the *Holy Family*, Marx sometimes referred to society in a similarly abstract and undifferentiated manner as 'the natural basis'[7] of the state. Entities derived from society are still related to it here in the same way as Spirit is to nature in Feuerbach. A passage of the *Holy Family* directed against the Left Hegelians brings out with particular clarity the fact that for Marx a naturalistic materialism constitutes the concealed precondition for a correct theory of society:

Or does critical criticism believe that it has even begun to grasp historical reality when it continues to exclude from the movement of history the theoretical and practical relations of men to nature, natural science and industry? Or does it think it has in fact already understood any period without having understood for example the industry of that period, the immediate mode of production of life itself? Of course spiritualistic, theological critical criticism knows only (at least it imagines it does) the main political, literary and theological events of history. Just as it separates thinking from the senses, the soul from the body, and itself from the world, so it separates history from natural science and industry, and sees history's point of origin not in coarse *material* production on the earth, but in vaporous clouds in the heavens.[8]

What is remarkable about this passage is that Marx does not simply attack the Left Hegelians for their false interpretation of history, in which material production and the impact of the natural sciences are left out of account, but tries to show that they necessarily had to arrive at this conception of history as philosophical idealists. He who separates thought from the senses, the soul from the body, is incapable of grasping the connection between the content of culture and the sphere of material production.

Marx was helped towards the concept of the 'basis' in his theory of history by the anthropological materialism contributed by Feuerbach. Feuerbach was concerned not with the mechanical movement of atoms but with the qualitative multiplicity of nature and with man as a sensuous and objective being. It was Feuerbach who, through his materialist inversion of Hegelian speculation, went beyond the purely internal criticism of idealism which was characteristic of the Left Hegelians. In the words of Marx, he abandoned 'drunken speculation' and went over to 'sober philosophy'.[9] The Paris Manuscripts emphatically indicate Feuerbach's significance:

Positive humanist and naturalistic criticism dates first from Feuerbach. Feuerbach's writings are the only works since Hegel's *Phenomenology* and *Logic* to contain a genuine theoretical revolution, and the quieter their impact the more certain, deep, extensive, and lasting it has been.[10]

With his abstract rejection of idealism Feuerbach laid the foundation of a new, non-idealist starting-point for Marx's thought.[11] Indeed, at this stage Marx temporarily abandoned certain important dialectical motifs to which he later returned. In some passages of the *Holy Family* it appears as if Marx agreed with Feuerbach in identifying the dialectic itself with idealism. However in the *German Ideology*, the *Theses on Feuerbach*, and the whole of his later work Marx returned to Hegelian positions, albeit mediated through Feuerbach's critique of Hegel.

The traditional interpretations of the relationship between Marx and Feuerbach are mainly restricted to an investigation of how far Feuerbach's atheistic critique of religion and spiritualist metaphysics suggested Marx's critique of Hegel or first made it possible. The naturalistic and anthropological basis of Feuerbach's critical endeavours is less emphasized, even though it had a much greater significance than is commonly assumed for the origins of the materialist dialectic. Erich Thier[12] is one of the few people to have pointed out that Feuerbach's influence on Marx did not rest so much on his atheism, which was already familiar to a man who knew both the thought of the French Enlightenment and the biblical criticism of the Left Hegelians, as on his emotional feeling for nature and man. Feuerbach's works of the years 1842 and 1843 (the *Vorläufige Thesen zur Reform der Philosophie* and the *Grundsätze der Philosophie der Zukunft*) are more important for the understanding of the Marxist concept of nature than the book picked out by Engels in *Ludwig Feuerbach*, namely *The Essence of Christianity*.

Feuerbach's critique of Hegel started at the crux of any

idealist system, the concept of nature. For Hegel, nature, as opposed to the Idea, was something derivative:

Nature comes first in time, but the Absolute Prius is the Idea; this Absolute Prius is the last thing, the true beginning, the Alpha is the Omega.[13]

Hegel's philosophy of nature is, in Hegelian terminology, the science of the Idea in its other-being. In nature the Idea confronts us in an immediate form not yet purified to become the Concept. It is the Concept posited in its lack of conceptual content. Nature is not a being possessing its own self-determination, but the moment of estrangement which the Idea in its abstract-general form must undergo in order to return to itself completely as Spirit. One of the strangest and most problematic transitions in the whole of Hegel's philosophy, criticized equally by Feuerbach and by Marx, is the transition from the *Logic* whose conclusion is the pure Idea, to the *Philosophy of Nature*, that is to say from thought to sensuous-material being:

The absolute freedom of the Idea is that it . . . *decides* to release freely from itself, as its own mirror-image, the moment of its own Specificity, and of the first determination or other-being, the Idea Immediate, i.e. nature.[14]

How far does the Idea, so to speak, lose its dialectical character in the course of its transformation into nature? How, in view of the fact that, as 'absolute', the Idea is always present to itself, does it come to estrange, to destroy itself in a world of objective-material existence? These questions remain shrouded in darkness in Hegel. Moreover, after having been brought forth by the Idea, nature gradually supersedes all natural determinations, and passes over into Spirit as its higher truth. The way in which Hegel presents this transition from nature to Spirit recalls the immaterial culmination of the dialectic of knowledge and the known in the *Phenomenology* at the stage of absolute knowledge which Marx precisely criticized. This is how Hegel put it:

We have shown, in the introduction to the *Philosophy of the Spirit*, how nature itself supersedes its externality and particularity, its materiality, as something untrue, something which is not in accordance with the

Concept internal to it, and through this attains to immateriality by going over into the Spirit.[15]

Holding the view that nature progressively lays aside its externality and brings forth the soul, Hegel believed that he could deduce from this the immaterial character of nature in general:

Everything material is superseded by the Spirit-in-itself working in nature, and this supersession culminates in the substance of the soul. The soul therefore appears as the ideality of all the material, as *all* immateriality, so that everything called material (however much it deludes common sense into accepting its independence) is recognized as dependent in relation to the Spirit.[16]

To this natural philosophical idealism of Hegel's, Feuerbach – as we saw – counterposed his own naturalism. For Feuerbach, Hegel's philosophy is philosophy from the standpoint of the philosopher, while he is a philosopher from the standpoint of non-philosophy. Instead of beginning with philosophy in order to end with philosophy, he wanted to begin with non-philosophy in order through philosophy to return to non-philosophy. In the *Vorläufige Thesen*, Feuerbach gave the following outline of his programme of a 'negation of all school philosophy':[17]

The philosopher must accept into the *text* of philosophy what in Hegel is degraded to the level of a *note*, namely what in man does *not* philosophize, what is rather *opposed* to philosophy and abstract thought. . . . Philosophy has therefore to begin not with itself but with its *antithesis*, with *non-philosophy*. This is our internal essence, which is unphilosophical, absolutely *anti-scholastic*, and distinct from thought. This is the principle of *sensualism*.[18]

The new philosophy no longer claimed any special position as against the other sciences but had its presupposition, like them, in nature. Feuerbach's conception, appropriately transformed, can be traced in Marx himself right through to *Capital*:

All the sciences must be founded on nature. A theory is no more than a *hypothesis* until its basis in nature is found.[19]

Nature, without which reason would lack matter, is grounded in itself. 'Being is from itself and through itself.'[20] Nature is the *causa sui*. Feuerbach's main criticism was directed against Hegel's view that nature is the Absolute Idea in estrangement:

> The Hegelian view that nature, reality, is posited by the Idea is only the *rational* expression of the theological teaching that nature is created by God, that material being is created by an immaterial, that is an abstract, being. At the end of the *Logic* the Absolute Idea even contrives to come to a nebulous 'decision', in this way itself documenting its origin in the theological heaven.[21]

Feuerbach turned Thought, Spirit, from an absolute Subject into a human quality alongside other natural qualities. All consciousness is the consciousness of corporeal men. The understanding of man as a needy, sensuous physiological being is therefore the precondition of any theory of subjectivity:

> Man alone is the *groundwork* of the Fichtean Ego, of the Leibnizian monad, of the Absolute.[22]

In the concluding stage of classical German philosophy the supra-empirical Ego, 'consciousness in general', finally proved to be an abstraction from the particular finite Subjects. The problem of the relation between the transcendental Ego and the empirical-psychological Ego was already very difficult in Kant's philosophy. Kant ought, in accordance with his programme, to have insisted strictly on the distinction between the two Egos. However, in concretely implementing the critique of reason, he could not avoid blurring this distinction and allowing the two Egos to merge. Owing to this even his transcendental Subject took on a certain anthropological colouring. In Feuerbach, who stood at the end of this whole movement of thought, man became the unique theme, precisely as an empirical and natural being:

> The new philosophy makes *man* (*including nature*, as the basis of man) into the *sole*, the *universal*, and the *highest* object of philosophy. It therefore makes anthropology, including physiology, into the universal science.[23]

Just as Feuerbach in his critique of religion sought to comprehend the content of religion as an alienation of man as a sensuous being, so here he viewed the absolute Spirit as an alienation of the finite human mind. Hegel's view that the logical categories existed before the creation of the world and of a finite Spirit, is in this way rejected and logical forms are declared to be the functions of transient human beings:

Metaphysics or logic is only a *real, immanent* science when it is not separated from the so-called *subjective Spirit.* Metaphysics is *esoteric psychology.*[24]

This idea of proceeding not from the absolute spirit but from the corporeal man is also of great importance for the Marxist theory of subjectivity. Marx is in agreement with the following passage from Feuerbach:

The *reality,* the *Subject* of *reason* is only *man.* It is *man* who thinks, not the *Ego* or *Reason.*[25]

The indissoluble distinction between concept and reality was indeed recognized by Hegel, but at the same time devalued by being allocated to the Subject side as a mere thought-determination. This distinction necessarily resulted from Feuerbach's reduction of the absolute Spirit to the human mind. It is not possible to gain a grasp of 'the real' through an unbroken chain of deductions. Feuerbach expressed this idea in a very penetrating manner:

The *real* cannot be represented in thought in whole numbers, but only in fractions. This distinction is a reasonable one, for it rests on the nature of thought, whose essence is generality, as opposed to reality, whose essence is individuality. What prevents this distinction from becoming a literal contradiction between the thought and the real is the fact that thought does not proceed in a straight line, in identity with itself, but is interrupted by sense-perception. Only thought which determines and rectifies itself by means of sense-perception is real, objective thought: the thought of objective truth.[26]

Marx went beyond Feuerbach in bringing not only sensuous intuition but also the whole of human practice into the process of knowledge as a constitutive moment. In doing this he also fulfilled Feuerbach's requirement that the new philosophy must differ '*in toto genere* from the old'.[27] Only by showing that they are dialectical moments of practice do Feuerbach's authorities, man and nature, arrive at concreteness. Marx, like Feuerbach, wrote of 'the priority of external nature',[28] although with the critical reservation that any such priority could only exist within mediation.

Marx defined nature (the material of human activity) as that which is not particular to the Subject, not incorporated in the modes of human appropriation, and not identical with men in general. He did not mean that this extra-human reality was to be understood ontologically in the sense of an unmediated objectivism. In Feuerbach, man the species-being, provided with merely natural qualities, confronts the dead objectivity of nature passively and intuitively rather than actively and practically, in a subjectivity which remains empty.[29] What Feuerbach described as the unity of man and nature related only to the romantically transfigured fact that man arose out of nature, and not to man's socio-historically mediated unity with nature in industry. The latter type of unity, however, is at all stages just as much a differentiation, the appropriation of something external, and a separation. Feuerbach's man does not emerge as an independent productive force but remains bound to pre-human nature. Physical activity does, it is true, presuppose this natural basis as a counter-block to man's transcending consciousness. All work is work on a fixed being which nevertheless proves transitory and penetrable under the action of the living Subjects. Feuerbach's anthropological accentuation of man as opposed to the rest of nature was always abstract. Nature as a whole was for Feuerbach an unhistorical, homogeneous substratum, while the essence of the Marxist critique was the dissolution of this homogeneity into a dialectic of Subject and Object. Nature was for Marx both an element of human practice and the totality of everything that exists. By unreflectively stressing the totality alone Feuerbach succumbed to the naive-realist myth of a 'pure nature'[30] and, in ideological fashion,[31] identified the immediate existence of men with their essence. It was not Marx's intention simply to replace Hegel's 'World Spirit' with a material 'World Substance' which would be an equally metaphysical principle. He did not reject Hegelian idealism abstractly like Feuerbach, but rather saw in it truth expressed in an untrue form. Marx accepted the idealist view that the world is mediated through the Subject. He considered however that he could bring home the full significance of this idea by showing what was the true pathos of 'creation' as presented by philosophers from Kant to Hegel: the creator of the objective world is the socio-historical life-process of human beings. In modern times extra-human natural existence has been reduced more and more to a function of human social organization. The philosophical reflection of this is that the determinations of objectivity have entered in greater and greater measure into the Subject, until at the culminating point of post-Kantian speculation they become completely absorbed in it. As a result, in Hegel too, the process of production remains in general an action of the Spirit, despite his magnificent empirical insights in points of detail. As Feuerbach said, in Hegel's logic thought is 'in uninterrupted unity with itself; the objects of thought are only its determinations. They are entirely incorporated in the Idea and have nothing of their own which could remain outside thought.'[32] The contradiction between the Subject and the Object is superseded in Hegel within the Subject as the Absolute. However much non-identity is the driving force of the dialectical process in its individual stages, it is idealist identity which triumphs at the end of the system. In the Marxist dialectic the reverse is the case: it is non-identity which is victorious in the last instance, precisely because Marx, unlike Feuerbach, fully recognized the significance of the Hegelian dialectic:

Hegel's dialectic is the basis of any dialectic, but only *after* its mystical form has been cast off.[33]

Marx meant by the 'mystical form' of the Hegelian dialectic the idealist interpretation of the idea of the mediacy[33a] of everything immediate. He retained Feuerbach's naturalistic monism to the extent that he regarded both Subject and Object as 'nature'.

At the same time he overcame the abstractly ontological character of this monism by relating nature and all natural consciousness to the life-process of society. Since the mediating Subjects, finite, temporally determined men, are themselves a part of the reality of things mediated through them, the idea of the mediacy of the immediate does not in its Marxist version lead to idealism. In fact for Marx, the immediacy of nature, in so far as, in opposition to Feuerbach, he regarded it as socially stamped, does not prove to be a vanishing appearance but retains its genetic priority over men and their consciousness.

Marx described extra-human reality which is both independent of men and mediated or, at least, capable of being mediated with them, by using the following synonymous terms: 'material', 'nature', 'stuff of nature', 'natural thing', 'earth', 'objective moments of labour's existence', 'objective' or 'material (*sachlich*) conditions of labour'. Since men constitute a component of this reality, the concept of 'nature' is identical with the 'whole of reality'[34] in the Marxist view. This concept of nature as the whole of reality did not result in an ultimate *Weltanschauung* or a dogmatic metaphysic but simply circumscribed the horizon of thought within which the new materialism moved. Materialist philosophy consists, in the words of Engels, in explaining the world from the world itself.[35] This concept of nature was 'dogmatic' enough to exclude from the theoretical construction anything Marx called mysticism or ideology; at the same time it was conceived undogmatically and broad-mindedly enough to prevent nature itself from receiving a metaphysical consecration or indeed ossifying into a final ontological principle.

Nature in this broad sense is the sole object of knowledge. On the one hand, it includes the forms of human society; on the other, it only appears in thought and in reality in virtue of these forms. In taking this view Marx showed himself to be rooted in the sensualism of Feuerbach, and in fact he proceeded from sense experience as the 'basis of all science'.[36] Materialist theory was for him identical with a scientific attitude in general:

Science is only genuine science when it proceeds from sense experience, in the two forms of *sense perception* and *sensuous* need; i.e. only when it proceeds from nature.[37]

The sensuous world and finite men in their existing social setting (the essence and the appearance at the same time) are the only quantities taken into account by Marxist theory. At bottom, there existed for Marx only 'man and his labour on the one side, nature and its materials on the other'.[38] On the basis of the objective logic of the human work-situation, he attempted to comprehend the other areas of life as well:

Technology discloses man's mode of dealing with nature, the process of production by which he sustains his life, and thereby also lays bare the mode of formation of his social relations, and of the mental conceptions that flow from them.[39]

Men construe the world, in the various spheres of their culture, on the model of their contemporary struggle with nature. Holding this view, both Marx and Feuerbach regarded all notions about supra-natural regions of existence as expressions of a negative organization of life. The historical movement,[40] they said, is a mutual relation between men and men, and between men and nature. It is true that the 'world-material' comprises both Subject and Object. However, what is essential is that historically the incompatibility of man with nature, i.e. in the last analysis the necessity of labour, triumphs over the unity of man and nature.

Nature interested Marx mainly as a constituent element of human practice. Hence the following decisive emphasis in the Paris Manuscripts:

. . . nature, taken abstractly, for itself, *rigidly* separated from man, is *nothing* for man.[41]

As long as nature remains unworked it is economically valueless, or rather, to be more precise, has a purely potential value which awaits its realization:

The material of nature alone, in so far as *no* human labour is embodied in it, in so far as it is mere material and exists independently of human labour, has no value, since value is only embodied labour. . . .[42]

The references to the history of philosophy in the *Holy Family* provide further examples of philosophical motives not otherwise made explicit by Marx. Here we meet with a general characterization of the Hegelian system which shows that Marx's materialism is not to be understood ontologically:

In Hegel there are three elements, Spinoza's Substance, Fichte's Self-consciousness, and the necessarily contradictory Hegelian unity of both, the Absolute Spirit. The first element is metaphysically travestied nature severed from man; the second is the metaphysically travestied Spirit severed from nature; the third is the metaphysically travestied unity of real man and the real human race.[43]

Here Marx was conducting a battle on three fronts. In attacking Spinoza's concept of Substance, he attacked the notion that nature exists 'in-itself' without human mediation. In criticizing Fichte's Self-consciousness, that is to say the concept of the Subject held by German idealism in general, he criticized the attribution of independence to consciousness and its functions in relation to nature. The mediating Subject is not simply 'Spirit', but man as a productive force. Finally, in Hegel's Absolute, in the unity of substance and Subject, he saw a unity of the two moments which had not been concretely and historically established but 'metaphysically travestied'. Nature cannot be separated from man; man and the accomplishments of his spirit cannot be separated from nature. Man's capacity for thought is a product of nature and history. Marx therefore characterized the process of thought as a process of nature:

Since the process of thought itself grows out of the situation, itself is a process of nature, truly conceptual thought is in the same position, and can only differentiate itself gradually, in accordance with the level of development, including that of the organ of thought.[44]

It would be quite wrong to see in materialism a uniform idea in whose history there has been only an immanent intellectual development.[45] If one disregards certain formal characteristics of materialist philosophy in general, it can be shown that materialism is subject to socio-historical change in its method, its specific interests and, finally, in its substantial features. Something which is of the highest importance for materialism in one century can appear peripheral in the next. However, like all philosophy, it is always an intellectual aspect of the human life-process:

The same spirit that builds philosophical systems in the brain of the philosopher builds railways with the hands of the workmen. Philosophy does not stand outside the world any more than man's brain is outside him because it is not in his stomach; but, of course, philosophy is in the world with its brain before it stands on the earth with its feet, whereas many another sphere of human activity has long been rooted in the earth by its feet and plucks the world's fruits with its hands before it has any idea that the 'head' too belongs to the world, or that this world is the world of the head.[46]

Matter in its physical or physiological determinateness is the central preoccupation of the materialism of the bourgeois Enlightenment of the seventeenth and eighteenth centuries. Hence, in a form of materialism, the essential content of which consists in the critique of political economy, matter must appear as a social category in the broadest sense. The metaphysical and scientific phrases, e.g. those of mechanics, on which with few exceptions all pre-Marxist materialism was based, do not rest on original formulations but are entirely derivative. In his excursus into the history of philosophy in the *Holy Family*, Marx showed how much physical materialism was bound up with the historically limited problems of the social emancipation of the bourgeoisie, both in the direction of its interests and in its dogmatic utterances about reality. As a result he placed the traditional objects of materialist thought in the background in so far as he conceived them in their social function and genesis. The obvious philosophical theses of any materialism also have their place in Marx, not of course as isolated assertions but essentially as superseded in the dialectical theory of society, through which alone they can be fully comprehended. In *Capital* Marx explicitly criticized previous materialism for its failure to see the relation of its formulations to the historical process:

The weak points in the abstract materialism of natural science, a materialism that excludes history and its process, are at once evident from the abstract and ideological conceptions of its spokesmen, whenever they venture beyond the bounds of their own speciality.[47]

Marx's polemic against Feuerbach in the *German Ideology* is an absolutely classic demonstration of the point that the natural sciences, a main source of materialist assertions, provide no immediate consciousness of natural reality at all, because man's relation to reality is not primarily theoretical but practical and modificatory. In their field of vision, their methodology, even in the content of what they regard as matter, the natural sciences are socially determined. The above-mentioned polemic against Feuerbach, which must be understood in the context of the *Theses on Feuerbach* written at the same time, bears the marks of Marx's own passage from the 'contemplative' to the 'new', i.e. the dialectical, materialism. Marx showed that Feuerbach's statements about nature do not constitute conclusive findings but are just as highly mediated as nature itself:

Feuerbach refers particularly to the view of natural science, he mentions secrets only revealed to the eye of the physicist or chemist; but where would natural science be without industry and trade? . . . Even the objects of the simplest 'sensuous certainty' are only given him through social development, industry and commercial intercourse. . . . Even this 'pure' natural science is provided with an aim, as with its material, only through trade and industry, through the sensuous activity of men. So much is this activity, this unceasing labour and creation, this production, the basis of the whole sensuous world as it now exists, that, were it interrupted only for a year, Feuerbach would not only find an enormous change in the natural world, but would very soon find that the whole world of men and his own perceptive faculty, nay his own existence, were missing.[48]

Although for Marx the sensuous world was not 'a thing given direct from all eternity, remaining ever the same, but the product of industry and of the state of society',[49] this socially mediated world remained at the same time a natural world, historically anterior to all human societies. Thus, even after the importance of the social moment has been recognized, 'the priority of external nature remains unassailed, and all this has no application to the original men produced by spontaneous generation; but this distinction [between pre-social and socially mediated nature, A.S.] has meaning only in so far as man is considered to be distinct from nature. For that matter, nature, the nature that preceded human history, is not by any means the nature in which Feuerbach lives, it is nature which today no longer exists anywhere (except perhaps on a few Australian coral-islands of recent origin) and which, therefore, does not exist for Feuerbach.'[50] The fact that Marx here asserted the priority of external nature, and thus of its laws, over the factor of social mediation, is of great epistemological importance and will later be discussed exhaustively.

It is not just because the working Subjects mediate the material of nature through themselves that is is impossible to speak of matter as a supreme principle of being. Men are not concerned in their production with matter 'as such', but always with its concrete, quantitatively and qualitatively determined forms of existence. Its general form, i.e. its independence of consciousness, exists only in particular shapes. There is no fundamental matter, no fundamental ground of being. Material reality can no more provide an ontological principle in the 'being for the other' it owes to its relativity to men, than it can in its 'being-in-itself'. There is even less justification for describing dialectical materialism as a 'philosophy of origin' than there is in the case of Hegel's dialectical idealism. Dialectical materialism admits no autonomous substance such as could exist independently of its concrete determinations. Engels expressed himself in the following manner on the concept of matter in his notes to *Anti-Dühring*:

N.B. Matter as such is a pure creation of thought and an abstraction. We leave out of account the qualitative distinctions between things in subsuming them as corporeally existing things under the concept 'matter'. Matter as such, as opposed to definite, existing pieces of matter, is therefore something which has no sensuous existence.[51]

He dealt again with the question of matter in the *Dialectics of Nature*:

Matter and motion *cannot* . . . be known in any other way than through the investigation of the separate material things and forms of motion, and by knowing these we also, in the same measure. know matter and motion *as such*.[52]

The latest attempts to systematize dialectical materialism dispense just as explicitly with the concept of matter as a substantial 'bearer' of secondary accidents. Neither Spirit nor matter is a uniform, 'fundamental' principle for explaining the world:

In opposition to metaphysical materialism, dialectical materialism rejects the notion of a 'final', immutable essence of things, of an 'absolutely fundamental substance', from whose 'ultimate' properties and appearances everything that exists can be derived. In nature there is nothing immutable and no absolutely fundamental substance.[53]

This dialectical interpretation of the concept of matter shows that Engels (and following him, present-day Soviet philosophy) was aware of the danger of an ontology and wished to avoid it. However, one cannot succeed in this if at the same time one uses the concept of matter to make the origin of the universe comprehensible. Wherever matter is brought in to provide an all-embracing, metaphysical explanation of the world, one is compelled willy-nilly to proceed from it as a universal principle and not from one of its concrete modes of existence. Engels pointed this out himself in a fragment of the *Dialectics of Nature*:

Final cause: matter and its inherent motion. This matter *not an abstraction*. Even in the sun the different substances are dissociated and without distinction in their action. But in the gaseous sphere of the nebular cloud all substances, although present separately, *become merged in pure matter as such*, and operate only as matter, not with their own specific properties.[54]

Only by recognizing, as Marx does, that material reality is from the beginning socially mediated, is it possible to avoid ontology and to do justice to Engels's formulation that matter as such is an abstraction, that matter is really present only in definite modes of existence.

The traditional philosophical problem of the meaning of history and of the world is very important for the understanding of the connection between Marxist materialism and philosophical materialism in general. The materialist dialectic is non-teleological, however peculiar that assertion may at first sound. History is here neither a chaotic collection of facts, as in Schopenhauer, nor is it connected together to form a whole with a uniform, spiritual meaning, as in Hegel. Marx did not give history a pantheistic 'independence'. His thinking came closest to adopting an air of justificatory idealism when, like Hegel, he pointed out the unavoidable necessity of domination and terror in 'prehistory'. It is true that the social formations which replace each other according to a law bring something like an all-embracing structure into human history. But this is not to be understood in the sense of an immanent 'teleology'. Marx did not regard the world as a whole as subject to any uniform idea which might give it meaning. There is only present in his work what Hegel called the 'finite-teleological standpoint':[55] the finite goals of finite, spatially and temporally limited men confronting limited areas of the natural and social world. Death as the anti-utopian fact *par excellence* 'demonstrates the powerlessness of all meaning-giving metaphysics and any theodicy'.[56] All goals and purposes arising in reality can be traced to men, acting in accordance with their changing situations. There is no meaning in isolation from these situations. Only where, as in the case of the Hegelian Spirit, the Subject is given an infinite, universal extension, can its purposes be simultaneously those of the world itself. For Hegel the 'finite-teleological standpoint' was something restricted, to be superseded in the theory of Absolute Spirit. Marx, on the contrary, knew of no other purposes in the world than those determined by men. The world could therefore, he said, contain no more meaning than men themselves have succeeded in realizing by the organization of the conditions of their life. Even when a better society had been brought about, this would not justify mankind's tortured path towards it:

That history has brought forth a better society out of one less good, that it can bring forth a still better one in its course, is a fact; but it is another fact that history's route lies across the sorrow and misery of individuals. There is a series of explanatory connections between these two facts, but no justificatory meaning.[57]

Because Marx did not proceed from the conception of a total meaning prior to man, history became for him a succession of constantly recurring individual processes, only to be grasped by a philosophy of fragments of the world which consciously abandons the appeal to unbroken deduction from a principle. He who grasps previous history has by no means made sense of the world in general. A formulation like the following, from Hegel's *Die Vernunft in der Geschichte*, would be completely unthinkable for Marx:

We must seek out in history a general purpose, the final goal of the world, not a particular purpose of the subjective Spirit or the mind. We must comprehend it through reason, which cannot make any particular finite purpose its interest, but only the Absolute.[58]

Ernst Bloch's far too metaphysical interpretation of Marx is characterized among other things by the thesis, which appears again and again in his writings, that Marxist philosophy also contains the notion of a final goal of the world. Bloch has written in an entirely Hegelian manner of the 'well-founded and real problem of a "meaning" of history, bound up with a "meaning" of the world',[59] which dialectical materialism has the task of solving. The consequences for his concept of utopia of Bloch's assumption that there is a meaning to the world in Marx will be discussed later in the section dealing with Marx's utopian vision of the relation between man and nature.

Here, however, in connection with the problem of the meaning of the world, we must draw attention to another consideration. Marx defended his implacable atheism not just on the basis of the discoveries of modern natural science,[60] or on the basis of a critique of ideology. For Marx, like Sartre, the non-existence of a 'sense-giving' God is the only guarantee of the possibility of the freedom of man. The essence of man is not something fixed. Man's essence has still not appeared in its entirety. On the contrary, in history up to the present, which is designated as 'prehistory' by the fact that men are not in control of their own powers in relation to nature, the essence of man has been brutally subsumed under the material conditions for the mainten-ance of his existence. The human species only attains a real reconciliation of its essence with its existence in so far as it comprehends itself at first theoretically as the cause of itself. The Paris Manuscripts in particular elaborate this point:

A being does not regard himself as independent unless he stands on his own feet, and he first stands on his own feet when he owes his *existence* to himself. A man who lives by the grace of another considers himself a dependent being. But I live completely by the grace of another when I owe to him not only the continuance of my life but also *its creation*; when he is its *source*. My life has necessarily such a cause outside itself if it is not my own creation.[61]

Marx rejected the *ontologically posed* question about the creator of the first men and of nature as a 'product of abstraction':[62]

Ask yourself how you arrive at that question. Ask yourself whether your question does not arise from a point of view to which I cannot reply because it is an absurd one? . . . If you ask a question about the creation of nature and man you abstract from nature and man. You suppose them *non-existent* and you want me to demonstrate that they *exist*. I reply: give up your abstraction and at the same time you abandon your question. Or else, if you want to maintain your abstraction, be consistent, and if you think of man and nature as non-existent, think of yourself too as non-existent, for you are also man and nature. Do not think, do not ask me any questions, for as soon as you think and ask questions your abstraction from the existence of nature and man becomes meaningless.[63]

This peculiarly emphatic passage is typical of Marx's attitude to all *prima philosophia*, and once again makes plain his main concern. Questions directed to the pre-human and pre-social existence of nature should not be posed 'abstractly'; in each case they presuppose a definite stage of the theoretical and practical appropriation of nature. All putatively primeval substrata are always already involved with what is supposed to emerge from their activity, and are for precisely that reason by no means absolutely primeval. The question of the 'act of creation'[64] of man and nature is therefore less a metaphysical than a historico-social question:

In that . . . for socialist man the *whole of what is called world history* is nothing but the creation of man by human labour, and the emergence of nature for man, he therefore has the evident and irrefutable proof of his *self-creation*, of his own *process of origination*. Once the essentiality of man and of nature, man as a natural being and nature as a human reality, has become evident in practice, and sensuously, the quest for an *alien* being, a being above nature and man (a quest which is an avowal of the inessentiality of nature and man) becomes impossible in practice.[65]

Marxist atheism, which is basically post-atheist, is against any devaluation of man and nature.[66] For idealism, the supreme being is God; for the materialism which is identical with humanism, it is man. The concept of God is the most abstract expression of domination, always combined with the dogmatic assertion that the world has a total, uniformly spiritual meaning. If God exists, revolutionary man no longer comes into the picture as the maker, not – admittedly – of a world meaning, but of a meaningful social whole in which each individual is uplifted and honoured. It is no accident that Prometheus was the most distinguished saint in Marx's philosophical calendar. Human self-consciousness, he wrote in his dissertation, must be recognized as the 'supreme divinity'.[67] If theory proceeds historically from the mediating connection of man and nature in social production, atheism is no longer a purely 'ideological' position:

Atheism, as a denial of this inessentiality [of nature and man, A.S.] is no longer meaningful, for atheism is a *negation of God*, and asserts by this negation the *existence of man*. Socialism as socialism no longer requires such a mediation; it begins from the theoretical and practical sensuous consciousness of man and nature as essential beings.[68]

However problematic materialism may have shown itself to be in the history of philosophy when it was presented as a comprehensive explanation of the world, its most significant representatives were not primarily interested in assembling a collection of dogmatic metaphysical theses. Where these have been put forward their accentuation has been entirely different from that of their counterparts in the camp of idealism. For the materialist there do not arise, except indirectly, any ethical maxims from the view that everything material is real and everything real is material.

Marxist materialism, although externally connected with the theologico-metaphysical formulations characteristic of Hegelian philosophy, should not be interpreted in the first place as an answer to the central questions traditionally asked by metaphysics. Like the great Encyclopedists, Marx was as tolerant in dealing with the ultimate questions of metaphysics as he was inexorable in relation to the necessities which arise from men's immediate practice. In the *German Ideology* there is a passage, originally drafted by Moses Hess, in which the idealists are summed up in the drastic manner of the eighteenth-century Enlightenment:

All idealists, philosophic and religious, ancient and modern, believe in inspirations, in revelations, saviours, miracle-workers; whether their belief takes a crude religious, or a refined philosophic, form depends only upon their cultural level. . . .[69]

If Marxist materialism engaged in abstract ideological proclamations of the kind still customary in the Soviet

Union and Eastern Europe today, it would differ in no respect from the bad idealism commented on above. Not the abstract nature of matter, but the concrete nature of social practice is the true subject and basis of materialist theory. The eighth thesis on Feuerbach accords with this interpretation:

Social life is essentially practical. All mysteries which mislead theory into mysticism find their rational solution in human practice and in the comprehension of this practice.[70]

Instead of dealing with the question of the spiritual or material nature of the soul, which can have at times an idealist, that is to say a diversionary, function in society even when the reply to it is a materialist one, Marxist materialism is primarily concerned with the possibility of removing hunger and misery from the world. Marx shared a eudemonistic impulse with the ethical materialists of antiquity, while even the idealist Hegel was close to their views on pleasure. On the one side, materialism is not initially a moral attitude and does not consist in the idolization of the crude sensual pleasures; on the other, it cannot be reduced merely to a theory or a method. 'The materialist is concerned not with absolute reason but with happiness (including its despised form, pleasure), and not so much with so-called inner happiness, which all too often allows itself to be complacent about outer misery, but with an objective condition, in which curtailed subjectivity comes into its own again.'[71]

In his essay on Feuerbach,[72] Engels scoffed at the supposed 'philistine prejudice' which understands materialism not just as a theory but also associates it with sensual pleasures. But what is the value of men's immense and not only theoretical efforts to transcend capitalism, if one of the objects aimed at is not pleasure, and the attainment of the satisfaction of the senses? Engels's formulation contains something of that asceticism, perceived by Heine already in the early days of the socialist movement, which was later one of the sources of an anti-human practice. He who has nothing much to eat, it is implied, should at least not be without a 'scientific conception of the world'.

The theoretical attempt to ensure that no man in the world should suffer material or intellectual need any longer is something which does not need any metaphysical 'ultimate justification'. Critical materialism disdains to continue the tradition of mere philosophizing by investigating 'the riddles of the world' or, with unflinching radicalism, putting itself continually in question in the style of modern ontology. Its intellectual construction was undertaken by finite men and grew out of the definite historical tasks of society. Its aim is to help men out of their self-made prison of uncomprehended economic determination.

Although the materialist theory seeks out the social bases of even the most delicate cultural artefacts, it is still far from being the positive 'world view' which is made out of it today in communist countries. Basically it is a unified critical judgment on previous history, to the effect that men have allowed themselves to be degraded into objects of the blind and mechanical process of its economic dynamic. Ernst Bloch is therefore right to say that so far 'no human life has existed, but only an economic life which has "driven" men, turned them away from their true selves, and made them into slaves and exploiters'.[73] Economic factors are as sharply emphasized by the theory as by social reality itself. However neither the economy nor the proletariat was for Marx a metaphysical principle of explanation. The economy was to be brought back again from its all-powerful position to a subordinate role. The 'materialist' character of Marxist theory does not amount to a confession of the incurable primacy of the economy, that anti-human abstraction achieved by the real situation. It is rather an attempt to direct men's attention towards the ghostly internal logic of their own conditions, towards this pseudo-physis that makes them commodities and at the same time provides the ideology according to which they are already in control of their own destinies.

Horkheimer characterized the anarchy of capitalist production in the following way:

The process is accomplished not under the control of a conscious will but as a natural occurrence. Everyday life results blindly, accidentally, and badly from the chaotic activity of individuals, industries and states.[74]

Since capitalist society is ruled by its own life-process, its rationality takes on an irrational, mythical, and fateful character, as indicated by Thalheimer:

Capitalist society stands in the same relation towards its own economy as does the Australian savage towards thunder, lightning, and rain.[75]

In a wrongly organized society, the control of nature, however highly developed, remains at the same time an utter subjection to nature.

He who denounces an evil is interpreted again and again as if he is glorifying or propagating it. A textbook example of a complete misrepresentation and distortion of what the critics of political economy call materialism is Peter Demetz's book, *Marx, Engels, and the Poets*.[76] Demetz writes as if Marx had invented everything his teaching opposes. It is not Marxist materialism which has, in the words of Demetz, 'robbed the figure of the artist of the element of freedom and thus degraded him to the impersonal servant of economic processes',[77] but the real development of a system of production alienated from men because un-controlled. It is not because Marx is a primitive economist that in his writings, even in draft programmes and the like, he renounced all moralizing and idealistic turns of phrase with a positively ascetic vigilance. One of the letters to F. A. Sorge is characteristic of his attitude. In it he complained about the emergence of a 'rotten spirit' in the Party, and spoke of a 'whole gang of half-mature students and super-wise doctors who want to give socialism a "higher, idealis-tic" orientation, that is to say, to replace the materialistic basis (which requires serious, objective study from anyone who wants to make use of it) with modern mythology, with its goddesses of Justice, Liberty, Equality, and Fraternity'.[78] It is precisely in refusing to allow the importance of the material problems to be belittled that Marx is truer to the human kernel concealed beneath the shell of idealistic phrases than those who pretend that history's still out-standing tasks have already been accomplished. Not all that is spiritual is ideology for Marx, only its unfulfilled claim to be social reality.

Hegel described the first nature, a world of things existing outside men, as a blind conceptless occurrence. The world of men as it takes shape in the state, law, society, and the economy, is for him 'second nature',[79] manifested reason, objective Spirit. Marxist analysis opposes to this the view that Hegel's 'second nature' should rather be described in the terms he applied to the first: namely, as the area of conceptlessness, where blind necessity and blind chance coincide. The 'second nature' is still the 'first'. Mankind has still not stepped beyond natural history.[80] This fact explains the closeness of the method of Marxist sociology to that of natural science (*Naturwissenschaft*). Many critics of Marx regard this method as inappropriate, but in fact the 'nature-like' constitution of its object of investigation ensures that it is not a human science (*Geisteswissenschaft*). When Marx treated the history of previous human society as a 'process of natural history',[81] this had first of all the critical meaning that 'the laws of economics confront men in all . . . planless and incoherent production as objective laws over which they have no power, therefore in the form of laws of nature'.[82] Marx had in mind the experience gained in the course of the perennial 'prehistory' of man that, in spite of all technical triumphs, it is still always nature which is victorious in the last resort and not man. 'All the contrived machinery of modern industrial society is merely nature tearing itself to pieces'[83] in that it is not socially controlled.

However, in addition to this accentuation of its critical aspects, Marx used the concept of natural history in the broader sense given to it by the evolutionist theories of the nineteenth century, i.e. as the history of the whole of reality. When he reproached the 'abstract materialism of natural science' for excluding the 'historical process',[84] he had in mind nature just as much as society.[85]

As in most of the mechanical materialists of the eighteenth century, so also in Hegel, who saw in nature the material separation of mutually indifferent existences, there exists in the strict sense no natural history:

Thinking reflection must rid itself of such nebulous, and basically sensuous, notions as in particular the so-called *emergence* e.g. of plants and animals out of water and then the *emergence* of the more developed out of the lower kinds of animal.[86]

For Marx, on the other hand, the regular emergence and separation of natural forms was so obvious as not to need discussing. His conception of development owes as much to Darwin as to Hegel. Engels pointed this out in his review of the first volume of *Capital*, in which he had this to say about Marx's method:

In so far as he endeavours to show that the present society, considered economically, is pregnant with another, higher form of society, he is simply striving to establish the same gradual process of transformation demonstrated by Darwin in natural history as a law in the social field.[87]

Marx's approach, in which 'the development of the economic formation of society' was conceived 'as a process of natural history,[88] meant that he viewed the historical process in its strict necessity, without engaging in aprioristic constructions or using psychological principles of explanation. He understood individual behaviour as a function of the objective process. In history so far individuals have appeared not as free Subjects but as 'personifications of economic categories'.[89]

In his pamphlet *What the 'Friends of the People' are and How they Fight against the Social Democrats* (1894), which is important for the understanding of historical materialism, Lenin discussed in particular the 'natural-historical' character of the Marxist method of investigation and its relation to Darwinian evolutionism:

Just as Darwin put an end to the view that animal and plant species are unconnected, that they arose fortuitously, 'created by God', and are immutable, just as he was the first to place biology on a fully scientific foundation by establishing the mutability and the succession of the species, so Marx put an end to the view that society is a mechanical aggregate of individuals, in which the desired changes can be brought about at the will of the authorities (or, if you like, of society and the government), and which emerges and changes casually, and was therefore the first to place sociology on a scientific foundation by laying down the concept of the economic formation of society as the totality of existing productive relations, and by establishing that the development of such formations is a process of natural history.[90]

Marx replaced all abstract reasoning about society and progress in general with the concrete analysis of one society, namely bourgeois–capitalist society. Marxist materialism does not contain a total explanation any more than

Darwin's theory does. It is rather the attempt to grasp the historical process in accordance with the facts, without resorting to metaphysical dogmas:

And just as . . . transformism by no means claims to explain the 'whole' history of the origin of species, but only to have placed the methods of this explanation on a scientific basis, so materialism in history has never claimed to explain everything, but merely, in Marx's words, to indicate 'the only scientific' method of explaining history.[91]

Marx himself, while recognizing the specificity of social laws, was aware of the relation of his theory to Darwin:

Darwin has interested us in the history of nature's technology, i.e. in the formation of the organs of plants and animals, which organs serve as instruments of production for sustaining their life. Does not the history of the productive organs of man, of organs that are the material basis of all social organization, deserve equal attention? And would not such a history be easier to compile, since, as Vico says, human history differs from natural history in this, that we have made the former, but not the latter?[92]

Engels distinguished natural from human history in a very similar manner in the *Dialectics of Nature*:

The whole of nature also is now merged in history, and history is only differentiated from natural history as the evolutionary process of *self-conscious* organisms.[93]

Natural and human history together constitute for Marx a differentiated unity. Thus human history is not merged in pure natural history; natural history is not merged in human history.

It is true, on the one hand, that the history of society is a *'real'* part of *natural history'*,[94] in that facts characteristic of pre-human history continue to exist in human society. Marx was thus able to describe the instruments of production, by whose construction and application men are essentially distinguished from animals, as 'extended bodily organs'.[95] Men, like animals, must accommodate themselves to their surroundings. Horkheimer and Adorno remarked on this as follows in the *Dialektik der Aufklärung*:

The cerebral organ, human intelligence, is robust enough to constitute a regular epoch in world history. The human species, including its machines, chemicals, and powers of organization (and why should one not include these, in the way that one includes the teeth in the bear, since they serve the same purpose and simply function better?) is in this epoch the *dernier cri* of adaptation.[96]

On the other hand, one should not neglect the specific difference between the course of history in nature and in society. This difference makes impermissible the simple translation of natural laws to social relations, as in the many varieties of Social Darwinism. In a letter to Kugelmann, Marx sharply criticized the attempt by F. A. Lange to ride roughshod over the richness of human history in the abstract manner of natural science:

Herr Lange has . . . made a great discovery. The whole of history can be brought under a single great natural law. This natural law is the *phrase* (in this application Darwin's expression becomes nothing but a phrase) 'struggle for life', and the content of this phrase is the Malthusian law of population, or rather overpopulation. So, instead of analysing the 'struggle for life' as represented historically in various definite forms of society, all that has to be done is to translate every concrete struggle into the phrase 'struggle for life', and this phrase itself into the Malthusian 'population fantasy'.[97]

It is only possible to speak of natural history when one presupposes human history made by conscious Subjects. Natural history is human history's extension backwards and is comprehended by men, as *no longer* accessible nature, with the same socially imprinted categories as they are compelled to apply to *as yet* unappropriated areas of nature.

It was Darwin's work which made plain what an extraordinary mass of presuppositions underlie all statements about nature and its history. Marx was well aware of this, although his mode of reflection on society was 'natural-historical'. This emerges clearly from a letter to Engels in which he wrote:

It is remarkable how Darwin recognizes among beasts and plants his English society with its division of labour, competition, opening up of new markets, 'inventions', and the Malthusian 'struggle for existence'. It is Hobbes's 'bellum omnium contra omnes', and one is reminded of Hegel's *Phenomenology*, where civil society is described as a 'spiritual animal kingdom', while in Darwin the animal kingdom figures as civil society. . . .[98]

In accord with this, Engels showed in a letter to P. L. Lavrov that certain theories, borrowed from bourgeois relations and their reflection in the realm of ideas, were applied to the development of organic nature, and then put forward by the Social Darwinists as supposedly pure natural laws of society:

The whole Darwinist teaching of the struggle for existence is simply a transference from society to living nature of Hobbes's doctrine of 'bellum omnium contra omnes' and of the bourgeois-economic doctrine of competition together with Malthus's theory of population. When this conjurer's trick has been performed, . . . the same theories are transferred back again from organic nature into history and it is now claimed that their validity as eternal laws of human society has been proved.[99]

Within the Marxist school of thought, the Social Darwinist method of approaching history played a great part in Karl Kautsky's work *Die materialistische Geschichtsauffassung*. By making the unity of human with pre-human history into an absolute fact about reality, Kautsky reached the conclusion 'that the history of humanity merely constitutes a special case of the history of living beings, with peculiar laws, which are however related to the general laws of living nature'.[100] These 'peculiar laws' of society themselves are forgotten in Kautsky's subsequent discussion. Whereas the history of cosmic and biological development forms only the 'natural-scientific basis'[101] of Marx's conception of history, and its main area of application is the history of society, Kautsky turned this relationship upside down. Human history according to Kautsky is an appendage of natural history, its laws of motion merely forms of appearance of biological laws. Karl Korsch, one of the few authors in the extensive literature on Marx who understood the complex dialectic of nature and history, emphatically criticized Kautsky's distortion of the Marxist theory of history:

It is not nature, or organic nature and the history of its development in general, nor is it the historical development even of human society in general, but rather modern 'bourgeois society' which forms for Marx and Engels the real point of departure, from which all earlier historical forms of society are to be grasped materialistically.[102]

The question of the relation between natural and human history also has its relevance for Marx's critique of ideology.

The falsification of socio-historically conditioned events like wars, pogroms, and crises so that they appear as un-avoidable natural facts, has up to the present been a solid component of the defence of authority. Marx was thinking primarily of class relations when he wrote:

Nature does not produce on the one side owners of money or com-modities, and on the other men possessing nothing but their own labour-power. This relation is not one of *natural history*, neither is it a *social* relation common to all historical periods. It is clearly the result of a past historical development, the product of many economic upheavals, of the extinction of a whole series of older forms of social production.[103]

Marx accepted no rigid facts about man, either of a spiritual or a biologico-material nature. His critique of Max Stirner in the *German Ideology* shows this:

Just as, previously, Sancho explained all crippling of individuals, and so of their conditions, by means of the fixed ideas of school-masters, without worrying about the origin of these ideas, so now, he explains this crippling by the merely natural process of generation. He has not the slightest idea that the ability of children to develop depends on the development of their parents and that all this crippling under existing social conditions has arisen historically, and in the same way can be abolished again in the course of historical development. Even differ-ences that have arisen naturally within the species, such as racial differences, etc., about which Sancho has nothing to say, can and must be abolished in the course of historical development.[104]

Finally, this question of the relation between nature and history has yet another aspect: its relevance for the method and theory of science. It has become customary, since the work of Dilthey and the neo-Kantians of South-West Germany, to assign to the historical and the natural sciences modes of investigation which are different in principle. While Dilthey distinguished between the method of causal 'explanation' peculiar to the natural sciences, and the method of intuitive 'understanding' peculiar to the historical, human sciences, Windelband and Rickert cut reality still more radically into two entirely distinct parts. Nature was conceived in Kantian fashion as the existence of things subject to laws. The 'nomothetic' character of the natural sciences corresponded to this conception. History was said to consist of a profusion of value-oriented, basically unconnected 'individual' data, only accessible to a descriptive 'ideographic' method. It thus became something beyond all rational analysis.[105]

Marx admitted no absolute division between nature and society, and hence no fundamental methodological distinction between the natural sciences and historical science. As he wrote in the *German Ideology*:

We know only a single science, the science of history. History can be contemplated from two sides, it can be divided into the history of nature and the history of mankind. However the two sides are not to be divided off; as long as men exist the history of nature and the history of men are mutually conditioned.[106]

An 'opposition between nature and history'[107] is created by the ideologists in that they exclude from history the productive relation of men to nature. Nature and history, said Marx in criticizing Bruno Bauer, are 'not two separate "things"'.[108] Men always have before them a 'historical nature and a natural history'.[109]

The reproach that Marx proceeded too 'naturalistically' when he wrote in *Capital* of the historical process of the economic formation of society as of a process of natural history, misses the mark because it dogmatically presupposes precisely the thesis criticized here; the thesis that there is a fundamental methodological distinction between the attitude of the researcher into nature and that of the researcher into history. Scientific thought cannot recognize any area *sui generis* absolutely inaccessible to explanation in accordance with uniform laws.

The methodological dualism of Dilthey, Windelband and Rickert, despite all the efforts of these authors to deal with history, rests on abstractions foreign to history. This attitude itself had at the outset the critical meaning that the door was not to be opened wide to interpretations of history, that arbitrary schemes of meaning were not to be imposed on data themselves indifferent to meaning. However, the essential point was lost as a result, and it then appeared as if the course of history was entirely without structure and only accessible to intuition and ideographic description.

In the review entitled *Die moralisierende Kritik und die*

kritische Moral, Marx mounted an attack upon the undialectical alternatives we have already discussed, in a manner highly instructive for the understanding of his method. He denied that it was necessary to choose between allowing history and nature to merge into each other, and making the distinction between them absolute:

It is characteristic of the entire crudeness of 'common sense', which takes its rise from 'the full life' and does not cripple its natural features by philosophical or other studies, that where it succeeds in seeing a distinction it fails to see a unity, and where it sees a unity it fails to see a distinction. If 'common sense' establishes distinct determinations, they immediately petrify surreptitiously, and it is considered the most reprehensible sophistry to rub together these conceptual blocks in such a way that they catch fire.[110]

Just as in Marx's view there is no purely immanent succession of ideas such as 'intellectual history' might investigate, so also pure historically unmodified nature does not exist as an object of natural-scientific knowledge. Nature, the sphere of the regular and the general, is in each case related both in extent and composition to the aims of men organized in society, aims which arise from a definite historical structure. The *historical practice* of men, their bodily activity, is the progressively more effective connecting link between the two apparently separate areas of reality. Indeed, the Marx of the Paris Manuscripts looked forward to an amalgamation of natural science and historical science (described here as the science of men) as a result of the reconciliation of nature and history through practice under communism:

Natural science will one day incorporate the science of man, just as the science of man will incorporate natural science; there will be a *single* science.[111]

Single because, within its diversity, the '*social* reality of nature'[112] and the simultaneously developing natural reality of man will become more and more appropriate to each other, through industry. The '*natural science of man*' will be identical 'with *human* natural science'.[113]

B. TOWARDS A CRITIQUE OF ENGELS'S DIALECTICS OF NATURE

In making the attempt to present Marx's concept of nature, one cannot avoid discussing Engels's formulations of a dialectical materialist theory of nature. As a strict historical materialist, Engels took the view that phenomenal nature, as also all scientific and philosophical knowledge of nature, was always related to the changing forms of social practice. Like Marx he repeatedly tried to show that natural science, in the materials it works on, the method it uses, and the way it poses questions, is at once the expression and the instrument of the progress of the forces of production.[114]

In what follows, we shall show that where Engels passed beyond Marx's conception of the relation between nature and social history, he relapsed into a dogmatic metaphysic. This occurred despite his refusal to admit that by introducing dialectics into the natural sciences he was inventing a philosophy of nature.

Instead of immediately dismissing Engels's opinion *a limine* as sheer nonsense (like some of his critics) we must first situate the whole problem in the history of ideas, since this will allow us to see how Engels arrived at his solution. However, a mere reference to the party-tactical or political need for a world conception on the part of the working-class movement, of the kind made by Fetscher,[115] is completely insufficient, since it would be an underestimation of the specificity of Engels's philosophical development.

The collapse of classical philosophy had two consequences. On the one hand, all understanding of the problematic of idealism, and hence of the dialectic, was lost. On the other, the flatly mechanical 'tub-thumping materialism', which expressed the final separation of natural science from philosophy, became more and more influential in the 1850s. Engels was concerned to uphold a conception of nature which is certainly materialist, but which does not simply relinquish the achievement of the dialectic. As he wrote in *Anti-Dühring*:

Marx and I were just about the only people who salvaged the conscious dialectic from German idealist philosophy, and we transferred it into the materialist conception of nature and history.[116]

This 'salvaging' refers not only to the first confrontation with Hegel, brought to a close by the *German Ideology* and the *Theses on Feuerbach*, which document the actual birth of dialectical materialism, but also to the very important *second appropriation of Hegel*,[117] which began, for Engels as for Marx, in the year 1858.[118]

It is hardly possible to speak of a difference between the theoretical views of Marx and Engels up to the *Theses on Feuerbach*. The routes taken by the two authors did however diverge partially towards the end of the 1850s. They both turned to positive science, but in very different ways.

In the great historical and economic analysis of *Capital*, Marx put in concrete form the jointly compiled programme of the *Theses on Feuerbach*. In doing this he also came to grips with the question, essential for the *German Ideology*, of the relation between nature and social practice, by trying 'through the critique of a science [namely political economy] to bring that science to the point where it can be presented dialectically'.[119]

Engels, however, proceeded differently. He interpreted the results of modern natural science, which already lay to hand in a finished form, with the help of dialectical categories. Whereas Marx, in very Hegelian fashion, allowed the dialectically presented science to emerge first from the criticism of its present state, and therefore at no point detached the materialist dialectic from the content of political economy, Engels's dialectic of nature necessarily remained external to its subject-matter. This appears particularly clearly when for example he 'applies' Hegelian categories to the biological concept of the cell, quite regardless of their idealist-speculative presuppositions:

The cell is the Hegelian being-in-itself and in its development undergoes precisely the Hegelian process, until finally there develops out of it the 'idea', in each case the completed organism.[120]

As we are here essentially concerned to establish the distinction between the Marxist concept of nature and that of Engels,[121] we shall confine ourselves to stating the basic metaphysical theses of the late Engels,[122] in order to extract from them the outlines of a critique.

It should first be stated that Engels's view of nature is not, as Fetscher claims, 'a more subtle version of the vulgar materialist and monist conceptions then generally current',[123] but is rather an attempt to extend the materialism of the French Enlightenment in its systematic form with the help of dialectics. In the essay *Ludwig Feuerbach and the End of Classical German Philosophy*, Engels wrote of his undertaking, clearly alluding to Holbach, as 'a "System of Nature" sufficient for our time'.[124] Alongside this, the romantic philosophy of nature, with its qualitative-dynamic character, also played a not unimportant part.[125]

The metaphysical view of nature, compulsory in Soviet materialism almost to the present day, consists of the following theses, developed in *Anti-Dühring*:

1. The unity . . . of the world consists in its materiality.[126]
2. The basic forms of all being are space and time, and a being outside time is just as nonsensical as a being outside space.[127]
3. *Motion is the mode of existence of matter.* Never and nowhere has there existed, or can there exist, matter without motion. The statement that all rest, all equilibrium is only relative, only has meaning in relation to this or that definite form of motion.[128]

What distinguishes this materialism from all the mechanical materialisms, from Democritus to Holbach, is its *nonreductive* character. Engels recognized differences of form within the material unity of the world. Matter's higher forms of existence and motion emerge admittedly from its lower forms, but they cannot be reduced completely to the latter. There is no final and fundamental form of material motion. Mechanical, chemical, biological and psychic forms of motion are *qualitatively* distinct from each other, and yet they are modes of appearance of the one material essence of the world. Engels endeavoured to make sense of the progress from the lower to the higher with the aid of the dialectic which he defined in the following way:

The dialectic is . . . the science of the general laws of motion and development of nature, human society, and thought.[129]

As appears from the *Dialectics of Nature*, the most mature philosophical work of his late period, Engels believed that he could abstract three fundamental dialectical laws from the three above-mentioned areas. These laws have entered into Soviet Marxist theory:

1. The law of the transformation of quantity into quality and vice versa;
2. the law of the interpenetration of opposites;
3. the law of the negation of the negation.[130]

To do him justice it should be remarked that Engels, unlike his present-day followers in the East, was by no means intent on recommending the dialectic to natural scientists as a *direct* method of research. What he basically had in mind was an encyclopedic reworking of the material of modern natural science:

Empirical research into nature has heaped up such an immense mass of positive knowledge that the necessity of ordering it systematically and according to its internal logic in each individual area of investigation has become absolutely imperative.[131]

Engels returned to reflections of his early period with the intention of unifying the history, and the system, of nature and natural science. He saw the first model of such a unity in the work of the French Encyclopedists. This appears from a passage in an article he wrote in 1844 on the eighteenth century:

The idea of the Encyclopedia was characteristic of the eighteenth century; it rested on the awareness that all these sciences were interconnected, yet no one was capable of making the transitions, and hence the sciences could only be placed side by side.[132]

While Diderot and d'Alembert, following Francis Bacon, had still divided up the sciences according to the appropriate faculty of perception, the nineteenth century saw the victory of the trend towards ordering them according to their content. This is the case in the scientific hierarchies of Saint-Simon and Comte, by which Engels was certainly influenced. But it was Hegel he followed in particular, the man 'whose . . . comprehensive treatment and rational grouping of the natural sciences is a greater achievement than all the materialistic nonsense [such authors as Büchner, Vogt, etc., A.S.] put together'.[133] Engels showed this when he attempted to classify the natural sciences on the basis of matter's different forms of motion, starting with Mathematics, continuing with Mechanics, Physics, and Chemistry, and ending with Biology:

Just as one form of motion develops out of another, so too must their reflections, the different sciences, necessarily proceed from one to the other.[134]

To return to the abstract metaphysical theses and dialectical laws mentioned earlier, these are at best a possible way of presenting and interpreting the results of scientific research. However, they have absolutely no connection with the method of natural science itself, which is oriented towards formal logic and is undialectical in the sense that it does not reflect the historical mediation of its objects.

Marx expressly discussed the question of the relation between a science's mode of research and its mode of presentation in *Capital*:

Of course the method of presentation must differ in form from that of inquiry. The latter has to appropriate the material in detail, to analyse its different forms of development, to trace out their inner connection. Only after this work is done, can the actual movement be adequately described. If this is done successfully, if the life of the subject-matter is ideally reflected as in a mirror, then it may appear as if we had before us a mere *a priori* construction.[135]

In the case of a man-made object like social history, methods of inquiry and presentation are, despite all their formal differences, internally related to each other, whereas the interpretation of a nature separated from all human practice must ultimately remain a matter of indifference to that nature.

The early Engels took issue with the materialism of the eighteenth century for merely presenting 'nature to men as an absolute, as a replacement for the Christian God'.[136] His own later philosophy could be criticized on precisely the same lines. To the extent that its assertions about nature are isolated from the living practice of men, they are subject to the criticisms in the *Theses on Feuerbach* against Feuerbach's view of nature. For Engels, nature and man are not united primarily through historical practice; man appears only as a product of evolution and a passive reflection of the process of nature, not however as a productive force. If the materialist conception of nature, as Engels wrote in *Ludwig Feuerbach and the End of Classical German Philosophy*, is nothing other 'than a simple conception of nature as it presents itself to us, without any external trimmings',[137] this means, in comparison with Marx's own position, a relapse into naïve realism.[138] It is not just a matter of the absence in Marx of a line dividing the sensuous world in general into the originally given elements and the 'external trimmings' mediated through practice. There is the further point that Marx was clearly aware that one can only speak of the 'material substratum' of particular commodity-entities 'furnished by nature without the help of man'[139] by abstracting from all mediating, useful labour.

In Engels's conception, external reality took on the rigid shape of mere 'facts'. This is shown for example by his attempt, made in a letter to Conrad Schmidt, to state the difference between the idealist and the materialist dialectic:

The inversion of the dialectic in Hegel rests on this, that it is supposed to be the 'self-development of thought', of which the dialectic of facts is therefore only a reflection, whereas the dialectic in our heads is in reality the reflection of the actual development going on in the world of nature and of human history in obedience to dialectical forms.[140]

Engels failed to appreciate that there can only be a 'dialectic of facts' when the 'world of nature and the world of human history' are not considered as two separate spheres. On the other point, the movement of thought in Marx is by no means limited to a mere mirroring of the factual. The uncritical reproduction of existing relationships in consciousness has precisely an ideological character for Marx. In Chapter Three, section C, we shall show that the reflective consciousness was for Marx simultaneously a moment of man's 'practical-critical' activity.[141] The thought always enters into the reality mirrored by it as an essential component. The objective dialectic of economic forces, which according to Marx carries the cultural burden with it, already harbours the spirit of active Subjects.

Whereas in Marx nature and history are indissolubly interwoven, Engels saw two different 'areas of application'[142] of the method of the materialist dialectic. In Engels's version, the moments of the dialectic are divorced from the concrete historical situation, and shrink down into the three hypostatized 'fundamental laws' laid down in the *Dialectics of Nature*, laws which stand over against reality. Hence the dialectic becomes a *Weltanschauung*, a positive principle for explaining the world, something it most definitely was not for Marx.[143]

We have already shown in the previous section that Engels insisted on the one hand that 'matter as such' is an *ens rationis*, since matter only exists in particular forms of being, but that on the other hand, when the cosmological problem has to be solved, matter no longer appears in its particular determinations but becomes the supreme principle. In the final analysis, then, Engels's concept of nature is indeed ontological. This could not be said of Marx, even by his Catholic interpreters who tend in general to represent dialectical materialism as an ontology, provided that they take seriously the specific difference between Marx and Engels. In his book *Der technische Eros*, Jakob Hommes criticized Marxist materialism for destroying its own realistic epistemological position by using the dialectical method. This is an objection directed basically against the subjective moment, against transforming practice, which Marx carried over from German idealism into his theory. Hommes is right when he says that the real things, which according to Marx are reflected in human consciousness, 'no longer represent nature as such existing independently of men'.[144] In Marx, says Hommes, the Object is not posited by the theoretical action of men, but the objective world loses its character as an independent creation, and becomes ultimately merely the embodiment of human action.

The 'ontological' trait in Engels's understanding of nature emerges readily from the basic metaphysical theses cited above. As we attempted to show in the previous section in connection with the natural sciences, these theses do not result from any 'original' problematic but are all socio-historically mediated.

Thus the first comment on Engels's thesis that the unity of the world consists in its materiality must be that the very problem of the unity of the world belongs to idealist philosophy. In Kant, the formal unity of self-consciousness produced the consciousness of the unity of the phenomenal world. The Hegelian dialectic overcame the rigid opposition between the form and the material of knowledge character-istic of Kant's philosophy and thus came a step nearer to what even Kant essentially presupposed, namely the organizing role of social labour. Nature, made to serve the processes of the Spirit, became in fact a unity, identical with the Spirit, a mere 'substratum of domination'.[145] The fact that in post-Kantian idealism the Spirit became a general Subject, not bound to the individual Ego, testifies to the rational, systematizing character of social labour.[146] Marx saw in social production the 'truth' of abstract-idealist production and therefore restored the notion of such a supra-individual Subject. This occurs in *Capital*, for instance, where the self-reproducing whole is described as a 'collective labourer',[147] and where individual labourers figure as the mere organs of this collective labourer.[148]

What brings into existence the concept of world unity? It is real domination, not just a 'long and protracted development of philosophy and natural science',[149] as Engels considered, however much the latter is a component of the former. To speak of the materiality of the world is therefore to say nothing positive. It is only to give a naïve expression to the totally material character of what is naturally given. Being is always 'viewed under the aspect of manufacture and management'.[150]

As far as the thesis of the spatial and temporal character of all natural existence is concerned, it is certainly true that space and time cannot be conceived without things, and *vice versa*. In Marx, nature only appears through the forms of social labour. The school of Durkheim has gone beyond this and, despite the difficulties involved, has endeavoured to show that given the most exacting conditions of know-ledge, space and time are also of social origin.

The situation is similar in the case of the thesis that motion is matter's mode of existence. Like all materialism, dialectical materialism also recognizes that the laws and forms of motion of external nature exist independently and outside of any consciousness. This 'in-itself' is however only relevant in so far as it becomes a 'for-us', i.e. in so far as nature is drawn into the web of human and social purposes.[151]

Engels's attempt to interpret the area of pre- and extrahuman nature in the sense of a *purely objective* dialectic must in fact lead to that incompatibility between the dialectic and materialism which has been repeatedly emphasized by a number of critics.[152] If matter is presented as being, within itself, dialectically structured, it ceases to be matter in the sense required by the exact natural sciences. But it is precisely this type of matter which was supposed, by Engels and his Soviet followers, to provide a basis for their viewpoint.

Discussions on the philosophy of Bloch have shown that the idea of a dialectic of nature working itself out independently of human mental activity and production must necessarily lead to the pantheistic-hylozoic conception of a 'nature-Subject', and hence of course to the abandonment of the materialist position.[153]

The essential categories of Engels's dialectics of nature, such as quality, quantity, measure, continuity, discreteness, etc., are all taken from the first part of Hegel's *Logic*, the 'Logic of Being', which Hegel significantly described as the 'ontological logic' in the *Propaedeutic*. A kind of 'presubjective' dialectic is possible there because in the course of its development the 'logic of being' *shows* itself to be mediated through the 'logic of essence' and finally through the 'logic of the Concept'. Nature passes over into Spirit, objectivity passes over entirely into subjectivity, transitions which are naturally denied to the materialism of Engels.[154]

If the absolute self-realizing Concept ceases to be the motive force of the contradictions (as in Marx), it leaves behind only historically limited men to be the bearers of the Spirit. There can then be no question of a dialectic of external nature, independent of men, because all the essential moments of a dialectic would in that case be absent. Lukács was the first interpreter of Marx to make this criticism, in *History and Class Consciousness*:

The misunderstandings that arise from Engels's dialectics can in the main be put down to the fact that Engels – following Hegel's mistaken lead – extended the method to apply also to nature. However, the crucial determinants of dialectics – the interaction of subject and object, the unity of theory and practice, the historical changes in the reality underlying the categories as the root cause of changes in thought, etc. – are absent from our knowledge of nature.[155]

Before the existence of human societies, nature could only achieve polarities and oppositions of moments external to each other; at best interactions, but not dialectical contradictions. Engels's 'System of Nature', like Holbach's, was a system of mere interactions:

Reciprocal action is the first thing that we encounter when we consider matter in motion as a whole from the standpoint of modern natural science.[156]

But the category of reciprocal action, or interaction, stands, as Hegel said, 'on the threshold of the Concept, so to speak',[157] i.e. above causal-mechanical and below dialectically-conceptual thought. In its strange alternation between the old mechanics and the strict dialectics of Hegel and Marx, Engels's concept of dialectics corresponded to the pre-dialectical character of nature itself.

As only the first intimations of the dialectic are present in nature, those elements in Engels which point beyond the old mechanical materialism do not entirely come into their own. In relation to the naked and in itself undialectical objectivism upheld by Engels in the theory of knowledge, the question as to whether nature's laws of motion are of a mechanical or a dialectical kind pales into insignificance.

These critical remarks on Engels's concept of nature do not imply the view that the concept of a dialectic of nature has entirely to be rejected. We shall rather attempt to show that the Marxist theory itself already contains the dialectic of nature with which Engels believed it had to be supplemented.

In the Marxist view, all natural being has already been worked on economically, and hence *conceived*. The question of the dialectical or non-dialectical structure of this being, since it is 'isolated from practice' is 'a purely *scholastic* question'.[158] The concept of nature cannot be separated, either in philosophy or in natural science, from the degree of power exercised by social practice over nature at any given time. Although even Marx occasionally used the concept of matter alongside that of nature, the 'practical' character of his theory ensured from the outset that materialist economics, not physical factors or speculative notions, determined the reality which these concepts covered. In the *Critique of the Gotha Programme*, nature is described as 'the primary source of all the instruments and objects of labour'.[159] In *Capital*, Marx referred to nature as the basis of 'the material forms of existence of constant capital',[160] the provider of the means of production, and this includes also living labour, i.e. man himself.

Nature becomes dialectical by producing men as transforming, consciously acting Subjects confronting nature itself as forces of nature.[161] Man forms the connecting link between the instrument of labour and the object of labour. Nature is the Subject-Object of labour. Its dialectic consists in this: that men change their own nature as they progressively deprive external nature of its strangeness and externality, as they mediate nature through themselves, and as they make nature itself work for their own purposes.[162]

Since this relationship between man and nature is the precondition for the relationship between man and man, the dialectic of the labour-process as a natural process broadens out to become the dialectic of human history in general.

Chapter Two

The Mediation of Nature through Society and Society through Nature

A. NATURE AND THE ANALYSIS OF COMMODITIES

Nature, as the material with which men are faced, can only be regarded as unformed material from the point of view of the purposes of human activity. The stuff of nature, which Marx equated with matter, is in itself already formed, i.e. it is subject to physical and chemical laws, discovered by the natural sciences in constant cooperation with material production. Man's aims can be realized by the use of natural processes, not despite the laws of nature but precisely because the materials of nature have their own laws. The content of these aims is not just limited by history and society but equally by the structure of matter itself. Which of the possibilities immanent in matter are realized, and to what degree, always remains a function of the level of the material and intellectual forces of production, just as the structure of matter is not eternally fixed. The concept of matter has been continuously enriched in the course of the history of the natural sciences, a history very closely interwoven with that of social practice. For this reason Lenin rejected mechanical materialism's concept of matter, dependent as it is on assertions bound in their content to a historically determined state of scientific consciousness. He adhered rather to Marx's own concept of matter, the dialectical-materialist view that men, whatever historical conditions they live in, see themselves confronted with a world of things which cannot be transcended and which they must appropriate in order to survive.

At the turn of the century when the 'disappearance of

matter' and the future impossibility of a philosophical materialism was being mooted in connection with epoch-making discoveries in physics, Lenin pointed out in *Materialism and Empirio-Criticism* that the philosophical concept of matter is not affected by the historically changing views of physicists on the *structure* of matter. 'For the *sole* "property" of matter whose recognition philosophical materialism requires is its property *of being objective reality*, of existing outside our consciousness.'[1]

Lenin took the view that it was not materialism in general which had become untenable, but only its traditional mechanical form. Mechanics, for centuries a total explanation of the world, had been reduced by the progress of natural science to a mere moment of knowledge, indeed a mere moment of the physical world itself:

'Matter is disappearing' means: the limit within which we have hitherto known matter is disappearing. Our knowledge is penetrating deeper; properties of matter are disappearing which formerly seemed absolute, immutable and primary (impenetrability, inertia, mass, etc.) and which are now revealed to be relative, and characteristic only of certain states of matter.[2]

This epistemological definition of matter as objective reality existing outside and independently of all consciousness corresponds entirely to the definition of matter given by the young Marx in the *Holy Family* from the point of view of social labour:

Man has not created matter itself. And he cannot even create any productive capacity if the matter does not exist beforehand.[3]

In the Paris Manuscripts he adopted a similarly objective viewpoint:

The fact that man is a *corporeal*, living, real, sensuous, objective being and a force of nature, means that he has *real, sensuous objects* as the object of his being and the expression of his life, or that he can only express his life through real, sensuous objects.[4]

. . . A being which does not have its nature outside itself is not a *natural* being and does not share in the being of nature.[5]

Nature is defined here in an entirely Hegelian manner as externality. Nature has essentially the character of things. Man too is a natural thing. Marx, at every stage of his development, owed much to Feuerbach in this connection, in the sense that Feuerbach, whatever criticisms may be made of him, transcended existing materialism, with its largely mechanical or physiological standpoint, by grasping man and nature qualitatively and objectively. For Marx, Feuerbach's superiority over the 'pure materialists' consisted in this realization 'that man too is a "sensuous object" '.[6] Man objectifies himself in his labour, without however 'positing' the objectivity of nature as such. For Marx, to mediate is not the same as to posit.[7] The human essence, he wrote:

only creates, posits *objects*, because it is posited through objects, because it is fundamentally *nature*. In the act of positing, it does not therefore descend from its 'pure activity' into the *creation of objects*; its *objective activity*, its activity as an objective, natural essence.[8]

Themes of this kind are again taken up in *Capital*. Here the economic analysis presupposes the philosophical-materialist view that labour is a process between *things*:

Man himself, viewed as a mere item of labour-power, is a natural object, a thing, although a living conscious thing, and labour itself is the material manifestation of this power residing in him.[9]

Elsewhere, Marx described labour-power as 'the material of nature transferred into the human organism'.[10] Labour, itself only the manifestation of a natural force, is always dependent on a substratum which cannot be reduced to labour alone. Marx dealt with this natural basis of labour in systematic form in *Capital*, too, precisely in his analysis of the two-fold character of the commodity and of the labour embodied in it. The commodity is a unity composed of mutually opposed determinations. As the 'cell'[11] of bourgeois society, it reflects the relation between nature and the historical process at an advanced stage of development of the forces of production. It contains nature as 'being-in-itself' and as 'being-for-others'.

As a determinant of exchange-value, labour is abstract, general and undifferentiated; as a determinant of use-value it is concrete, particular and composed of many distinct modes of labour. The exchange-value of a commodity has no natural content whatsoever. It is indifferent to its natural qualities because it is the embodiment of human labour in general measured by the time outlaid, and all the determinations of nature are extinguished in it.[12] If exchange-value is a 'non-natural characteristic'[13] typical of the bourgeois form of production, in the use-value the commodity confronts us in its 'plain, homely natural form'.[14] The present investigation is particularly concerned with the latter form of the commodity. Use-values are specific natural materials, mediated through specific purposive actions which serve to satisfy specific human needs. Marx defined them more closely in the following manner:

The use-values coat, linen, etc., in short the bodies of commodities, are combinations of two elements, material and labour. If we subtract the total sum of useful labour embodied in the coat, linen, etc., a material substratum is always left, which is furnished by nature without the help of man.[15]

If labour is the formal 'creator of value', the stuff of nature is its material creator. Hence, through what we have already said of the character of labour, the division of natural material and labour cannot be absolute. At the level of the individual use-value, it may *in abstracto* be possible to make a distinction between what derives from labour, i.e. from the activity of men, and what is provided by nature as the 'material substratum' of the commodity. But as far as the world of experience as a whole is concerned, the material provided by nature cannot be distinguished from the practico-social modes of its transformation. The question of the quantitative and qualitative share of man and the material of nature in the creation of the product of labour is one to which there is no general answer for Marx. The fact that this relation cannot be fixed formally is an indication of the dialectical nature of the process.[16] Once created, the world of use-values compounded of labour and natural material (i.e. humanized nature) confronts men as something objective, existing independently of them. The material of nature itself confronted men in the same way in its first immediacy, when it had not yet been penetrated by men. Human productive forces stamp the material of nature intellectually and practically. This process however completely confirms nature's independence of consciousness rather than destroys it. The materials of nature, having undergone the labour-process, remain components of the sensuous world:

The form of wood, for instance, is altered when one makes a table out of it. Yet, for all that, the table continues to be that common, sensuous thing, wood.[17]

The immediacy of nature asserts itself at ever higher stages of the process of production, though now humanly mediated through men. Marx had this relationship in mind when he wrote:

While the labourer is at work, his labour constantly undergoes a transformation: from the form of flux to that of being, from the form of motion to that of objectivity.[18]

In the finished thing which is the result of labour, the motion which mediates it is extinguished. But inversely if the product of labour undergoes further processes, it is reduced again to a mere moment of the mediating motion. What is immediate at one stage of production is mediated at another:

Though a use-value issues from the labour-process as a *product*, other use-values, products of previous labour, enter into it as *means of production*. The same use-value is both the product of a previous process, and a means of production in a later process. Products are therefore not only results, but also *essential conditions* of the labour-process.[19]

This 'objectification as loss of the object'[20] which defines the labour-process has in addition a more general theoretical content. As against Engels's assertion that 'the world is not to be comprehended as a complex of ready-made *things*, but as a complex of *processes*',[21] Marx did not make the idea of the dialectical process an abstract alternative to reified consciousness. One cannot, without falling into error, conceive things in a metaphysically rigid way as finished and unchangeable. Equally however, one cannot dissolve things completely into the moments of the social process which mediates them, for this would amount to the same metaphysical error with reversed premisses. It is a matter rather of unfolding the concrete dialectic of the immediacy and mediacy of objective being in its appropriate forms.

The section in *Capital* which deals with the 'Fetishism of Commodities and the Secret thereof'[22] has, in particular, given rise to mistaken idealist interpretations. Marx showed that capitalist production, in transforming the products of labour into commodities, bestows a 'ghostly objectivity'[23] on the underlying social relations. The commodity-form of the products of labour 'has absolutely no connection with their physical properties and with the material relations arising therefrom. There it is a definite social relation between men, that assumes, in their eyes, the fantastic form of a relation between things.'[24] The products of labour become commodities, and therefore no longer incorporate the living interaction between men and nature, but emerge as a dead and thing-like reality, as an objective necessity by which human life is ruled, as by a blind fate.

Deceived by the 'objective appearance'[25] which results from the social transformation of the products of labour into commodities, the economists have engaged in long-winded and inevitably fruitless discussions about the role played by nature in the creation of exchange-value. In doing this they inverted the real relationship between use-value and exchange-value. It appears to false consciousness that 'the use-value of objects belongs to them independently of their material properties, while their value, on the other hand, forms a part of them as objects'.[26] The natural determination of the commodity appears as social, its social determination appears as an inherent natural determination. The economists are disconcerted,

when what they thought they had just crudely defined as a thing suddenly appears as a social relation, and then reappears to tease them again as a thing, when they have just defined it as a social relation.[27]

Production is always social. It is always 'the appropriation of nature by the individual within and *through the mediation of* a definite form of society',[28] even if the individuals at first pursue their private labours independently of each other. The use-value of the things produced by them is realized without exchange 'by means of a direct relation between the objects and man'.[29] The social character of the private labours which have taken place independently of each other is first revealed in the exchange of the products of labour, i.e. in the total social process. The pre-bourgeois forms of production, whose essence consists in personal relations of dependence between men, are transparent enough to prevent labour and the products of labour from taking on 'a fantastic form different from their reality'.[30] The products of labour do not become commodities. The fundamental form of social labour is here the concrete, particular, 'natural form of labour',[31] and not abstract, general and equal labour.

The specifically Marxist discovery that historical relations are objectified in the form of the commodity can be misinterpreted so as to produce the idealist conclusion that, since Marx reduces all economic categories to relationships between human beings, the world is composed of relations and processes and not of bodily material things.[32] One of the main endeavours of Marxist analysis is no doubt to penetrate the surface of economic reality which has hardened into things in order to get at the essence behind it – the social relations of men. But as we have already revealed, for Marx these relations are not something final and absolute. It emerges from the analysis of the process of production, on which rests the sphere of circulation, that human labour does not constitute the sole 'creator' of material wealth. The mode of existence of abstract-general labour, its 'form of appearance',[33] is always the concrete-particular, and presupposes a natural substratum irreducible to human social determinations. All social relations are mediated through natural things, and *vice versa*. They are always relations of men 'to each other and to nature'.[34]

Nature can neither be dissolved into the moments of a metaphysically conceived 'Spirit' nor can it be reduced to the historical modes of its appropriation in practice. Lukács succumbed to this neo-Hegelian 'actualist' view in *History and Class Consciousness*, in other respects important for the history of the interpretation of Marx. In the course of his comprehensive discussion of the philosophical aspects of the fetishism of commodities, he remarks about Marx's concept of nature:

Nature is a societal category. That is to say, whatever is held to be natural at any given stage of social development, however this nature is related to man and whatever form his involvement with it takes, i.e. nature's form, its content, its range and its objectivity are all socially conditioned.[35]

Lukács pointed correctly to the socio-historical conditioning of all natural consciousness as also of phenomenal nature itself. But in Marx nature is not *merely* a social category. It cannot be totally dissolved into the historical processes of its appropriation in respect of form, content, extent and objectivity. If nature is a social category, the inverted statement that society is a category of nature is equally valid. Although nature and its laws subsist independently of all human consciousness and will for the materialist Marx, it is only possible to formulate and apply statements about nature with the help of social categories. The concept of a law of nature is unthinkable without men's endeavours to master nature. The socially imprinted character of nature and nature's autonomous role constitute a unity within which the Subject by no means plays the part of 'creator' assigned to it by Lukács. The material world, 'filtered'[37] through human labour and not actually created by it, remains that repeatedly mentioned 'substratum . . ., which is furnished without the help of man'.[38] The theoretical and practical supersession of alienation (*Entfremdung*) aimed at by Marx did not signify, as with Hegel, the supersession of objectivity as such, but rather of its alienated character.[39] In the *Phenomenology*, the Hegelian Spirit, in the course of its advance to ever higher stages of development, grasps the external world of object-forms as mere appearance, grasps the world as something posited by itself, until finally, at the stage of absolute knowledge, reflecting on the totality of the moments it has traversed, it returns completely from its alienation (*Entäusserung*) into itself. Marx, viewing the Spirit solely in its relation to finite and transient human beings (a view held also by Feuerbach), criticized Hegel's philosophy as a colossal subjectivism, according to which absolute self-consciousness lies at the basis of all objectivity.[40] Hegelian speculation, Marx thought, was concerned less with the fact that the human essence objectifies itself in a manner opposed to itself (Marx was thinking here of the real division between the products of labour and their producers) than with the fact that it 'objectifies itself by distinction from and in opposition to abstract thought' – constitutes 'the essence of alienation as it is posited and as it has to be superseded'.[41]

As opposed to this, the Marxist view is that the supersession of alienation takes place not in philosophy but with socialism, since socialism is the highest form of real mediation between man and nature. With socialism, nature's objectivity does not simply disappear, even when it is adequate to men, but remains something external, to be appropriated. In other words, men will always have to work:

So far, therefore, as labour is a creator of use-values, i.e. is useful labour, it is a necessary condition, independent of all forms of society, for the existence of human beings; it is an eternal nature-imposed necessity, through which is mediated the metabolic interaction between man and nature, i.e. human life itself.[42]

Marx made still more use of philosophical categories in the *Grundrisse*,[43] where he developed the theme of the indissoluble connection between nature's dependence on men, and its independence.

In their formative and functional activity, men transcend the natural-born, abstract immediacy of material existence. Marx, like Hegel, regarded productive activity as consumption as well, which used up both the material worked on and the activity of work.[44] Work is not just a spiritual but also a physical negation of the immediate, a negation which is also a negation of the negation, since nature's material objectivity is restored after it has undergone men's theoretical and practical activity.

The process of production has three abstract moments: raw material and the instruments of labour (which together comprise matter in this context), and form which, as labour, constitutes a material relation among moments themselves material. Not only the raw material worked, but also the instrument applied to it are translated from possibility to actuality through labour and absorbed through labour's relation to the material. The three moments of the process are as much annihilated as reproduced in the 'neutral product'[45] of labour:

The whole process appears therefore as *productive consumption*, i.e. as consumption which ends neither in *nothing* nor in the mere subjectification of the objective, but is itself again posited as an *object*. The consumption is not a simple consumption of the material, but a consumption of consumption itself; in the supersession of the material it is the supersession of this supersession and hence the *positing* of the same. The FORMATIVE [this word is written in capitals in Marx's text, A.S.] activity consumes the object and consumes itself, but it only consumes the given form of the object, in order to give it a new objective form, and it consumes itself only in its subjective form as activity. It consumes the objective character of the object (its indifference towards the form) and the subjective character of the activity. It forms the one, while materializing the other. However, as a *product* the result of the process of production is a *use-value*.[46]

All materials of nature appropriated through labour are use-values. But not all use-values are appropriated, i.e. humanly mediated, materials of nature. Air, water and so on, are furnished without human intervention, just like the rest of nature. Their useful character for men does not depend on labour. The means of labour, the instrument of production, is in general 'a thing or a complex of things which the labourer interposes between himself and the object of his labour, and which serves to *conduct* his activity to that object'.[47] The instrument of production is itself already a use-value, a 'combination of natural substances with human labour'.[48] As, however, the labour-process originally only takes place between man and the earth, the 'universal object'[49] of labour, there always enter into it means of production which are not themselves products, and therefore do not present any combination of natural substances and human action, although the whole of nature only takes on significance in the particular historical framework of social processes. These means of production bring forth use-values without at the same time bringing forth exchange values.

All labour begins by 'separating things from their immediate connection with the environment',[50] by felling timber or by extracting ores from their veins. Most of the objects of labour men deal with are however already 'filtered'[51] through previous labour. They are 'raw material'. The raw materials can now contribute to the creation of a product as the 'principal substance' or as an 'accessory'.[52] Whether a use-value functions as raw material, means of labour or product, depends entirely on the role it plays in the labour-process.

A use-value attains to its actual determination by being negated. It maintains itself while being consumed. If it enters into further processes of production as already modified material, it shows itself to be still as it were an 'untrue existence' of nature for man, to be still insufficiently mediated, still inadequately adapted to his needs. The labour which is here already objectified, rigidified into a thing, is revivified when the material in which it was incorporated is subjected to further treatment. The previous mediated immediacy is dissolved, submerged, in the new, richer use-values,[53] the 'more mediated immediacies':

Living labour must seize upon these things, awaken them from the dead, and transform them from merely possible to real and effective use-values. Bathed in the fire of labour, appropriated as its organic parts, and made alive for the performance of their conceptual and utilitarian functions in the process, they are in truth consumed, but consumed with a purpose. Their purpose is to act as the constituent elements of new use-values, of new products, which are capable of entering, as means of subsistence, into individual consumption, or, as means of production, into some new labour-process.[54]

While individual consumption consumes use-values as the means of subsistence of the living individual, productive consumption consumes them as 'the means whereby labour, the labour-power of the living individual, is enabled to act'.[55] In order to maintain the products of past labour in their objective existence as use-values, it is necessary for them to remain in contact with living labour, to be 'thrown'[56] (as Marx put it) into the labour-process as the results and the conditions of existence of that process.

If the possibilities inherent in a use-value are realized neither in the sense of individual nor in that of productive consumption, if it is not put to the service of human purposes, it reverts to the sphere of the 'metabolism of nature'.[57] The artificial, humanized, 'second' nature which was erected on the basis of the first nature is transformed back into the latter. The 'transformation' of the materials of nature by men is undone by the destructive force of the extra-human influences exerted by nature. Every breakers' yard confirms the Marxist notion that 'the continuous absorption of the individualized [i.e. what has been appropriated by man, A.S.] into the elemental is just as much a moment of the natural process as is the continuous individualization of the elemental'.[58]

Marx interpreted this natural process of the decay of use-values not applied to human purposes in another way as well, which is just as relevant for the understanding of his philosophy. We have repeatedly pointed out so far that for Marx use-values are combinations of two elements, the stuff of nature and the labour which shapes it. It is true that nature has 'slumbering powers', and that its own forms can be reshaped by man. However, this does not mean that the combined concept of matter and nature (both of which are included in pre-human nature) becomes a 'semi-mythical Nature-Subject',[60] and thus restores the Hegelian identity of Subject and Object, which Marx criticized, indeed, from a materialist point of view. Nature, the material of the world, which comprises both the Subject and the Object of labour, is not a homogeneous substratum. The moment of non-identity is retained under all social conditions, precisely on the basis of labour, which nevertheless, on the other hand, unites the Subject and the Object. The view that physical nature's 'meaning . . . has at the present not yet appeared' and that this meaning 'like that of men is still in a position of utopian latency'[61] only has a place in an eschatologically oriented metaphysic such as that of Bloch.

In relation to the problem we are discussing here, the non-identity of Subject and Object has the consequence that the human form is indifferent towards the stuff of nature, that it remains external to it. This is particularly noticeable when a use-value is subjected to the process of natural decay.

Marx strongly emphasized this mutual indifference of form and material. He wrote in the *Grundrisse* of the distinction between the natural form of the material, which all labour must take as its starting-point, and its determinate form, as mediated through men:

The indifference of material towards form develops from mere objectified labour-time, in whose objective existence labour only continues to subsist as the vanished, *external form* of its natural substance. The form is itself external to the substance (as the form of the table is external to the wood, or the form of the roller is external to the iron), in other words it merely exists in the external form of the material. The material does not maintain its form through any living, immanent law of reproduction, in the way that the tree maintains its form as a tree. The form exists only as a form external to the material, or only Materially [Marx's capitalization]. For example, wood maintains itself in the definite form of a tree, because this form is a form of wood; whereas in the case of a table its form is an accidental property of the wood, not the immanent form of its substance. When the material is destroyed, therefore, the form is destroyed along with it.[62]

With the destruction of the use-value, the quantum of labour embedded in its material is similarly lost.

We are dealing here, of course, with a merely relative indifference of form towards material. In the above-mentioned instance, where a product composed of natural material and labour is incorporated into further labour-processes, the amount and type of labour already concealed within the product is by no means a matter of indifference:

The quantity of *objectified labour* is maintained by the maintenance of its *quality as a source of use-values for further labour* through contact with living labour.[63]

It is characteristic of the simple process of production that in it the qualitative determinacy of the labour already expended continues to be upheld. This maintenance of quality in the process of creating value simultaneously involves the maintenance of the quantity of labour. It is true that living labour adds a new quantity of labour to that already objectified. But it is not the added quantity of labour which maintains the objectified labour, rather it is labour's quality as living labour in general. When added to the product, it transcends the mutual indifference of the form and the material subsisting within it:

The objectified labour ceases to exist as something dead, a form external to, indifferent to the material, since it is again posited as a moment of living labour; as a relation of living labour to itself in an objective material, as the *objectivity* of living labour (as Means and Object) (the *objective* conditions of living labour). In this way living labour, through its realization in the material, transforms it, and this transformation (which is determined by the purpose of the labour and the activity engaged on with a view to achieving that purpose, and which does not, as in a dead object, posit the form as external to the material, a mere fading reflection of its existence) maintains the material in a definite form, and subjects changes in that form to the purpose of the labour. Labour is the living, shaping fire; it represents the impermanence of things, their temporality, in other words their formation in the course of living time.[64]

The material which has been worked on assumes a form more suitable to human consumption as stage follows stage in the process of production, 'until at last it acquires a form in which it can be the direct object of consumption, in which the consumption of the material and the abolition of its form results from its enjoyment by man, and in which its transformation is its utilization'.[65]

The material's highest form of mediation is at the same time the highest form of its immediate existence as a use-value for men. As far as possible, human labour transforms the in-itself of nature into a for-us.

B. THE METABOLISM OF MAN AND NATURE: HISTORICAL DIALECTIC AND 'NEGATIVE' ONTOLOGY

In the Paris Manuscripts, while under the influence of Feuerbach and Romanticism, Marx portrayed labour as a process of progressive humanization of nature, a process which coincided with the naturalization of man. He therefore saw in history, stamped as it is with the imprint of human labour, a clearer and clearer equivalence between naturalism and humanism.[66] The later, and more critical, Marx of the economic analyses took the view that the struggle of man with nature could be transformed but not abolished. In this connection, he made use of the term 'metabolism',[66a] which, for all its scientific air, is none the less speculative in character. This 'metabolism' is subject to laws of nature anterior to man. Any attempt to form the stuff of nature must take heed of the regularities proper to matter. 'Man can only proceed in his production in the same way as nature itself, that is he can only alter the *forms of the material*.'[67] The alteration of the forms can itself only take place with the help of natural forces, amongst which Marx also counted the active human Subjects.

By releasing the 'slumbering powers'[68] of the material of nature, men 'redeem' it: changing the dead 'in-itself' into a living 'for-itself', they so to speak lengthen the series of objects brought forth in the course of the history of nature, and continue it at a qualitatively higher level. Nature propels forward its process of creation by the agency of human labour. Revolutionary practice therefore assumes a 'cosmic'[69] as well as a social significance.

It is very remarkable that here, where Marx described human labour as the alteration of the form of matter in accordance with its natural laws,[70] he also had in view a very general philosophical state of affairs: the world is matter in motion in definite forms. Marx agreed with Engels[71] on this point, at least *in abstracto*. This appears from his selecting the following quotation from the book *Meditazioni sulla Economia Politica*, by the Italian economist Pietro Verri, published in 1773, as corroboration of the view quoted above, that man can only proceed in his production in the same way as nature itself:

All the phenomena of the universe, whether produced by the hand of man or by the general laws of physics, are not in fact *newly-created* but result *solely* from a transformation of existing material. *Composition* and *division* are the only elements, which the human spirit finds again and again when analysing the notion of reproduction; and this is equally the case with the reproduction of value ... and of riches, when earth, air, and water become transformed into corn in the fields, or when through the hand of man the secretions of an insect turn into silk, or certain metal parts are arranged to construct a repeating watch.[72]

While natural processes independent of men are essentially transformations of material and energy, human production itself does not fall outside the sphere of nature. Nature and society are not rigidly opposed. The socially active man

confronts the material of nature as one of her own forces. He sets in motion arms and legs, head and hands, the natural forces of his body, in order to appropriate the material of nature in a form suitable for his own needs. By thus acting through this motion on the nature which is outside him and changing it, he at the same time changes his own nature.[73]

The content of this metabolic interaction is that nature is humanized while men are naturalized. Its form is in each case historically determined. Labour-power, that 'material of nature transferred to a human organism',[74] acts on the materials of nature which are outside man; it is therefore through nature that nature is transformed. Men incorporate their own essential forces into natural objects which have undergone human labour. Through the same process, natural things gain a new social quality as use-values, increasing in richness in the course of history.

In referring to 'the motion of man on nature' Marx was seeking to express the view that the things which serve to satisfy human needs undergo a qualitative change. For dialectical as opposed to mechanical materialism, motion, that essential category of dialectical thought, is 'not merely a change of place, but also, in fields higher than mechanics, a change of quality'.[75]

There is thus a qualitative distinction between appropriated natural materials and those not yet subjected to human activity. We must remember, however, that even the most ingenious human discoveries can only unfold the possibilities latent within nature. Only on this basis can there take place the 'transformation', the 'composition and division' referred to by Verri. Only in this way can quantitative lead to qualitative changes. Nature is, and remains, the only substance *by means of which* and *in which* man's labour can be embodied'.[76]

With the concept of 'metabolism' Marx introduced a completely new understanding of man's relation to nature. At first he shared Bacon's view, which was inherited and developed by the Enlightenment, that nature should be seen essentially from the point of view of its usefulness to man. However, when he engaged on his analysis of the social life-process, thus concretizing the concept of appropriation, Marx went far beyond all the bourgeois theories of nature presented by the Enlightenment. The epoch of the Enlightenment was incapable of analysing labour as the means of appropriation, of moving from this to the necessity of the division of labour and the accompanying class divisions, and finally of revealing with this analysis the class character of bourgeois society, since this was an epoch 'when the bourgeoisie posited itself as an absolute, and viewed the concept of class, if it did so at all, purely as a moment of past history'.[77] Hence the real background of the Marxist concept of metabolism did not even enter the field of vision of the Enlightenment. Nature was seen as something immediately given, instantly capable of apprehension, whereas Marx stated that:

The object of labour can only become raw material when it has already undergone a change mediated through labour.[78]

The whole of nature is socially mediated and, inversely, society is mediated through nature as a component of total reality. The hidden nature-speculation in Marx characterizes this side of the connection. The different economic formations of society which have succeeded each other historically have been so many modes of nature's self-mediation. Sundered into two parts, man and material to be worked on, nature is always present to itself in this division.[79] Nature attains self-consciousness in men, and amalgamates with itself by virtue of their theoretical-practical activity. Human participation in something alien and external to them appears at first to be something equally alien and external to nature; but in fact it proves to be a 'natural condition of human existence', which is itself a part of nature, and it therefore constitutes nature's self-movement.

Only in this way can we speak meaningfully of a 'dialectic of nature'. Unlike Engels (who agreed for once with Feuerbach on this), Marx the nature-dialectician did not limit himself to contemplating pre-human nature and its history, viewing reality only 'in the form of the Object',[80] nor, despite his admiration for Hegel, did he view reality 'in the form of the Subject'. He insisted instead on the indivisibility of the two moments. The awareness of this indivisibility lies at the core of Marx's materialism.[81] Marx's

Subject-Object, in contrast to Hegel's, is never entirely incorporated into the Subject.

The nature-speculation inherent in Marx referred to above is nothing but an attempt, which runs through the whole of his work, to provide an appropriate concept for the mutual interpenetration of nature and society within the natural whole. To this end Marx used new and in part peculiarly biological metaphors, of which the expression 'metabolism', used throughout *Capital*, seems finally to have been chosen as the best formulation.

Nature appears in the Paris Manuscripts, with reference to Hegel's *Phenomenology of Mind*, as 'the *inorganic body* of man; that is to say nature, excluding the human body itself'.[82] It is his body, 'with which he must remain in continuous interaction in order not to die'.[83] Just as in living nature assimilation changes the inorganic into the organic, so man assimilates that 'inorganic body' in his work and converts it in an ever-increasing measure into an 'organic' part of himself. Man can only do this, however, because he himself belongs *directly* to nature, which is by no means a purely external world entirely separated from his internal characteristics:

The interdependence of the physical and mental life of man with nature has the meaning that nature is interdependent with itself, for man is part of nature.[84]

Whereas the animal is bound, in his appropriation of the world of objects, to the biological peculiarities of his species, and hence confined to definite regions of the world, the universality of man is signified by the fact that he can appropriate, at least potentially, the whole of nature. Through labour he can make nature 'his inorganic body, both as a direct means of life and as the matter, the object, and the instrument of his life-activity'.[85] Whether as the end-product or the starting-point of labour, nature retains its 'inorganic', self-sufficient objectivity. Yet man, unlike the animal, 'is free in the face of his product',[86] because his relation to nature does not consist purely in the satisfaction of immediate physical needs:

Animals construct only in accordance with the standards and needs of the species to which they belong, while man knows how to produce in accordance with the standards of every species and knows how to apply the appropriate standard to the object. Thus man constructs also in accordance with the laws of beauty.[87]

Man 'lives' from nature; this point has not only a biological but also and above all a social significance. It is only the social life-process which makes possible man's biological species-life.

In the *Grundrisse*, as well as in the final version of *Capital*, Marx used terms of a somewhat ontological flavour to describe the appropriation of the material world. The earth is described in the *Grundrisse* as the 'laboratory',[88] the 'primitive instrument',[89] and the 'primitive condition of production',[90] and in *Capital* as 'the original larder' and 'the original tool house'.[91] Moreover, the theme of the Paris Manuscripts that nature is the inorganic body of man appears again in the *Grundrisse* in a remarkably more concrete form in the course of the analysis of the origin of property:

What M. Proudhon calls the *extra-economic* origin of property . . . is the pre-bourgeois relation of the individual to the objective conditions of labour, and first of all to the *natural* objective conditions of labour; because, as the working Subject is a natural individual, having a natural existence, the first objective condition of his labour appears as nature, i.e. as earth, his inorganic body. The individual himself is not only the organic body of nature, but also *this inorganic nature as a Subject*.[92]

Marx's statement that man is as yoked to his natural existence as to his body is not applied here to the labour-process in general, but only to its pre-bourgeois forms. Under slavery and serfdom there is basically no division between labour and its natural preconditions. Both moments merge to form an undifferentiated *natural basis* for the existence of the slave-owner or the feudal lord:

The slave stands in absolutely no relation to the objective conditions of his labour; it is rather the *labour* itself, in the form of the slave as of the serf, which is placed in the category of *inorganic condition* of production alongside the other natural beings, e.g. cattle, or regarded as an appendage of the earth. . . . These *natural conditions of existence*, to which he is related as if they were his own inorganic body, are of a twofold, that is to say of a subjective and an objective nature. He finds he is a member of a family, a clan, a tribe, etc. . . . and as such a member

he is related to a definite area of nature . . . as his own inorganic existence, as the condition for his production and reproduction.[93]

This original and, precisely on that account, abstract
identity of man with nature, goes so far that man not only
appears as a mode of nature's organic existence, but nature
appears inversely as 'its own inorganic existence'.[94] With
the emergence of bourgeois conditions of production, this
identity changes into its equally abstract opposite: the
radical divorce of labour from its objective natural conditions. In so far as the unity of man and the stuff of nature is
retained even under bourgeois relations of production, in
the shape of use-values, this is something self-evident for
Marx and does not require any explanation since it is
'common to the most disparate epochs of production'.[95]
What the critique of political economy is interested in and
wishes to explain is something only typical of bourgeois
society, namely the '*division* between these inorganic conditions of human existence and this active existence itself, a
division first posited in its completeness in the relation
between wage-labour and capital'.[96]

Under capitalism the worker is eliminated as an objective
condition of production, and enters for the first time in a real
sense into a 'relationship' with production; for the slave and
the serf this was not the case, since they were merely accidental properties of the material earth. The capitalist does
not appropriate the worker directly, as he would a natural
thing, but through the mediation of exchange, as the bearer
of abstract labour. The worker thus becomes a 'purely
subjective power of labour, lacking in objectivity',[97] and this
power meets its negation 'as a value existing for itself'[98] in
the alienated and objective preconditions of labour.

Marx presented here a significant side of the much-dis-
cussed dialectic of the transition from the antique-feudal to
the bourgeois era. As long as nature is appropriated through
agriculture and is therefore absolutely independent of men,
men are abstractly identical with nature. They lapse, so to
speak, into natural existence. However, where men succeed in
universally mastering nature technically, economically and
scientifically by transforming it into a world of machines,
nature congeals into an abstract in-itself external to men.[99]

On this basis we may glance briefly at the problem of utopia, to be dealt with in detail in Chapter Four: the just society would be a process in which men would neither simply coincide with nature nor be radically distinct from it.[100]

It was pointed out earlier that the analysis of the division of wage-labour and capital in Marx amounts to an analysis of the exchange-value character of the commodity, which is independent of its use-value. This analysis is particularly directed towards the commodity-form of the products of labour in bourgeois relations of production, a fact which allows us to explain what in Marx the dialectician would otherwise be a peculiar circumstance: wherever he described the labour-process as a metabolic interaction between man and nature, he confined himself to an enumeration of its moments, 'purposive activity of labour', 'object', and 'instrument',[101] moments which are abstract because they are valid for all stages of production, and disregarded their specific historical determinations. Where labour appears as the creator of use-values, it is for Marx 'a necessary condition, independent of forms of society, for the existence of man; an eternal natural necessity, which mediates the metabolism between man and nature, and hence makes possible human life in general'.[102]

In Marx's view, the general nature of the production of use-values was not altered by the fact that it took place in the service of the capitalist, and he therefore considered the labour-process 'independently of the particular form it assumes under given social conditions'[103] as a process 'in which man through his own acts mediates, regulates and controls the metabolism between himself and nature'.[104] This does not mean, however, that the Thomist philosopher Marcel Reding, who views dialectical materialism as an ontology, is right to interpret this passage in the sense that for Marx 'the most general structures of man and labour are supra-historical and timeless'.[105]

The change from one historical epoch to another is by no means without impact on the moments of the labour-process. In *A Contribution to the Critique of Political Economy*, Marx insisted that all work done on nature is only done 'within and *through the mediation of* a definite form of society'.[106] Thought fixes general determinations which are common to all economic formations, 'but the so-called general conditions of all production are nothing but these abstract moments, which do not refer to any real stage of production'.[107]

The general, whenever Marx uses this term as anything more than an abbreviated expression for the purposes of inquiry, is always a 'concrete' in the Hegelian sense. It contains within itself an accumulation of particular determinations.[108] When Marcel Reding asserts that Marx describes the 'structure of labour and the labouring man'[109] as invariant, he is losing sight of the equally important historical moment, without which what Marx says remains empty and impotent. It is possible to point to a very striking example of how seriously Marx took the historical dialectic of the identity and non-identity of man and nature. History itself projects into the physiological structure of the human being:

> Hunger is hunger. But the hunger which is satisfied with cooked meat eaten with knife and fork is another hunger than that which swallows raw meat with the aid of hands, nails, and teeth. The mode of production produces, both objectively and subjectively, not only the object consumed but also the manner of its consumption.[110]

Human nature, this 'totality of needs and drives',[111] is only to be conceived as a historical process, involving not the unmediated coexistence of a constant and a variable component, but rather the constitution of the life of the general through the particular.[112] The essence of man arises in each case from a definite form of society; it is 'not an abstraction inherent in each single individual' but rather 'the ensemble of social relations'.[113]

Marx was not a positive ontologist. Yet Reding's ontological misunderstanding is no accident. It is reinforced by Marx's occasional failure to explain the relation between nominalism and conceptual realism, as it is mirrored in his way of handling the relation between the general and the particular laws of historical development. Thus Adorno when pointing out that the dialectical theory does not in fact completely transcend Comte's dichotomy between social statics and social dynamics, had the following comment to make:

Marx confronts the invariant natural laws of society with the specific laws of a definite stage of development, 'the higher or lower level of development of social antagonisms' with the 'natural laws of capitalist production'.[114]

Marx distinguished between the laws valid in general for a social formation and their more or less developed forms of appearance. Beyond this, he emphasized, in a still more trenchant manner, the 'eternal nature-imposed necessity'[115] of the metabolism between man and nature in its abstract moments as opposed to its concrete historical forms. We are not confronted here with a problem to be decided purely theoretically, a problem of the insufficiently determined dialectic of the particular and the general. We have rather to deal with the fact that our historical reality itself, understood at the outset as 'pre-history', is ruled by eternal categories which are relatively independent of all change, so that according to Marx wage-labour has within it moments of slavery and serfdom, just as slavery and serfdom have within them moments of wage-labour: the distinction consists in this, that in the one case labour-power is reproduced directly, in the other case indirectly, through the market. There existed very well-nourished slaves in antiquity; while at present there exist in the most highly developed countries itinerant labourers below the poverty line.[116] What is decisive is that serfdom and slavery can only arise at a certain stage of productivity.

If the labourer needs all his time to produce the necessary means of subsistence for himself and his dependants, he has no time left in which to work *gratis* for others. Without a certain degree of productiveness in his labour, he has no such superfluous time at his disposal; without such superfluous time, no surplus-labour, and therefore no capitalists, no slave-owners, no feudal lords, in one word, no class of large proprietors.[117]

Marx criticized the attempt to connect 'mystical notions'[118] with this naturally conceived productivity of labour, developing instead the view that surplus-value has a 'natural basis' only 'in the very general sense', and that 'there is no natural obstacle absolutely preventing one man from disburdening himself of the labour required for his own existence and burdening another with it, any more, for instance, than unconquerable natural obstacles prevent one man from eating the flesh of another'.[119]

Furthermore, if the productivity of labour is considered in the context of the specific capital relation, it must be remembered that this starting-point is not simply 'a gift of nature, but rather of a history embracing thousands of centuries'.[120]

However, even if the naturally determined productivity of labour ceases to form the equally naturally determined source of the domination of man over man, even if what arose historically can no longer perpetuate itself as something 'natural', life still remains determined by its most general necessity, the metabolism between man and nature.

It is true that this necessity will then have been mastered, and that men will no longer be struggling amongst themselves, but with material nature. Nevertheless, the continuance of this struggle means that classless humanity will also be confronted with something ultimately non-identical with itself, so that, in an ironic way, Reding's thesis of the timelessness of the structure of labour is in fact correct. There is in fact in Marx something like an ontology, although this is to be conceived in a negative sense.[121]

Marx liked to illustrate the necessity of social processes in a somewhat drastic manner by using the model of natural relations. The best example of this is the concept of metabolism, at present under discussion. Like Engels, Marx took a great interest in the advance of natural science in the nineteenth century and its philosophical implications for the further development of the theory of society. The preparatory work for *Capital* took place in the decade between 1850 and 1860, a period in which there flourished in Germany the natural scientific materialism associated with Büchner, Vogt, and Moleschott. Marx and Engels repeatedly and severely criticized this dogmatic and, in general, crudely mechanical form of materialism.[122] This does not however exclude the possibility that Marx owed certain insights to this materialism. As emerges from a passing remark, Marx was entirely familiar with the use made of the concept of metabolism by Jacob Moleschott, the spokesman of the materialist movement. Moleschott, who is today almost entirely forgotten, was first influenced by Schelling's philosophy of nature and Hegelianism, but later (partly through his acquaintanceship with Feuerbach) became an investigator into nature and a physiological materialist with social leanings. In his later years, having himself come more and more under the influence of natural-scientific materialism, Feuerbach regarded Moleschott's work as the fulfilment of his own earlier programme of a 'philosophy of the future'.[123]

Let us take, for example, such popular writings of Moleschott's as the *Physiologie des Stoffwechsels in Pflanzen und Tieren* (1851), *Der Kreislauf des Lebens* (1857), and *Die Einheit des Lebens* (1864). The materialism put forward in these books, and supported with a mass of empirical material, portrays nature, on the model of human physiology, as a vast process of transformation and metabolism. This materialism is still imbued with speculative elements. Since in his view all the being of things was presented through properties, Moleschott did not accept that a thing could have a property which did not simply manifest itself through the fact that this thing was in a relation with another thing.[124]

We shall only quote certain statements from *Der Kreislauf des Lebens*, from which it may be concluded with some certainty that Marx made use of Moleschott's theory of metabolism, not, of course, without altering it:

What man excretes nourishes the plant. The plant changes the air into solids and nourishes the animal. Carnivorous animals live on herbiverous animals, to fall victim to death themselves and so spread abroad newly germinating life in the plant world. The name 'metabolism' has been given to this exchange of material. We are right not to mention this word without a feeling of reverence. For just as trade is the soul of commerce, the eternal circulation of material is the soul of the world.[125]

. . . The quintessence of all activity on earth is the movement of the basic materials, combination and division, assimilation and excretion.[126]

. . . The wonder lies in the eternal existence of the material throughout its changes of form, in the change of the material from form to form, in metabolism as the fundamental basis of earthly life.[127]

... I make no bones about stating this: the pivot about which the wisdom of the present-day world turns is the theory of metabolism.[128]

One point of interest here is that the concept of metabolism, although it relates to the natural context, was clearly suggested to Moleschott by the analogy with the social sphere.[129] Moreover, Moleschott's formulations are strongly reminiscent of the passage from Pietro Verri's *Meditazioni sulla Economia Politica*, quoted approvingly by Marx in *Capital*, where it is similarly stated that 'all the phenomena of the universe' are based on 'transformation of the material', and on 'composition and division'.[130] Finally, and this is the most important point, Marx, like Moleschott, lent the concept of metabolism the somewhat 'ontological' dignity we have mentioned before, when he described it as an 'eternal nature-imposed necessity'.[131]

In order to understand Marx's concept of metabolism we must also refer to the crypto-materialist elements in the philosophy of Schelling. Marx showed that he was familiar with these in a letter of 1843 to Feuerbach, in which he contrasted Schelling's philosophy of nature as 'the genuine conception of his youth' with the 'positive' philosophy of his later years, which he encouraged Feuerbach to attack.[132] He thought Feuerbach's naturalism marked the realization of the 'fantastic youthful dream'[133] of Schelling's nature-speculation.

Moleschott's conception of nature as a process of circulation is also found quite frequently in the early Schelling.[134] 'The first transition to *individuality*,' according to Schelling, 'is the *forming* and *shaping* of matter.'[135] Things are disengaged from their immediate natural context through work, and they take on the imprint of individuality. The process of nature itself leads unconsciously to this imprinting by man. According to Schelling, there already exists an 'organizing process' in nature, which transcends inorganic matter by producing an 'infinite individualization of matter'.[136] Through the mediation of human labour, this individualization proceeds at a higher level:

In common life everything which has attained a *shape*, through itself or through the hand of man, is considered or treated as individual.[137]

In the *Grundrisse* Marx wrote, in entirely Schellingian language, of the 'constant individualization of the elemental', which is as much a moment of the natural process as the 'constant dissolution of the individualized into the elemental'.[138]

The labour-process is embedded in the great context of nature. In the final analysis, nature triumphs over all human intervention, since it is the higher unity of society and the particular segment of nature which has been appropriated. The materials of nature, despite their permeation by man, sink back into their original immediacy. Schelling pointed out correctly that raw matter can only be described as destructible 'in so far as it has assumed a definite form through human ingenuity'.[139]

The concept of the life-process, which is present in Marx's writings from the *German Ideology* onwards, is related in Schelling and Hegel only to organic nature. In the same way, the notion of external nature as the inorganic body of man, as it appears in the Paris Manuscripts, and the description of the labour-process as the metabolism between man and nature, as it dominates the preliminary studies and the final version of *Capital*, belong to the physiological rather than to the social sphere. These concepts of natural science attain a qualitatively new character by being applied to social situations, as a result of the Marxist transition from narrowly naturalistic to historical materialism; at the same time they remain closely tied to their origin, even in their socio-historical application. In the same way as the continued existence of an individual is bound up with the functions of the body, society too must stand in an uninterrupted productive contact with nature. Men pass through the materials of nature, while these materials pass through their hands in the form of use-values, only to be transformed back into mere nature. From Marx's criticism of the abrupt division between town and country typical of the capitalism of his time, it emerges unmistakably that he understood the concept of metabolism not only metaphorically but *also* in an immediately physiological sense. This division, Marx said, severely disturbed 'the metabolism between man and the earth, i.e. the return to the soil of its elements consumed by man in the form of food and clothing, and therefore violated the eternal natural condition for the lasting fertility of the soil'.[140] The conglomeration of great numbers of human beings in the towns had the result both of depriving the soil of an immense quantity of fertilizer, and of endangering the health of the town population. Marx had in view for the society of the future a 'higher synthesis . . . of agriculture and industry', which of course presupposes that the metabolism between man and nature comes about 'systematically, as a regulating law of social production, and in a form appropriate to the full development of the human race'.[141]

As we have tried to show, the Marxist distinction between general and specific laws of history does not imply the existence of two levels of reality, accompanying each other without mediation. Consequently, the *material* side of the metabolism between man and nature emerges more sharply in Marx, notwithstanding his recognition of the historical mutability of its formal determinations. The iron compulsion towards the production and reproduction of human life, which defines the whole of history, has in it something of the rigid cyclical form of nature.

The Subject and the Object of labour are ultimately determined by nature. On the objective side, men remain dependent on at least such basic materials as earth, water, and air, despite the artificiality of the kinds of objects they produce.[142] Apart from this, such an important phenomenon for the understanding of social processes as the division of labour does not simply result from the immanent development of the economy. It is also a response to a situation found in nature:

It is not the absolute fertility of the soil, but its differentiation, and the variety of its natural products, which form the natural foundation for the social division of labour, and which, by changes in the surroundings within which he lives, spur man on to the multiplication of his needs, his capacities, his means and modes of labour.[143]

Marx particularly emphasized that regions with certain geographical and climatic disadvantages tend at first to favour the development of industry more than regions which dispose of a rich supply of the means of subsistence, provided by nature without human activity:

A too prodigal nature 'keeps man in hand, like a child in leading-strings'. It fails to make man's own development a nature-imposed necessity. It is not the tropics with their luxuriant vegetation, but the temperate zone, that is the mother-country of capital.[144]

On the subjective side too, there are natural boundaries which limit historical change. In the *German Ideology*, Marx had already taken as his starting-point the 'bodily organization' of individuals, and their 'relationship with the rest of nature, determined by this'.[145] In *Capital* he dealt much more exhaustively with the question of how far the labour-process is bound to man's physiology:

... However varied the useful kinds of labour, or productive activities may be, it is a *physiological* fact, that they are functions of the *human* organism, and that each such function, whatever its form or content, is essentially the *expenditure* of *human* brain, nerves, muscles, sense-organs, etc.[146]

... A single man cannot operate upon nature without calling his own muscles into play under the control of his own brain. As in the natural body head and hand wait upon each other, so the labour-process unites the labour of the hand with that of the head.[147]

It is precisely modern industry which shows how much the working Subjects are bound to the presuppositions of the system of nature. Labour processes are, admittedly, significantly differentiated in modern industry, in that they change increasingly into 'consciously planned and systematically particularized applications of natural science to the attainment of given useful effects'.[148] However, technology simultaneously reveals

the few *main fundamental forms of motion*, which, despite the diversity of the instruments used, are necessarily taken by every productive action of the human body; just as the science of mechanics sees in the most complicated machinery nothing but the continual repetition of the simple mechanical powers.[149]

It is no accident that Marx should have introduced here a comparison with mechanics, an unhistorical model. In its material aspect, the labour-process does not undergo any change radically dividing the stages of production from each other. This is why Marx expressly stated that the stages of production are distinguished from each other not by *what* is produced but by *the way in which* it is produced.[150]

With the concept of metabolism Marx presented a picture of the social labour-process as a process of nature. We shall attempt to show how far Marx went in this direction[151] and how far he was justified in making use of such an analogy. Since classical times, and right up to Machiavelli and even Pareto, alterations in the configuration of society have been understood as part of a cyclical movement proceeding according to natural laws. We find, just as early, attempts to interpret the changes and mutual interactions of natural objects by means of social categories. A model which frequently appears in this connection is that of the exchange of commodities and money, or money and commodities. Thus, in the dialectics of Heraclitus:

> All things can be exchanged for fire, and fire can be exchanged for all things, in the same way as commodities exchange for gold, and gold for commodities.[152]

In Marx we meet with an analogous conception. The metabolism between man and nature – a special case of the general interaction of natural things – was placed by Marx in the category of exchange and, inversely, he had recourse to the concept of metabolism when characterizing the process of exchange. In the direct labour-process, i.e. the metabolism between man and nature, the *material side* triumphs over the historically determined form; in the process of exchange, which depends on the labour-process, the *historically determined form* triumphs over the material side.

In the Marxist representation of the metamorphosis of the commodity, it is the reduction of the different forms of concrete labour to qualitatively equal, abstract human labour in general conditioned by a specifically bourgeois society, which is dealt with, rather than the directly productive relation of men to nature (as the useful material of their use-values), i.e. the 'natural precondition of human existence'[153] which is characteristic of all forms of society. The commodity possesses exchange-value as the 'materialization' of abstract human labour, not through its subjective and objective determination by nature. The investigation of the creation of use-values through the labour-process does not at first require a characterization of the relations of production within which that process takes place. The historical specificity of an economic epoch appears first through the social relations of individuals in the process of exchange, which are distinct from those occurring in the labour-process.[154] Marx described the exchange of commodities under bourgeois relations of production in the following manner:

The exchange of commodities is the process, in which the social metabolism takes place, i.e. the exchange of the particular products of private individuals, as well as the creation of definite social relations of production through which the individuals enter into this metabolism.[155]

In the process of exchange, the use-value, which is a product of the direct exchange between man and nature, takes on an 'existence as an exchange-value or general equivalent, cut loose from any connection with its natural existence'.[156] Then, through the mediation of this social metabolism, the exchange-value returns to its former immediacy, again becomes a use-value. With the transition from circulation to consumption, the commodity's social determination becomes extinguished and is replaced with its natural determination, since its use-value is independent of the amount of time required for its manufacture.

Chapter Three

Society and Nature, and the Process of Knowledge

A. THE LAWS OF NATURE AND TELEOLOGY

Human nature is dependent on physical objects external to it. Marx never tired of emphasizing that men must remain in a continuous process of exchange with nature in order to reproduce their life. Men change the 'forms of the materials of nature'[1] in a manner which is the more appropriate to their needs, the better they know those forms. The process of knowledge is therefore not a purely theoretical, internal process. It stands in the service of life. Marx saw nothing but an expression of man's self-alienation in the notion that knowledge has a self-sufficient existence, cut off from life, as presented by all contemplative philosophy. In Marx's view, men must familiarize themselves, on pain of destruction, with the 'forms',[2] i.e. the laws, of the material on which they operate, and with the essential nature of the phenomena that surround them. All control over nature presupposes an understanding of natural connections and processes; this understanding grows out of the practical transformation of the world.[3]

The idea that men can only control nature by themselves submitting to nature's laws is already characteristic of the scientific outlook of the early bourgeois epoch. As Francis Bacon wrote in his *Novum Organon*, 'nature is only subdued by submission',[4] and theoretically recognized causes are converted into rules of practical behaviour.

At a more advanced stage of bourgeois society, Hegel[5] identified *homo sapiens* with *homo faber*. Even in his pre-phenomenological phase he was concerned with the relation between the regularities inherent in material and human aims. Labour unites the two moments.

The materialist version of the dialectic owes to Hegel its insight into the more general relation of necessity and freedom, which stands behind the relation of natural law and teleology. The materialist dialectic, however, transcended Hegel's conception of the problem by demonstrating that drives, desires, and aims, and indeed all forms of human interest in nature, are in each case socially mediated.

To attain an understanding of this socially mediated unity of the laws of nature and teleology, it is necessary first to discuss such categories as nature, matter, law, motion and purpose in more detail than in the earlier chapters of this book.

In his critique of Feuerbach, Marx described social production as 'the basis of the whole sensuous world'.[6] He insisted nevertheless that the social mediation of nature confirms its 'priority' rather than abolishes it.[7] Matter exists independently of men. Men create the 'productive capacity of matter only if matter is presupposed'.[8] Lenin was therefore in line with Marx's own thought when, in his pamphlet *The Agrarian Question and the 'Critics of Marx'*, he attacked the notion held by the vulgar economists that human labour could *replace* the forces of nature:

Speaking generally, it is as impossible to replace the forces of nature by human labour as it is to substitute pounds for yards. Both in industry and in agriculture, man can only utilize the forces of nature, once he has understood their mode of operation, and he can *facilitate* their exploitation by means of machinery, tools, etc.[9]

The laws proper to the material of nature, laws which all human social endeavours must reckon with, are neither ignored nor fetishized by dialectical materialism.[10]

There is considerable confusion in existing interpretations of Marx on the question of the self-determination of nature within its mediation. Jean-Yves Calvez attached too much weight to certain statements made by Marx in the Paris Manuscripts, where he is concerned to emphasize the moment of social mediation, as against materialists who have ignored human practice.[11] Thus, like Lukács in *History and Class Consciousness*, he dissolves nature, both in form and in content, into the social forms of its appropriation. Without being completely aware of it, Calvez adopts a curious idealism of procreation cloaked in sociology, which appears particularly in this question of the laws of nature. He writes:

Nature without man has no sense, no movement. It is chaos, undifferentiated and indifferent matter, hence ultimately nothing.[12]

It is hard to reconcile such a formulation with Calvez's statement, made in the same breath, and illustrated with certain passages from *Capital*, that human activity only takes place within the framework of laws inherent in the material of nature.[13]

The interpretation of the Marxist concept of nature given by Georges Cottier is similarly contradictory. On the one side, he correctly emphasizes the 'internal autonomy' of nature, the way in which it limits the possibilities for human action;[14] on the other side, however, and without reconciling this with the first statement, he describes nature, in the language of Aristotle and the scholastics, as '*materia prima*',[15] i.e. as a shapeless substratum, lacking the 'immanent form'[16] ascribed to it by Marx. It is true that Marx also referred to nature's 'slumbering powers'.[17] However, he did not have in mind an ontological substratum of mere possibilities, but rather the physical energies of man and the materials through which his purposes can be realized.

Let us return to the self-movement of matter, denied by Calvez, but unmistakably affirmed by Marx at many different points. The *dialectical* element of Marxist materialism does not consist in the denial that matter has its own laws and its own movement [or motion[17a]], but in the understanding that matter's laws of motion can only be recognized and appropriately applied by men through the agency of mediating practice. The dialectical movement between man and nature which takes place in production does not exclude the operation of the laws of nature (as it does in Hegel). In his sketch of Anglo-French materialism in the *Holy Family*, Marx characterized Bacon's not altogether mechanical concept of matter in the following way, which is reminiscent of Schelling[18] and on that account applicable to his own theory:

Motion is the first and most important inherent quality of *matter*, not only *mechanical* and *mathematical* motion, but still more, impulse, vital life-spirit, tension, or (to use Jakob Böhme's expression) the throes (*Qual*) of matter. The primary forms of matter are the living, individualizing *forces of being*, inherent in it and producing the distinctions between the species.[19]

As far as the consequences of mechanical materialism in the broader sense are concerned, they were not simply rejected by Marx but reduced to a moment of a theory of nature, the theory we discussed in the context of his theory of society.[20] Marx's thought is in fact as far away from bad idealism as from mechanical materialism. The recognition of the relative truth of the moment of naïve realism in nature does not therefore mean a regression to a purely mechanical materialism, as Calvez asserts.[21]

The fundamental materialist tenet could be summed up as follows: the laws of nature exist independently of and outside the consciousness and will of men. *Dialectical* materialism also holds to this tenet, but with the following supplement: men can only become certain of the operation of the laws of nature through the forms provided by their labour-processes. The connection between the independence and the social determination of the laws of nature, understood in the above sense, is what Marx had in mind when he wrote, in a letter to Kugelmann:

It is absolutely impossible to transcend the laws of nature. What *can* change in historically different circumstances is only the *form* in which these laws express themselves.[22]

Society is always faced with the same laws of nature. Its existing historical structure determines the form in which men are subjected to these laws, their mode of operation, their field of application, and the degree to which they can be understood and made socially useful. The power of nature cannot be broken entirely. Nature can only be ruled in accordance with its own laws. 'Far from assuming fatalism, determinism in fact provides a basis for rational action.'[23] As was pointed out in another connection, Marx considered that 'man can only proceed in his production in the same way as nature itself, i.e. he can only *change the forms of the material*'.[24] Engels, too, agreed closely with Hegel on the question of the laws of nature. As he wrote in *Anti-Dühring*:

Freedom does not consist in the dream of independence of natural laws, but in the knowledge of these laws, and in the possibility this gives of systematically making them work towards definite ends.[25]

Following the whole tradition of the Enlightenment, and indeed Hegel too, Marx opposed any kind of naïvely teleological interpretation[26] of extra-human nature. He praised Darwin's *Origin of Species* in a letter to Lassalle, on the ground that it 'not only dealt the death-blow for the first time to "teleology" in the natural sciences, but also empirically explained its rational meaning . . .'.[27] Marx understood the 'rational meaning' of teleology to be that there exists something like a 'natural technology'[28] in the plant and animal kingdoms. According to Marx's interpretation of Darwin the organs of plants and animals are developed in the process of adaptation to and exchange with external conditions, to become 'instruments of production'.[29] Primitive man did not pass beyond the 'first, instinctive, animal forms'[30] of purposive behaviour towards nature. The pre-human history of nature was in Marx's view the precondition for the struggle with nature consciously waged by socially organized men.

Although Hegel ridiculed the opinion which sees the hand of a purposeful Creator in all possible natural phenomena as 'childish',[31] his own idealist philosophy did nevertheless contain the idea of a 'final universal goal'.[32] We have already stressed in the first chapter that it is precisely the denial of such a final goal, and such a previously given meaning of the world, which unites Marxism with the tradition of philosophical materialism and scepticism since classical times, and with all anti-metaphysical, anti-rationalist philosophy in the wider sense. For Marx, the 'world' was not a metaphysically conceived universe, but the 'world of man'.[33] Purpose in the strict sense is therefore always a category of human practice, and here Marx limited himself, as a materialist, to what Hegel called the 'finite-teleological standpoint'. Hegel put it this way:

In practice man relates to nature as to something immediate and external. He himself is in this relation an immediately external and hence sensuous individual, who has however the right to conduct himself towards natural objects as their *purpose*.[34]

In *Capital*, Marx discussed exhaustively the way in which the 'purposive will'[35] of man triumphs over nature:

We presuppose labour in a form that stamps it as exclusively *human*. A spider conducts operations that resemble those of a weaver, and a bee puts to shame many an architect in the construction of her cells. But what distinguishes the worst architect from the best of bees is this, that the architect raises his structure in imagination before he erects it in reality. At the end of the labour-process, we get a result that already existed in the *imagination of the labourer* at its commencement, that was therefore already *ideally* present. He not only *effects a change* of the form of the natural basis; in it, he also *realizes his purpose*, which he *knows*, which determines the mode of his activity, and to which he must subordinate his will.[36]

In *A Contribution to the Critique of Political Economy*, where he presented the dialectic of consumption and production, Marx dealt with the anticipatory character of human intentions in a similar manner:

Consumption furnishes the impulse for production, as well as its object, which plays in production the part of its guiding aim. It is clear that while production furnishes the material object of consumption, consumption posits the object of production ideally, as its image, its impulse, and its purpose.[37]

Labour's purposes are subject to limitations, according to both Hegel and Marx. In the view of both thinkers, those purposes are limited objectively by the material at men's disposal and by its laws, subjectively by the structure of men's drives and needs. In relation to the subjective aspect, Marx went beyond Hegel by working out the socio-historical roots of human purposes, thus giving a concrete shape to his conception of it.

Man mentally anticipates the results of his activity. As Hegel said, this does not mean that man 'wanders around in empty thoughts and purposes',[38] but implies rather that he possesses a general knowledge of the structure of natural objects.[39] Anticipatory knowledge presupposes practical action which has already been completed and from which this knowledge proceeds, just as, inversely, it forms the precondition of any such activity.

Human action is not absolutely dependent on the material. It is true that the will which posits the purpose can only come to realization in and through the laws proper to the material, and that it can of itself add nothing to these laws; nevertheless the material of nature does possess a certain plastic quality. For example, the natural material called wood can form the basis of the most various use-values while remaining within the boundaries of its physical and chemical composition. In the same way, it is possible to invert this relationship to some extent and to create a use-value from many different natural materials, without impairing its usefulness.

A material remains independent of man's ways of shaping it, within the boundaries of its own determinate nature. This statement signifies that the purpose is subordinate to the material, but the material is also subordinate to the purpose. The remarks of Paul Valéry on the relation of the anticipatory consciousness and the given material are appropriate and have an astonishing affinity to the above-mentioned passages from Marx:

Man acts; he exercises his powers on a material foreign to him; he separates his operations from their material infrastructure, and he has a clearly defined awareness of this; hence he can think out his operations and coordinate them with each other before performing them; he can assign to himself the most multifarious tasks and adapt to many different materials, and it is precisely this capacity of ordering his intentions or dividing his proposals into separate operations which he calls intelligence. He does not merge into the material of his undertaking, but proceeds from this material to his mental picture, from his mind to his model, and at each moment exchanges *what he wants* against *what he can do*, and *what he can do* against *what he achieves*.[40]

When man emerges from his mythical subjection to nature, his labour casts off its 'first, instinctual form'.[41] In place of a naïve utilization of nature, solely through the medium of the organs of the body, there emerges conscious production directed to a purpose. This higher unity of man and nature, mediated through the tool, was what Marx understood by the word 'industry'. He agreed with Hegel and the Enlightenment in their estimation of the anthropological role of the tool:

The use and fabrication of instruments of labour, although existing in the germ among certain species of animals, is specifically characteristic of the human labour-process, and Franklin therefore defines man as a tool-making animal.[42]

Man has endeavoured in the course of history to increase his physical powers, taking as his starting-point the hand, 'the tool of tools',[43] as Hegel put it. In the case of the tool, 'nature itself becomes one of the *organs* of his activity, one that he annexes to his own bodily organs, adding stature to himself in spite of the Bible'.[44] With the development of artificial instruments of production, man's control of nature increases both extensively and intensively. It is 'the work of history', said Marx, 'to discover the various uses of things'.[45] Primitive tools and machines[46] are copies of human bodily organs. They show the strength of man's original orientation towards the model of his bodily form. Later tools depart from this model, develop their own forms, 'de-organize themselves'[47] (to use Bloch's fine expression), but remain bodily organs of man, even if artificial, as necessary to civilized life as hand and arm are to primitive life:

But just as man requires lungs to breathe with, so he requires something that is the product of man's hand in order to consume nature's forces productively.[48]

The tool is a portion of nature which has already been incorporated by man. With its help progressively more objects are transformed into 'results and receptacles of subjective activity',[49] more and more areas of nature are opened up. Consequently, the tool undergoes considerable changes in the course of the history of technology:

From being a dwarf implement of the human organism, it expands and multiplies into the implement of a mechanism created by man.[50]

There can be hardly any doubt that the most basic and abstract concepts have arisen in the context of labour-processes, i.e. in the context of tool-making.[51] Hegel, as well as Marx, was aware of the historical interpenetration of intelligence, language and the tool. The tool connects man's purposes with the object of his labour. It brings the conceptual element, logical unity, into the human mode of life. Hegel wrote in the *Jenenser Realphilosophie*:

The *tool* is the existent rational mean, the existent universality of the practical process; it appears on the side of the active against the passive, is itself passive in relation to the labourer, and active in relation to the object of labour.[52]

Marx followed this view in *Capital*, with his theory of the tool as the existing, the materialized mediator between the labourer and the subject of labour. Since man 'confronts the material of nature as one of nature's own forces',[53] the tool is the object through whose activity the material of nature is integrated with itself.

The labourer is not in an immediate connection with the object of his labour, unappropriated nature, but with the instrument of labour, which was for Marx identical with the tool, and which he defined in the following way:

The *instrument of labour* is a thing, or complex of things, which the labourer interposes between himself and the object of his labour, and which serves to *conduct* his activity onto it. He makes use of the mechanical, physical, and chemical properties of some things in order to set them to work on other things *in accordance with his purposes*.[54]

Here Marx directly adopted the theory of the 'cunning of reason' developed in Hegel's *Logic*. The passage he cited from Hegel runs as follows:

Reason is as *cunning* as she is *powerful*. Her cunning consists principally in her mediating activity, which by causing objects to act and react on each other in accordance with their own nature, in this way, without any direct interference in the process, carries out reason's own intentions.[55]

If we keep to the above-mentioned Marxist definition of the tool as the mediator between labour with a definite aim and its object, we can distinguish three forms of tool, according to the role played by each of them in the labour-process. The tool can maintain itself in its identical form, it can enter materially into the produce of labour and, finally, it can be completely consumed, without becoming part of the product of labour.

Unlike Marx, Hegel portrayed the labour-process *exclusively* in its abstract moments, although, as Marx said of Adam Smith, 'wearing from the start the character-masks of the period of capitalist production'.[56] In the *Science of Logic*, he wrote of the tool as a thing remaining external to the object to be worked on and having nothing to do with the product of labour itself. The tool maintains itself in 'external alteration, and precisely *through* this externality' with the result that 'as an *instrument*' it is '*something higher* than the *finite* purposes' which serve 'external expediency':

The plough is more honourable than the consumption it makes possible, and which is its purpose. The *tool* lasts while the immediate satisfactions pass away and are forgotten. In his tools, man possesses power over external nature, although in respect of his purposes he is, on the contrary, subject to it.[57]

Despite his awareness of the historical role of the tool, Marx had a far lower estimation of it than Hegel. He had no intention of deriving any arguments against the satisfactions of the senses from their transitory nature. He was wary of fetishizing the tool in relation to the immediate use-values created with its help, as Hegel had done. The latter's formulation presupposed a situation in which men were turned more and more into appendages of their own uncontrolled productive forces. Nevertheless, it had an element of truth in it, in that most tools remain the same in use, and are foreign to their product. Marx made the following implicit reply to Hegel in *Capital*:

The instruments of labour properly so-called, the material vehicles of the fixed capital, are consumed only productively and cannot enter into individual consumption, because they do not enter into the product, or the use-value, which they helped to create, but retain their independent form with reference to it until they are completely worn out.[58]

Since the tool is itself already a product, already *in itself* the '*unity* of subjective and objective'[59] which was to have been established by the product, and to which nature as a whole has not yet attained, it can also be consumed in the course of labour in such a way that it enters into the material of the product. Marx was thinking here above all of chemical manufacture, in which accessories are added to the raw material, 'in order to produce some modification thereof, as chlorine is added to unbleached linen, coal to iron, and dyestuff to wool'.[60] Like tools in general, such materials mediate between human purposes and the material of labour, without 'the *reappearance* of any of the raw materials used in the substance of the final product'.[61] Instrument of labour and object of labour here merge into each other. Accessory materials in the narrower sense are those not directly applied to the material, which without having anything to do with the product, 'are *consumed by the instruments of labour*, as coal under a boiler, oil by a wheel, hay by draft-horses . . .'.[62]

Lenin[63] stated correctly that Hegel was a precursor of historical materialism because he emphasized the role played by the tool both in the labour-process and in the process of cognition. Just as Hegel overcame the meta physical rigidity which dominated all pre-dialectical conceptions of the problem of freedom and necessity, so also he dissolved the reified opposition between teleology and natural causality. Marx took the view that the cunning of man consisted in his 'use of the mechanical, physical, and chemical properties of some things in order to set them to work on other things *in accordance with his purposes*'.[64] This idea is itself based on Hegel's examination, in the *Science of Logic*, of the categories Mechanism, Chemism, and Tele-ology. These categories are of the greatest importance for the understanding of the materialist dialectic.

Mechanism and Chemism are categories of objectivity, which Hegel regarded as subject to natural necessity[65] because both signify the submergence of the Concept in externality, as opposed to the third category, that of Tele-ology, or Purpose, in which the Concept has a 'being of its own'.[66]

The thesis of Mechanism consists in this, that the natural bodies, with all their differences, have one thing in common, namely that they are indifferent to each other and confront each other in an abstract, external manner. In Chemism, extended to cover a somewhat wider field than that of chemistry by Hegel, natural objects are only in-different in their pure, bare, mere relationship, in their metamorphoses, in which of course they retain their immediate independence. Hegel described the process of Chemism in the following way:

The process consists in passing to and fro from one form to another, which forms continue to be external as before. The specific properties, which marked off the extremes against each other, are superseded in the neutral product.[67]

The chemical process, in which these opposites are mediated but yet remain themselves within the mediation, is *in itself* already what the human labour-process is *for itself*. In view of this, it is not surprising that Marx also wrote of the 'neutral product'[68] in the *Grundrisse* when he wanted to express the fact that in the use-value the material of nature and human labour are bound up together, but at the same time remain external to each other. The neutral, in other words, is divisible.[69]

Nature can only combine with itself after the emergence of organic life,[70] and specifically of man as a self-conscious active Subject because, as Marx said, it is in labour that nature sheds a part of itself and confronts itself through the division into 'material of nature' and the purposeful 'force of nature'.[71] Man's existence for himself consists in his ability to exploit nature's Mechanism and Chemism in order to realize his purposes. Hegel saw in the teleology of labour the higher unity and 'truth' of Mechanism and Chemism.[72] The moments of the process of Chemism return again in labour at a higher level. The labourer and the subject of his labour are external to each other and yet related through the tool:

The teleological relation is a syllogism, in which the subjective purpose coalesces with the objectivity external to it, through a middle term which is the unity of both. This unity is on one hand *purposive activity*, on the other the means, i.e. the objectivity made *directly* subservient to purpose.[73]

Man's finite-teleological activity does not break out of the natural context; it does not need a transcendental principle to explain it, however much, because it is historical activity, it negates nature. Purposes at first foreign to nature do not simply make use of nature, but have themselves natural causes. Natural objects mediated with society are certainly 'transnatural' but not 'supra-natural', to use Merleau-Ponty's expressions.[74]

Hegel, like Marx, was aware of the bad infinity constituted by the compulsion of nature towards the reproduction of life. Hence the following passage from the *Logic* on the result of human labour:

Only an *externally* impressed form has arisen on the basis of the existing material, and it is also a contingent characteristic by reason of the limited content of the purpose. The goal attained is therefore only an Object, which again becomes the means or the material for other purposes, and so on until *infinity*.[75]

The product of labour, the realized purpose, remains 'internally flawed'.[76] The reconciliation of man and nature posited by it is not final. Most natural objects undergo a whole series of manipulations. From the point of view of the next higher phase of a labour-process, the formed material appears again to be unformed. Marx repeatedly emphasized this point:

When products enter as *means of production* into new labour-processes they lose their character of products. They continue to function merely as objective factors of living labour.[77]

This is valid both for the stages of transformation of a natural object, viewed in isolation, and for the relation of man and nature in the history of society in general.

In this structure of the work-situation, with its inter-locking moments of mutual indifference and relatedness, with the dependence of man on the objective world and its laws, and the nullity of this world in relation to man's transforming practice, is reflected the contradictory unity of the moments of knowledge in Marx discussed below, where we shall try to show how – mediated through historical practice – both epistemological realism and socially applied subjectivism make themselves felt in his thought.

B. MARX'S THEORY OF KNOWLEDGE

In discussing the concept of nature of a modern thinker in the strict sense, it is impossible to avoid dealing with his *epistemological position*. With the economic transition from medieval to bourgeois society, nature began to appear, epistemologically speaking, as 'made', rather than simply 'given'. As man's organized intervention into natural pro-cesses becomes more comprehensive, that conception knowledge which consists exclusively of the passive imita-tion of objective structures becomes more inadequate.

Kant's talk of nature as the existence of things subject to laws presupposed a transcendental-philosophical reflection upon the forms innate in the Subject, for only on this condition could an ordered world of experience come into existence. The idea of the conceptual mediation of the immediate through the Subject became a leading theme of post-Kantian speculation, in which the transcendental philosophy passed over into the idealist dialectic. Marx himself did not ignore this problematic, but in his case it is the historical life-process of finite men rather than an infinite Spirit which mediates.

The present work is concerned with the main moments of the historical process between nature and society. However, since the Subject and the Object of knowledge are not separable from each other in Marx, we have repeatedly been brought up against problems which belong to the sphere of epistemology.

An attempt must now be made to go beyond what has been said as yet, and to reflect *explicitly* upon Marx's epistemological position. This is the more necessary, in that the literature still produces a considerable number of misinterpretations. One such misinterpretation identifies Marx with the 'reflection theory' propagated today in popular tracts in the Soviet Union and elsewhere. Another is the view that the critique of the philosophical attitude as such, which undoubtedly accompanied Marx's critique of idealism, implies that he had no interest in or understanding of epistemological questions. Finally, there is the view that ignores Marx's philosophically essential utterances because they are not couched in the phraseology of traditional academic philosophy.

In what sense can we speak of a theory of knowledge in Marx? This question must be answered because his critical theory has been ransacked again and again in search of an epistemological 'foundation',[78] which Marx neither wished nor needed to give, in view of the advanced stage of philosophical consciousness provided already by Hegel's system. Konrad Bekker pointed out correctly in his dissertation that the very criticist question of the conditions of possible knowledge is 'abstract' in the Hegelian sense and lost any object for Marx through Hegel's critique of Kant.[79]

The highest form of epistemology, for Marx as for Hegel,

is the philosophy of world history. The process of cognition should not be described as a relation of Subject and Object which can be fixed for all time. The theory of the unity of theory and practice which is peculiar to classical German philosophy and, in modified form, to the materialist dialectic means that different theoretical reflections should correspond to the different historical forms of man's struggle with nature, and that the theoretical reflection of the struggle should be at once its constitutive moment and its expression.

The abstract moments of any labour-process ('*purposive activity* or *labour itself*, its *object* and its *means*')[80] compose a unity in diversity which is formed anew in each historical epoch. In the same way sensuousness and understanding, intuition and concept come together in changing constellations. The moments of knowledge change as men enter into new productive relationships with each other and with physical nature. The 'division of labour from the objective factors of its existence – the instrument of labour and the material to be worked' on is '*superseded*'[81] in the process of production, and in the same way the theoretical method cannot be separated from its subject.

The knowing consciousness is a form of the social consciousness, and should not therefore be viewed in isolation from psychology and human history.[82] Both the sensuous and rational theoretical functions are an aspect of the human essence which is unfolded in the course of history through labour. In the Paris Manuscripts, Marx remarked on this:

It can be seen that the history of industry, and the developed *objective* existence of industry, is the *open book* of the *forces of the human essence*, the human *psychology* which is present to our senses. . . . No psychology for which this book, i.e. the most tangible and accessible part of history, remains closed, can become a *real* science with a genuine content.[83]

This corresponds exactly to what he said about sensuousness when distinguishing his views from those of Feuerbach:

The cultivation of the five senses is the work of all previous history.[84]

In our discussion of the role of the tool in the previous section, we have already emphasized that the capacity for rational knowledge, called by Marx 'the transformation of perception and imagination into concepts',[85] does not imply that consciousness is a fixed datum, but something springing from history subject to historical change. In the *Dialectics of Nature* Engels underlined the great significance of practical mastery over nature for the development of the capacity of thought:

Natural science and philosophy have up to now quite ignored the influence of man's activity on his thought. They know only nature on the one side, ideas on the other. But it is precisely the alteration of *nature by men*, not nature as such in isolation, which is the most essential and immediate basis of human thought. Man's intelligence has increased proportionately as he has learned to transform nature.[86]

In one of his last works, the *Randglossen zu Adolph Wagners Lehrbuch der politischen Ökonomie* (1879/80),Marx gave a kind of genealogy of conceptual thought. This has still not yet been properly appreciated despite its great relevance for the theory of knowledge. The whole remarkable passage deserves reproduction:

For the doctrinaire professor, man's relation to nature is from the beginning not practical, i.e. based on action, but theoretical. . . . Man stands in a relation with the objects of the external world as the means to satisfy his needs. But men do not begin by standing 'in this theoretical relation with the objects of the external world'. Like all animals they begin by eating, drinking, etc., i.e. they do not stand in any relation, but are engaged in activity, appropriate certain objects of the external world by means of their actions, and in this way satisfy their needs (i.e. they begin with production). As a result of the repetition of this process it is imprinted in their minds that objects are capable of 'satisfying' the 'needs' of men. Men and animals also learn to distinguish 'theoretically' the external objects which serve to satisfy their needs from all other objects. At a certain level of later development, with the growth and multiplication of men's needs and the types of action required to satisfy these needs, they gave names to whole classes of these objects, already distinguished from other objects on the basis of experience. That was a necessary process, since in the process of production, i.e. the process of the appropriation of objects, men are in a continuous working relationship with each other and with individual objects, and also immediately become involved in conflict with other men over these objects. Yet this denomination is only the conceptual expression of something which repeated action has converted into experience, namely the fact that for men who already live in certain social bonds (this assumption follows necessarily from the existence of language), certain external objects serve to satisfy their needs.[87]

Marx's first point against Wagner here, in line with his philosophical development after the *Theses on Feuerbach*, was that man's relation to nature cannot as such be fixed abstractly, that it is not initially theoretical and reflective but practical and transforming. Nowhere else in the whole of Marx's work are the ideas which follow formulated so sharply. They also show that Marx was not, as is sometimes said, a wholly unpsychological thinker.

Production comes into existence as a result of sensuous needs. All those human functions which go beyond the immediacy of the given develop with production. Nature appears at first to be an undifferentiated, chaotic mass of external materials. From repeated intercourse with nature, which is common to men and animals alike, there emerges an initial crude classification of natural objects according to the yardstick of the pleasure or pain produced by them. The elementary theoretical achievement of this level of development is the establishing of distinctions, the isolation of the objects with pleasurable associations from the others. The nominalist classification[88] of natural objects, with the intention of exerting genuine control over them, corresponds to the economically more advanced and hence more organized human group and the contradictions emerging in it. The particular is subsumed under the abstract-general. In the view of Marx (as of Nietzsche) man's 'will to power' over things and his fellows originally underlies his intellectual activity. The Spirit is originally empty. The concepts formed by it are the product of accumulated practical experience.[89] Its value is limited to the instrumental. Despite the materialism of this view, we must insist that Marx did not see in concepts naïvely realistic impressions of the objects themselves, but rather reflections of the historically mediated relations of men to those objects.

If, by their very make-up and interconnection, the moments of knowledge turn out to be differently determined products of history, it follows that a formal analysis of consciousness in the Kantian sense, i.e. knowledge about knowledge, isolated from problems of *fact and content*, is no longer possible. One can only establish what the tool of perception is capable of by applying it concretely to history.

Hegel and his materialist pupils were at one in criticizing the traditional view of the theory of knowledge. It is only necessary to recall the introduction to the *Phenomenology*, which contains the programme for a historical dissolution of the problem of knowledge. According to Hegel, the rich content of the possible relations between Subject and Object is unfolded in the course of the history of phenomenal knowledge.

Marx took this Hegelian idea further by defining the *Phenomenology*'s central concept of labour[90] more closely as concretely socially determined, and by identifying the relation of the Subject and Object of knowledge still more directly than Hegel did with the relation of Subject and Object in the work-situation.

The epistemological side of Marx's thought has formed the subject of much recent research in France. Pierre Naville for example, in his book *Psychologie, marxisme, matérialisme*, emphatically brings out the concrete historical position of the problem of knowledge in dialectical materialism:

> The problem of knowledge – if this problem truly exists by itself – cannot be separated from a whole ensemble of more or less well-defined historical conditions. There is no 'problem' of knowledge until the concrete, practical functions of knowledge have been exercised; and this exercise does not occur by chance or 'in itself', but in the situations which give it its form.[91]

Lenin (who had already concerned himself with the problem of the philosophical content of *Capital* even before Lukács) similarly underlined what previous literature had insufficiently appreciated: the *epistemological* character of the dialectic in its Hegelian as in its Marxist version:

> In *Capital*, Marx applied to a single science [political economy, A.S.] logic, dialectics, and the theory of knowledge of materialism (three words are not needed: it is one and the same thing). Materialism has appropriated everything valuable in Hegel and developed it further.
> . . . Dialectics *is* the theory of knowledge of (Hegel and) Marxism. This is the 'aspect' of the matter (it is not 'an aspect' but the *essence* of

the matter) to which Plekhanov, not to speak of other Marxists, paid no attention.[92]

In the next section, which deals with the content of the problem of knowledge in Marx, we shall show how the historical practice of man in its totality constitutes the logical unity, not only of the subjective human faculty of knowing, but also of the world of experience which corresponds to it.

C. HISTORICAL PRACTICE AND THE CONSTITUTION OF THE WORLD

Nothing distinguishes authentic from vulgar Marxism so much as its relation to the problems resulting from the movement of thought from Kant to Hegel. Marx was very deeply indebted to German Idealism for his whole approach, despite all his critical attacks on philosophy in general.

Thus, in the *Theses on Feuerbach*, he criticized all previous materialism for conceiving reality one-sidedly as an object given in intuition, 'but not as *sensuous human activity, practice*, not subjectively'.[93] Idealist philosophy, in its Kantian form, had shown that the intuitively given world of experience was not something ultimate, but rather the result of the shaping and unifying activities of the Subject. As a result, Marx was aware that a materialist critique must avoid falling back into a primitive objectivism. He therefore had to undertake a non-idealist reconstruction of the problem of the possible coexistence of an objective world of experience and a unified consciousness of it, instead of abstractly denying the idealist view as such.

For materialism, the 'truth' of the idealist concept of subjectivity is organized social labour, the 'real Subject',[94] the 'general intellect'[95] taking shape in the life-process, the effect of 'the labourer in general'[96] who is a composite of the action of individuals.

The abstract conception of the moment of subjective activity had been extended further and further in the course of the development from Kant to Hegel, until it became a speculative construction of the world. A necessary consequence of this, according to Marx, was the loss of the other moment, correctly pointed to by previous materialism, the fact that being and thing-like structure cannot be reduced to thought. The problem of the constitution of the world returned in a materialized form in Marx's theory, since Marx was attempting, by means of the concept of practice, to preserve both the idealist moment of creation and the moment of the independence of consciousness from external being. Marx argued against the old materialism in idealist fashion, and against idealism in materialist fashion. Sartre brought out in sharp relief the peculiar nature of this twofold combat in his essay *Matérialisme et Revolution*:

Idealism and materialism both lead to the disappearance of the real: the one because it suppresses the thing, the other because it suppresses subjectivity. In order to reveal reality, a man must fight against it; to put it succinctly, revolutionary realism equally requires the existence of the world and of subjectivity; better still, it requires a correlation between the one and the other such that one cannot conceive a subjectivity outside the world nor a world not illuminated by the effort of a subjectivity.[97]

Even before his critical confrontation with Feuerbach, Marx objected to the rigid dualism of the epistemological positions which had dominated modern thought since Descartes, and which German philosophy had tried to overcome on a speculative basis. This is how he put it in the Paris Manuscripts:

It is only in a social context that subjectivism and objectivism, spiritualism and materialism, activity and passivity, cease to be antinomies and thus cease to exist as such antinomies. The resolution of the *theoretical contradictions* is possible *only* through practical means, only through the practical energy of man.[98]

. . . We see . . . how consistent naturalism or humanism is distinguished from both idealism and materialism, and at the same time constitutes their unifying truth.[99]

What Marx still described here as 'naturalism' or 'humanism' was a great advance on Feuerbach, despite the Feuerbachian terminology employed, and already contained the epistemological kernel of the materialist dialectic. This dialectic is 'naturalistic', even though not in the sense of Feuerbach's philosophy, because in it nature and society are mutually mediated within nature, reality as a whole. The social Subject, through which all objectivity is filtered, is a temporally and spatially limited component of this objectivity.

Social practice unifies the moments of knowledge and mediates the transition from one to another. Men's theoretical approach is achieved in the forms prescribed by the structure of their work-situation. In their labour, men act at once as sensualist materialists and subjective idealists. They act as sensualist materialists because they have to stand the test of the material, which inflexibly preserves its autonomy, and are bound to the mechanical, physical, and chemical properties of this material.[100] Every physical action they undertake teaches them that they are dealing with real natural things and not with 'aggregates of sensation' as the Positivists or the Machists would have it.[101] They act as subjective idealists when they subject nature to their purposes, always following Marx's exhortation to go over from interpreting existing reality to changing it. 'Consciousness . . . not only reflects the objective world. It also creates it.'[102] By being transferred to industry, nature is annulled. As Hegel wrote in the *Phenomenology*, nature's 'being-in-itself descends to the level of empty appearance as a reality opposed to the active consciousness'.[103]

The basic positions of the modern theory of knowledge are reflected in this *practical* intertwining of objectivism and subjectivism, as it is seen in the dialectic of labour in Hegel and Marx. Inversely, it can be maintained that these basic positions reflect the practical stages of production and the historical transition from one to the other. This latter materialist conception is of course peculiar to Marx in this form.

Since men are forced to rely on material which exists independently of them, there is in fact nothing in their minds but what was previously present to their senses, as sensualist philosophers maintain. However, there is another side to this question, namely the fact that even the passive appropriation of nature signifies its transformation. This shows how Hegel's inversion of the sensualist principle that 'there is nothing in the senses which was not previously in the mind' becomes truer with the transition to the bourgeois era. Men do not passively allow their aims to be prescribed for them by nature, but subject nature to them from the very beginning. 'At the end of every labour-process, we get a result that already existed in the *imagination of the labourer*, i.e. that was already present *ideally*.'[104]

The pre-Marxist materialists, according to whom nature as such, separated from its practical alteration by society, counted as the source of the various forms in which it was reflected in consciousness, failed to realize that even the most simple perceptions presuppose abstraction and contain conceptual elements.[105] All abstraction is based on perception, and perception itself, either of real things or of things subject to anticipatory *modification* in the mind, is based on conceptual operations. It is not possible to distinguish what originates from mere nature and what originates from human intervention in the content of our perceptions. Marx's thesis is that psychology can only become a science with a real content if it is not separated from the history of industry. In connection with this, the psychologist S. L. Rubinstein has demonstrated the dependence of the world of perception and the modes of perception on the forms taken by man's activities towards natural objects:

If we look especially at human perceptions and their historical development, we see . . . the dependence of the form of reception on the form of activity as a dependence of specifically human perception and its development upon the development of social practice: social practice transforms nature and creates the objective being of humanized nature. In this way practice partly calls forth new forms of specifically human perception and partly develops existing ones. The specifically human forms of perception are not only the precondition of specifically human activity but also its product.[106]

Men in their practice do not stick fast at the immediacy of natural existence which they see before them, but go over to the more mediated industrial appropriation of nature. In the same way, they do not remain at the level of the sensuously concrete knowledge provided by perception, but pass on to conceptual knowledge. The latter uncovers the deeper levels of reality and thus proves itself to be 'more concrete' than sensuous knowledge, which is formally full of colour and life but abstract in content since it lacks determinations. Materialism shares with Hegel his insight into the concreteness of the concept, through which is revealed the abundance of the relations and regularities governing the object. One essential correction had to be made however. In materialism, the concept remains bound to the finite perceiving consciousness, and hence cannot appear as the 'demiurgos of the real world'.[107] In the course of his methodological remarks in the introduction to *A Contribution to the Critique of Political Economy*, Marx expressly insisted in opposition to Hegel, that the 'movement of the categories'[108] must be strictly distinguished from the reality reproduced through them. The economic analysis begins with the 'concrete' in its customary sense, with an accumulation of what the Positivists call 'facts'. Looked at more closely, these facts in their isolation turn out to be pure abstractions. Only when really conceptual thought has elaborated the many abstract and one-sided determinations of the given process does there arise something concrete:

The concrete is concrete, because it is the combination of many determinations, and therefore the unity of the manifold. It appears in thought therefore as a process of collection, as a result not a starting-point, although it is the real starting-point, and hence also the starting-point of perception and imagination.[109]

The first immediacy, the 'concrete' in the positivist sense, the starting-point, is identical with the 'concrete' of a higher order in so far as it is proved to be concrete after undergoing theoretical analysis. It does not follow from this that 'the comprehended world as such is the real'.[110] The operation of the concrete concept does not create its object:

Hegel fell . . . into the illusion that the real was the result of thought, which combined itself with itself, immersed itself in itself, and moved itself outside itself, whereas the method of ascending from the abstract to the concrete is only the manner in which thought appropriates the concrete for itself, and reproduces it in intellectual form. This process, however, does not lie at the origin of the concrete itself.[111]

Naturally Marx would have been the first person to admit that the process of knowledge not only represents a reproduction of material relations, but can also determine their character to a high degree. That is true not only for the theory of society, but also, in particular, for the natural sciences which develop into a 'direct force of production'.[112]

It was no accident that the beginnings of a genuine recognition of the laws of nature in the Renaissance coincided with the origins of the bourgeois world. The process of production became to an ever-increasing degree the planned application of the discoveries of natural science; finally it was itself transformed into 'experimental science',[113] as Marx put it in the *Grundrisse*. Individual achievements have less and less significance with the development of this 'experimental-scientific' character of production:

The special skill of each individual insignificant factory operative vanishes as an infinitesimal quantity before the science, the gigantic physical forces, and the mass of labour that are embodied in the factory mechanism.[114]

History compels the reconciliation of 'general social knowledge'[115] with material production. It makes it more and more unavoidable that the human life-process should be brought under the effective 'control of the general intellect'.[116]

Marx agreed with the bourgeois Enlightenment that thought which was not directed towards the accomplishment of practical tasks became merely whimsical. 'Man must prove the truth, i.e. the reality and power, the this-sidedness of his thinking in practice.'[117] Practice means not only the life-process of society as a whole and the revolutionary action which is to emerge out of its antagonisms, but also industry in the narrower sense and the experiments of natural science.

Industry and experiment together form an essential moment of the process of cognition, by providing the necessary checks. 'Hypotheses are not related to facts in the head of the academic but in industry.'[118] The truth or falsity of a particular theory is established, not within conceptual thought, but only through experiment. Hence Lenin, in accord with Marx, made the following demand:

The standpoint of life, of practice, should be first and fundamental in the theory of knowledge. . . . Of course, we must not forget that the criterion of practice can never, in the nature of things, either confirm or refute any human idea *completely*. This criterion too is sufficiently 'indefinite' not to allow human knowledge to become 'absolute', but at the same time it is sufficiently definite to wage a ruthless fight against all varieties of idealism and agnosticism.[119]

In his later study of Hegel, Lenin investigated the epistemological aspect of Marx's concept of practice more closely, and found that the seeds of this concept were already present in Hegel's thought:

Theoretical cognition ought to give the Object in its necessity, in its all-sided relations, in its contradictory movement, in- and for-itself. But the human Concept 'definitively' catches this objective truth of cognition, seizes and masters it, only when the Concept becomes 'being-for-itself' in the sense of practice.[120]

The turn of phrase which has crept into all textbooks of dialectical materialism since Lenin, according to which historical practice is the basis of knowledge and the criterion of truth, only retains its genuine meaning under certain conditions. On the one hand, misunderstandings of the pragmatic type must be avoided,[121] while on the other hand it must not be forgotten that the epistemological role of practice is not exhausted by its retroactive determination of the agreement or disagreement of thought with the Object. In other words, practice must not become a kind of external appendage to theory. In fact, practice in general can only be the criterion of truth because – as a historical whole – it *constitutes* the objects of normal human experience, i.e. plays an essential part in their internal composition.

Of course, the sensible world is also a product of industry. From the simplest object of everyday use to the most complicated machine, it is, in the words of the *Grundrisse*, 'natural material, transformed into organs for imposing man's will or activity on nature'.[122] A fixed, objective world, which makes itself independent of individual men, emerges from the relation of Subject and Object in labour. 'That which in the labourer appeared as motion, now appears in the product as a fixed quality, as being.'[123] The 'sensuous objects, really distinct from thought objects',[124] referred to by Feuerbach and other physical materialists, only take on their character as objects in the strict sense when men, in the course of consuming them productively, rob them of their 'natural' independence.

In so far as objectivity falls into the historically expanding realm of human intervention, it is the result of a process of composition; in so far as it falls outside this realm, it is at least mentally pre-formed. 'Even where one is dealing with the experience of natural objects as such, their natural character is determined by their contrast with the social world and is to that extent dependent on it.'[125] The model of objectivity is for Marx the individual product of labour, the use-value. Like the use-value, objectivity is constituted from two elements, a 'material substratum' which 'is furnished by nature without the help of man',[126] and formative labour. This differs, of course, from the neo-Kantian interpretation of the Austro-Marxists who believed that they had to add an external epistemological supplement to the Marxist theory of history. Nevertheless, there does exist between Marx and Kant a relationship which has not yet been sufficiently noticed. In Marx, as in Kant, the form and the matter of the phenomenal world can be separated *in abstracto*, but not in reality. It is ultimately meaningful to refer to the Kantian problem of constitution[127] when discussing Marx's dialectic, because Marx followed Kant in holding that form and matter are external to one another, despite the great difference between their views on the way the two elements interact. What Kant called 'transcendental affinity', assuming the subjective formedness of the sensuous material and its originally chaotic character, was for the Marx of *Capital* the social formedness of an already formed nature:

Man can work only as nature does, that is *by changing the form o, matter*.[128]

This idea links Marx directly with Hegel, who, also in relation to labour, expressed himself as follows in the *Philosophy of Right*:

Yet matter is never without an essential form of its own, and only because it has one is it anything. The more I appropriate this form, the more do I enter into actual possession of the thing.[129]

Marx adopted an intermediate position between Kant and Hegel, which can only be fixed with difficulty. His materialist critique of Hegel's identity of Subject and Object led him back to Kant, although again this did not mean that being, in its non-identity with thought, appeared as an unknowable 'thing-in-itself'. Kant wanted to use the concept of 'transcendental apperception' to demonstrate, as it were for eternity, how a unified world of experience comes into existence. Marx both retained Kant's thesis of the non-identity of Subject and Object and adopted the post-Kantian view, no longer exclusive of history, that Subject and Object entered into changing configurations, just as the unity of the subjective and the objective realized in the various products of labour nevertheless means that 'the proportions between labour and the material of nature are very diverse'.[130]

One can say in general of the historico-economic process of the transformation of Object into Subject and of Subject into Object, that under pre-industrial conditions the objective, natural moment is dominant, whilst in industrial society the moment of subjective intervention asserts itself in increasing measure over the material provided by nature.

The transition to industrial production means however not only a new attitude of the Subject to its material, but also an alteration of the extent and type of the material entering into the field of economic interest:

The external physical conditions fall into two great economic classes, natural wealth in the *means of subsistence*, i.e. a fruitful soil, waters teeming with fish, etc., and natural wealth in the *instruments of labour*, such as waterfalls, navigable rivers, wood, metal, coal, etc. At the dawn of civilization, it is the first class that turns the scale; at a higher stage of development, it is the second.[131]

In an agrarian economy, men take up a passively receptive attitude to nature, which appears directly as wealth in the means of subsistence:

Land is still regarded here as something which exists naturally and independently of man, and not yet as capital, i.e. as a factor of labour. On the contrary, labour appears to be a factor of nature.[132]

Marx also grasped the epistemological content of this

economic fact, as can be seen from the first thesis on Feuerbach. Marx's objection to Feuerbach and previous materialists was that they viewed nature as a fixed datum, and
knowledge as the mirror which reflected it. In economic
terms, this meant that materialism had not taken account of
the historical transition from agrarian to industrial production, and was oriented to a state of society in which land was
'still regarded as something natural which exists independently of man'. Feuerbach failed to recognize that nature had
meanwhile become 'a mere object for men'.[133] It had long
ceased 'to be recognized as a power for itself'.[134]

With the ever-increasing reduction of nature in modern
times to the level of a moment in social action, the determinations of objectivity entered progressively and increasingly into the Subject. This displacement of emphasis
within the labour relationship towards the subjective side
was conceptually expressed by the principle that only what
was 'made' by the Subjects was in a strict sense knowable.
This principle was at first understood in an abstractly
logical manner, from Descartes up to the German Idealists,
but was given a radically historical application by Vico and
by Marx.[135]

Men use largely the same ideas to realize their own
capabilities by the practical construction of an objective
world and to comprehend that world theoretically. From
this starting-point we can understand Lenin's methodological remark that, in the dialectic, the 'complete "definition" of an object must include the whole of human
experience, both as the criterion of truth and as the practical
indicator of its connection with human wants'.[136]

The question of the possibility of knowing the world only
had meaning for Marx on the assumption that the world was
a human 'creation'. We only really know what a natural
thing is when we are familiar with all the industrial and
experimental-scientific arrangements which permit its
creation.

This idea played a considerable part in the critique of
Kant's 'thing-in-itself' repeatedly undertaken by Engels.
He commented as follows in the *Dialectics of Nature* on the
statement that the thing-in-itself is unknowable:

It does . . . not add a word to our scientific knowledge, for if we cannot occupy ourselves with things, they do not exist for us.[137]

For the materialist theory, as for Hegel, the boundary between the in-itself and for-itself of things, and between the socially appropriated and the as-yet-unappropriated region of nature is relative and historical, rather than absolute. When men register the phenomena of nature, they always also register its essence. In his pamphlet on Feuerbach, Engels made this reply to the agnosticism of Hume and Kant:

The most telling refutation of this as of all other philosophical crotchets is practice, namely, experiment and industry. If we are able to prove the correctness of our conception of a natural process by making it ourselves, bringing it into being out of its conditions and making it serve our own purposes into the bargain, then there is an end to the Kantian ungraspable 'thing-in-itself'. The chemical substances produced in the bodies of plants and animals remained such 'things-in-themselves' until organic chemistry began to produce them one after another, whereupon the 'thing-in-itself' became a thing for us, as, for instance, alizarin, the colouring matter of the madder, which we no longer trouble to grow in the madder roots in the field, but produce much more cheaply and simply from coal tar.[138]

D. THE CATEGORIES
OF THE MATERIALIST DIALECTIC

The question of the relation of the successive historical categories in which nature is represented to its objective structure is part also of the wider problem of the epistemological role of practice. First of all we must distinguish Marx's economic categories in the narrower sense, such as 'Capital', 'Commodity', 'Value', from his logico-epistemological categories such as 'quality-quantity-measure', 'essence-appearance-phenomenon', which are utilized in the economic analysis and stem from Hegel's *Science of Logic*. Marx wrote of the categories of bourgeois economics:

They are forms of thought expressing with social validity the conditions and relations of a *definite, historically determined* mode of production, viz., the production of commodities.[139]

Whereas the economic categories lose their validity with the decline of the historical relations they express,[140] the logical categories, despite their empirical, human presuppositions, have a more general and comprehensive validity. They are historical sediments – that 'ideal' described, rather unhappily, in the Afterword to the second edition of *Capital*, as 'nothing else than the material world reflected by the human mind, and translated into forms of thought'.[141] The categories are mental stages and nodal points of the theoretical appropriation of nature which grow out of living practice.[142] They are always simultaneously the expression both of the structures of material reality and the stages of its practical-intellectual appropriation.

Historical materialism differs from sociologism in its analysis of substantial attitudes of thought, artistic movements, moral conceptions, and so on, in that Marx insisted that the social genesis and the title to truth of an intellectual creation cannot be identified with each other. This point is of still greater significance in connection with the social understanding of the most abstract categorical conditions of thought.

Arnold Hauser is right in saying that the essence of the materialist philosophy of history consists in the thesis that spiritual attitudes are anchored in conditions of production, and move within the range of interests, aims, and prospects characteristic of these; not that they are subsequently, externally, and deliberately adjusted to economic and social conditions.[143] This certainly does not mean, however, that for example all statements about nature only succeed in revealing something about the particular social order in which the statement was made, rather than something about the objective natural context itself. This was how Ernst Bloch represented it in *Erbschaft dieser Zeit*:

The concept of nature certainly expresses in the first place the society in which it appears; its order or disorder, the changing forms of its dependence. These forms return superstructurally in the concept of nature too: thus the primitive, the magical, the qualitatively ranked, and finally the mechanical concepts of nature, are to be understood in large part as ideology. Mechanical natural science was indeed to an especially great degree the ideology of the bourgeois society of its time, ultimately the ideology of the circulation of commodities.[144]

Marx and Engels themselves emphasized the element of correctness in such a view, giving the example of Darwinism.[145] However, it would hardly have occurred to them to say that the theory that nature had to undergo a definite historical development would become untenable with the disappearance of the social conditions under which it arose.

There are occasional remarks in *Capital* about the relation between the mechanistic mode of thought and the period of manufacture:

Descartes, in defining animals as mere machines, saw with eyes of the manufacturing period, while to eyes of the middle ages, animals were *assistants* to man, as they were later to Von Haller in his *Restauration der Staatswissenschaften*.[146]

It is true that in the same context Marx made the critical comment that 'Descartes, like Bacon, anticipated an alteration in the form of production, and the practical subjugation of nature by man, as a result of the altered methods of thought',[147] that in other words the philosophers remained unconscious of their own social basis. However this is not to say that the modern mode of thought was purely an ideology, without being simultaneously a reflection of real nature.[148]

In the *Dialectics of Nature*, Engels dealt with the most important category for the explanation of nature, the category of causality. The conception that two events follow each other with necessity according to a rule is not a mere projection borrowed from the human sphere. Nor is it possible simply to extract the causal law from nature in a naïvely realistic way. The circumstance that men are in a position in their production to establish causal connections, including those that do not otherwise exist in nature, fully confirms the objectivity of causality, according to Engels, rather than makes the category a relative one:

But not only do we find that a particular motion is followed by another, we find also that we can evoke a particular motion by setting up the conditions in which it takes place in nature, indeed that we can produce motions which do not occur at all in nature (industry), at least not in this way, and that we can give these motions a predetermined direction and extent. *In this way*, by *the activity of human beings*, the idea of *causality* becomes established, the idea that one motion is the *cause* of another. True, the regular sequence of certain natural phenomena can by itself give rise to the idea of causality: the heat and light that come with the sun; but this affords no proof, and to that extent Hume's scepticism was correct in saying that a regular *post hoc* can never establish a *propter hoc*. . . . If I am able to make the *post hoc*, it becomes identical with the *propter hoc*.[149]

Men grasp the objectively existing laws of nature through, and by means of, the historical forms of their practice.

Chapter Four

Utopia and the Relation between
Man and Nature

It may appear at first misleading even to wish to discuss the concept of utopia in connection with Marxism. In his own view Marx was not a utopian. He believed that he had accomplished the development of socialism from utopia to science, that he had advanced beyond all fanciful devices to secure perfect conditions for mankind. Throughout the whole of his life he criticized the Utopians: in his youth the Left Hegelians and early socialist authors like Proudhon, Owen, Hess and Grün; later on the system of Comte.

In making his criticisms Marx showed himself to be the pupil of Hegel, since the latter (especially in the preface to the *Philosophy of Right*) had opposed any depiction of a future situation, any empty exhortation counterposed to being without mediation.

What is remarkable is that Marx, precisely because he agreed with Hegel in rejecting the construction of abstract utopias, became probably the greatest utopian in the history of philosophy. As a pupil of Hegel, he was driven beyond the boundary Hegel himself had set for philosophy, which was considered too lofty to be concerned with the historical future.

In Marx's works, there is certainly no lack of comprehension and analysis of what is. This was the procedure recommended by Hegel, as against the elaboration of empty ideals. A serious approach to the given does not however exclude the possibility of making definite statements about the objective historical tendency of the given itself: theoretical statements, which in their content are strictly related to, and themselves form a moment of, the reality which is analysed in the course of its dialectical movement.

Ernst Bloch also understood Marx's unadmitted utopian

consciousness in this sense. It anticipates a future human reality in accordance with the real possibilities embedded in present existence. In his work, *Das Prinzip Hoffnung*, which can be described as a phenomenology and encyclopedia of the forms of utopian consciousness, Ernst Bloch attempted to preserve the concept of utopia, in itself foreign to Marxist thought. He pointed out that in Marx strict analysis of the situation and conscious anticipation of the future together form moments of a historical process, whereas the Utopians whom Marx correctly criticized remained abstract in their approach because they persisted in painting pictures of what was to come without theoretically dissecting the forces in reality which were to surmount its present form.[1]

It is interesting to note that the problem of utopia arose first in the work of Engels, not of Marx. In the *Outlines of a Critique of Political Economy* (1844), the book which, as its title suggests, first turned Marx's attention towards the problems of economics, Engels wrote of socialism that it was 'the reconciliation of mankind with nature and with itself'.[2]

There is no doubt that in writing the Paris Manuscripts Marx was influenced not only by Feuerbach's critique of Hegel but also by the views of Engels, who was then a Feuerbachian. In that work, he made the following comment on communism:

Communism is the positive abolition of private property, of human self-alienation, and thus the real appropriation of the human essence through and for man. It is, therefore, the return of man himself as a *social*, i.e. really human, being, a complete and conscious return which assimilates all the wealth of previous development. Communism as a fully developed naturalism is humanism and as a fully developed humanism is naturalism. It is the *definitive* resolution of the antagonism between man and nature, and between man and man. It is the true solution of the conflict between existence and essence, between objectification and self-affirmation, between freedom and necessity, between individual and species. It is the solution of the riddle of history and knows itself to be this solution.[3]

While stressing that the work of Marx does not fall into two unrelated parts, we can see in the problem of Utopianism how far in advance the later Marx was over the abstract and romanticizing anthropology of the Paris Manuscripts.

It was not by chance that they remained fragments and were therefore not published in Marx's lifetime. Despite his use of history and philosophy to concretize the Hegelian and Feuerbachian concept of alienation, Marx did not completely free himself from Feuerbach's idols, 'man' and 'nature', because he lacked an exact knowledge of economic history. In particular, when Marx celebrates man as a 'real, corporeal being, with his feet firmly planted on the solid ground, inhaling and exhaling all the powers of nature',[4] we catch a glimpse of Feuerbach's sensualist cult of nature, redolent of the atmosphere of *Vormärz*[4a] and also related to the contemporary lyric poetry of Heine. Just as the climate of such problematic joy in nature rapidly disappeared, so also did the remarks about 'man' which present-day critics have tried to fix onto Marx for good.[5] The critical comments on the 'true socialists' in the *German Ideology* and the *Communist Manifesto* can just as well be understood as a piece of self-criticism, and when Marx poked fun in the *Manifesto* at formulations such as 'alienation' and 'realization of the human essence',[6] he was also attacking his own use of them in the Paris Manuscripts. Marx gave up using such terms as 'estrangement', 'alienation', 'return of man to himself'[7] as soon as he noticed that they had turned into ideological prattle in the mouths of petty-bourgeois authors, instead of a lever for the empirical study of the world and its transformation.

The mordant sharpness with which Marx and Engels mount their attack in the *German Ideology* on the strongly Feuerbachian doctrines of the 'true socialists', plainly shows the distance which separated them, even at this time, not only from Feuerbach's anthropologism, his concept of alienation, but also his enthusiasm for nature. In connection with the last point, let us simply refer to the critique of the article 'Sozialistische Bausteine', in the *Rheinische Jahrbücher*, from which Marx and Engels gave the following insipid instance of the 'intimate confessions of a true socialist':[8]

. . . gay flowers . . . tall and stately oaks . . . their satisfaction, their happiness lie in their life, their growth and their blossoming . . . an infinite multitude of tiny creatures in the meadows . . . forest birds . . .

a mettlesome troop of young horses . . . I see (says 'Man') that these creatures neither know nor desire any other happiness than that which lies for them in the expression and the enjoyment of their lives.[9]

As opposed to such ingenuous enthusiasm, which pretends to see in nature nothing but 'a unity of life, movement, and happiness',[10] Marx and Engels did not permit themselves even the slightest lapse into naïvety. In the same way as Darwin, who came after them, they presented the pitiless struggles of living beings for their very existence through the medium of *social* categories. Their materialist understanding of social conflicts gave them a sharp eye for the interminable struggles which take place within organic nature. With biting irony, therefore, they completed the effusive declarations of the true socialist as follows:

'Man' could observe a quantity of other things in nature, e.g. the bitterest competition among plants and animals; he could see, for example, in the plant world, in his 'forest of tall and stately oaks', how these tall and stately capitalists consume the nutriment of the tiny shrubs, which might well complain: we are banned from earth, water, air and fire; he could observe the parasites, the ideologists of the vegetable world, he could further observe that there is open warfare between the 'forest birds' and the 'infinite multitude of tiny creatures', between the grass of his 'meadows' and the 'mettlesome troop of young horses'.[11]

Of course, Marx and Engels were not simply concerned in this passage to oppose to the true socialist's thesis of the harmonious unity of nature the empty antithesis that in reality there is much less harmony in nature than he supposed. They pointed out in addition the psychological and theoretical roots of such an illusion. His 'model of ingenuous philosophical mystification'[12] arose because he 'ascribed to *nature* itself the mental expression of a pious wish':[13]

The true socialist proceeds from the thought that the dichotomy of life and happiness must cease. To prove this thesis, he summons the aid of nature and assumes that in it this dichotomy does not exist; from this he deduces that since man, too, is a natural body and possesses all the general properties of such a body, no dichotomy should exist for him either. Hobbes had much better reasons for invoking nature as a proof of his *bellum omnium contra omnes*. Hegel, on whose construction our true socialist depends, actually perceives in nature the cleavage, the dissolute period of the absolute idea, and even calls the animal the concrete anguish of God.[14]

Marx's definitive renunciation of any kind of romantic Feuerbachian cult, whether of 'Man', 'Nature', or 'Woman', is revealed still more drastically in his review of Daumer's book *Die Religion des neuen Weltalters*, published in 1850 in the *Neue Rheinische Zeitung*. In this certainly classic case, Marxist analysis reveals in a penetrating manner the ideological character of a sentimentality about nature which has defended the opposite of its own assertions right up to the present day.

The reproduction of certain passages from Daumer's concoction is made unavoidable by the importance of this episode for the critique of ideology. This is Daumer's statement:

Nature and *woman* are the really divine, as opposed to the *human* and to *man*. . . . The sacrifice of the human to the natural, of the male to the female, is the genuine, the only true subjection and self-alienation, the highest, nay, the only virtue and piety.[15]

Here is Marx's reply:

We see here that the superficiality and ignorance of the speculating founder of a religion is transformed into very pronounced cowardice. Herr Daumer flees before the historic tragedy that is threatening him too closely to alleged nature, i.e. to mere rustic idyll, and preaches the cult of the female to cloak his own effeminate resignation.

Herr Daumer's cult of nature, by the way, is a peculiar one. He has managed to be reactionary even in comparison with Christianity. He tries to establish the old pre-Christian natural religion in a modernized form. Thus he achieves nothing but Christian-Germanic-patriarchal drivel on nature expressed, for example, as follows:

> *Nature holy, Mother sweet,*
> *In Thy footsteps place my feet.*
> *My baby hand to Thy hand clings,*
> *Hold me as in leading strings!*

'Such things have gone out of fashion, but not to the benefit of culture, progress or human felicity.'

We see that this cult of nature is limited to the Sunday walks of an inhabitant of a small provincial town who childishly wonders at the cuckoo laying its eggs in another bird's nest, at tears being designed to keep the surface of the eyes moist, and so on. There is no question, of course, of modern sciences, which, with modern industry, have revolutionized the whole of nature and put an end to man's childish attitude towards nature as well as to other forms of childishness. . . . For the rest, it would be desirable that Bavaria's sluggish peasant economy, the ground on which priests and Daumers likewise grow, should at last be ploughed up by modern cultivation and modern machines.[16]

Marx showed here that the ideological distortion of man's relation to nature has two complementary sides. One side, and this was of course in the backward Germany of 1850 the more important, was that the deification of the immediacy of elemental nature served the interests of a reactionary opposition to technical progress, which wished to maintain precapitalist forms of production. However, the other side of the ideology of nature was later to prove more effective. In those places where capitalist production had already triumphed, nature was glorified as a refuge in face of capitalism's ever more ruthless pillaging. From the level of a theoretical consciousness which has applied its concepts to the latest stages of the disastrous dialectic of industrial development, Horkheimer and Adorno say the following in their *Dialektik der Aufklärung*:

Precisely because the social mechanism of domination seizes onto nature as a wholesome contrast to society, nature itself is bartered away and rendered unwholesome. The pictorial assertion that the trees are green, the sky is blue, and the clouds move across it, makes them straight away into the coded equivalents of factory chimneys and petrol stations.[17]

The polemic against Daumer was directed first of all against patriarchal glorification of precapitalist production; the progress of capitalist technology was viewed initially as an advance in enlightenment. For historical reasons, Marx was not completely aware of the other aspect, the glorification of subjugated nature. That he had grasped the essence of this side of the problem is evident, however, from his sharp criticism of Daumer's cult of 'Woman':

Herr Daumer naturally does not say a word about the present social situation of women; on the contrary it is a question only of the female as such. He tries to console women for their social distress by making them the object of a cult in words which is as empty as it would fain be mysterious. Thus he puts them at ease over the fact that marriage puts an end to their talents through their having to take care of the children by telling them that they can suckle babes until the age of sixty, and so on. Herr Daumer calls this the 'sacrificing of the male to the female'.[18]

Real humanism is not concerned with ultimate metaphysical concepts, whether idealist or materialist. The social emancipation it strives for serves the interests of real, individual men. A letter of 21 June 1856 from Marx to his wife shows this in a very striking manner:

But love, not the love of Feuerbach's Man nor Moleschott's metabolism, nor again love of the proletariat, but love of the beloved and more particularly of you, makes a man a man again.[19]

In the years of his maturation and maturity, Marx devoted himself to the historical analysis of capitalist relations of production, unencumbered not only by Feuerbach's 'true man', or by the nature-worship of the natural-scientific materialists of his century, but also by any metaphysical transfiguration of the proletariat as the bringer of salvation.[20] In *Capital*, material investigation takes the place of the abstract talk of human self-alienation which has long since degenerated into the small change of present-day cultural conversation.

There is a certain current of thought today which interprets Marxian theory in line with imputed chiliastic and eschatological legends.[21] Measured against this view, the content of what one could call Marx's utopia of the relation of men to their own, and to external, nature is both more modest and more ambitious. More modest, because it takes seriously the inevitably finite nature of man and his possibilities in the world. More ambitious, because metaphysical declarations are replaced by a sober analysis of the possibility of concrete freedom. Concrete freedom, for Marx in close accord with Hegel, consisted in conceiving and mastering social necessity. The worker-philosopher Joseph Dietzgen formulated the meaning of the materialist conception of history very accurately in a letter to Marx:

You express for the first time in clear, irresistible, scientific form what will be from now on the *conscious* tendency of historical development, namely the subordination of the as yet blind natural power of the social process of production to human consciousness.[22]

We must return here to the remarks made in the first

chapter about the materialism of Marx. This materialism is critical, rather than a positive confession of faith. Economic relations are not glorified. It is intended rather that they should take on such a shape that their role in men's lives becomes unimportant. In the course of history so far, men have allowed themselves to be determined, as Engels said, by the 'alien rule'[23] of their own social forces, and for this reason cannot be said in the strict sense to have yet emerged from natural history.[24] As long as the economic relations are left to themselves, they act as incalculable natural forces. 'But once their nature has been grasped, they can be transformed in the hands of the associated producers from demoniacal masters into willing servants.'[25]

If men learn not only to see through the laws ruling their lives in theory, but also to control these laws in practice, they will be able to transcend the 'natural-historical' materialism to which they have fallen victim in past history. In view of the number of misunderstandings, even deliberate ones, on this point, it cannot be stressed too often that Marx's materialism is directed towards its own super-session. Marx and Engels were fully in accord here. Yet there does exist a distinction between the two authors, when one looks more closely at the way in which they describe the transition from bourgeois to socialist society.

Let us first quote the famous passage in *Anti-Dühring*, in order to make the comparison with Marx. Engels wrote:

The seizure of the means of production by society puts an end to commodity production, and therewith to the domination of the product over the producer. Anarchy in social production is replaced by conscious organization on a planned basis. The struggle for individual existence comes to an end. And at this point, in a certain sense, man finally cuts himself off from the animal world, leaves the conditions of animals behind him and enters conditions which are really human. The conditions of existence forming man's environment, which up to now have dominated man, at this point pass under the dominion and control of man, who now for the first time becomes the real conscious master of nature, because and in so far as he has become master of his own social organization. The laws of his own social activity, which have hitherto confronted him as external, dominating laws of nature, will then be applied by man with complete understanding, and hence will be dominated by man. Men's own social organization which has hitherto stood in opposition to them as if arbitrarily decreed by nature and history, will then become the voluntary act of men themselves. The objective, external forces which have hitherto dominated history, will then pass under the control of men themselves. It is only from this point that men, with full consciousness, will fashion their own history; it is only from this point that the social causes set in motion by men will have, predominantly and in constantly increasing measure, the effects willed by men. It is humanity's leap from the realm of necessity into the realm of freedom.[26]

Probably the most significant passage of *Capital* for the problem of utopia is the following:

In fact, the realm of freedom actually begins only where labour which is determined by necessity and mundane considerations ceases; thus in the very nature of things it lies beyond the sphere of actual material production. Just as the savage must wrestle with nature to satisfy his wants, to maintain and reproduce life, so must civilized man, and he must do so in all social formations and under all possible modes of production. With his development this realm of physical necessity expands as a result of his wants; but, at the same time, the forces of production which satisfy these wants also increase. Freedom in this field can only consist in socialized men, the associated producers rationally regulating their interchange with nature, bringing it under their common control, instead of being ruled by it as by the blind forces of nature; and achieving this with the least expenditure of energy and under conditions most favourable to, and worthy of, their human nature. But it nonetheless still remains a realm of necessity. Beyond it begins that development of human energy which is an end in itself, the true realm of freedom, which, however, can blossom forth only with this realm of necessity as its basis. The shortening of the working day is its basic prerequisite.[27]

Both authors were of the opinion that human happiness is not simply proportional to the measure of man's technical mastery of nature, but that it depends very much on the social organization of that technical mastery. The question, whether technical progress is for man's benefit or not, can only be answered in that context.

For Engels, the socialization of the means of production solves the problem. There follows the famous sudden leap from the realm of necessity to that of freedom. Marx, however, was both more sceptical and more dialectical in seeing that the realm of freedom does not simply replace that of necessity, but retains it as an inextinguishable internal moment. A more rational organization of the economy can certainly limit the labour-time necessary for the reproduction of life, but can never wholly abolish labour. This reflects the dialectical duality of Marxist materialism. It is capable of being transcended in non-transcendence. Marx reconciled freedom and necessity on the basis of necessity.[28]

Even when, in classless society, one section of mankind can no longer interpose the remainder, the great majority, between themselves and nature as a means of its appropriation, the problem of nature, as an object to be mastered, continues to exist for men in their new-found solidarity. As we have repeatedly mentioned, Marx did not make the demagogic promises imputed to him, or justified by the misuse of his words, but insisted at many different points in *Capital* that labour could never be abolished:

The labour-process . . . is human action with a view to the production of use-values, appropriation of natural substances to human requirements; it is the general condition for the metabolism between man and nature; it is the everlasting nature-imposed condition of human existence and therefore is independent of every social form of that existence or rather, is common to every such form.[29]

The metabolism between man and nature is thus independent of any historical form for Marx because it can be traced back into pre-social natural-historical conditions, and because 'as the expression and maintenance of life, it is common both to the man who is not in any way socialized and to the man who is in some way socially determined'.[30] As Marx wrote in the *German Ideology*, there will always exist the 'materialist connection of men with each other, which is conditioned by men's needs and their mode of production, and is as old as mankind . . .'.[31]

In the Marxist dialectic, as in the Hegelian, what is non-identical with the Subject is overcome stage by stage. Greater and greater areas of nature come under human control. In Marx, however, and this distinguishes him from Hegel's ultimate idealism, the material of nature is never totally incorporated in the modes of its theoretico-practical appropriation.

The philosophy of the Paris Manuscripts can only be fully assessed from the position of the mature Marx. Although the young Marx attacked the *Phenomenology of*

Spirit, in the manuscript entitled 'Critique of Hegel's Dialectic and General Philosophy', for ultimately equating objectivity and alienation; although the fact that the non-identical was merely to be comprehended conceptually did not mean that it became something purely conceptual; the moment of the identity of man and nature did nevertheless dominate Marx's thought at this stage. One need only recall the formulation cited already, that communism is the '*definitive* resolution of the antagonism between man and nature',[32] or the even more unequivocal statement that it is 'the accomplished union in essence of man with nature, the veritable resurrection of nature, the realized naturalism of man and the realized humanism of nature'.[33]

Only in later life did Marx seriously approach the problem of non-identity. When he did so, he accepted neither Hegel's equation of Subject and Object nor his own equation of humanism and naturalism. In his view, men are never completely alone with themselves in the objects they produce. Hegel wrote in the *Phenomenology* that self-consciousness only took 'that object to be *good* and *in-itself*, in which it found itself, and that object to be bad in which it found the opposite of itself' and, moreover, that 'the good' was 'the *identity* of objective reality with self-consciousness', while 'the *bad*' was 'their *non-identity*'.[34] Applying this to Marx's utopia, it must be said that it is heavily encumbered with 'the bad', i.e. the non-identity of man and the material to be appropriated.[35] The mass of matter that has to be assimilated and subjugated remains external to men even in classless society, although under more favourable conditions than in previous societies. In addition to this, human nature must continue to pay its tribute to the external material.

In his doctoral dissertation, Marx showed that he was already familiar, through Hegel, with the idea that man only attains consciousness of himself through labour. But labour presupposes the suppression of instincts. 'In order that man may become as man his only real Object, he must conquer his relative existence, the power of desire and of mere nature in himself.'[36] This idea, which links Marx with Freud's doctrine of the reality principle, shows that rather than being reckoned simply as a philosophical optimist, he deserves a place in the tradition of the great European pessimists. The indestructibility of the material moments of the dialectic of labour even after the disappearance of class antagonisms corresponds psychologically to the continued existence of a certain measure of necessary self-denial. The idea, almost excessively repeated by Marx, that mankind must always engage in metabolic interaction with nature, whatever the historical conditions, has an exact pendant in Freud's reality principle.[37]

The materialist dialectic and psychoanalysis are mirrored in each other. In dealing with the suggestion that Marx was an ontologist, because he said that the metabolism was independent of its historical forms,[38] the point was made that the supposed unhistorical character of the structure of labour was itself something *historically mediated*. In the same way, Herbert Marcuse made the following reply to the (in itself justified) criticism of Freud for his failure to consider the particular historical limits of the reality principle:

This criticism is valid, but its validity does not vitiate the truth of Freud's generalization, namely that a repressive organization of the instincts underlies *all* historical forms of the reality principle in civilization.[39]

It belongs essentially to the advance of civilization as more and more organized increasing domination, that nature takes revenge on the men who have degraded it to mere material for human aims, by ensuring that men can only buy their domination by an ever-increasing suppression of their own nature. The division of nature and man in labour is reflected in the irreconcilability of the pleasure principle and the reality principle. In Freud's case, the view that 'every civilization rests on a compulsion to work and a renunciation of instinct'[40] by no means led to an attitude of resignation, in spite of his psychologically grounded scepticism about socialism. The hidden utopia of psychoanalysis, indicated for example in *The Future of an Illusion*, is basically the Marxist utopia, 'viewed from within':

The decisive question is whether and to what extent it is possible to lessen the burden of the instinctual sacrifices imposed on men, to reconcile men to those which must necessarily remain and to provide a compensation for them.[41]

Precisely the problem of utopia shows once again absolutely clearly that, especially for the mature Marx, nature is not a positive metaphysical principle. In the *German Ideology* there is already the statement that the Spirit has the 'curse on itself of being "burdened" with matter'.[42] Since men are, as physiological beings, directly entwined with nature, organs of its circulation process, what befalls all creatures befalls them; like all animals they die, and nothing comes thereafter, as Brecht put it. If they wish to separate themselves off from nature as Subjects, they must tackle this problem in order to reproduce their life. They must work with nature, and negate it, and in all forms of society this means the sacrifice of pleasure, and self-denial. Whether man's relation to nature is considered from the point of view of unity or that of diversity, it is not possible to speak of an attempt to make nature metaphysical.

Hitherto in history, the result of man's control over nature has asserted itself as a natural force because of his inability to control society. If man were properly organized, it would be possible to a great extent to abolish this socially conditioned 'natural force'. In this situation, men would become, as Engels put it, 'the masters of their own socialization'.[43] The materialism which would nevertheless remain would no longer be 'the bourgeois materialism of indifference and rivalry; the bases would have disappeared of this coarse atomistic materialism, which' – notwithstanding all ideological declarations – 'was and is the actual religion of practice'.[44]

The content of the materialism which remains behind will be the removal of the world's misery. It will also bring with it a more honest attitude to what, in previous history, was described as culture and Spirit.

The attitude of the mature Marx has in it nothing of the exuberance and unlimited optimism to be found in the idea of the future society presented in the Paris Manuscripts. It should rather be called sceptical. Men cannot in the last resort be emancipated from the necessities imposed by nature.

In a more rational society, the realm of necessity will be mastered and its role will decline in relation to that of the cultural sphere. Despite this, Marx insisted that the arrangement of the human situation he was aiming at would by no means put an end to the distinction between one area of life which was determined by 'external expedience',[45] and another area in which 'the development of man's powers . . . would count as an aim for itself'.[46] Something beyond the sphere of material production remains in existence, however little labour-time may be required for the reproduction of life. In the history of class society, the distinction between the two areas of life is that between the economic basis and the ideological superstructure. The classless organization of society will also have material production at its base. Marx expressly retained this concept. The extra-economic sphere, Spirit and culture, should lose its superstructural character, despite being separated from the immediate world of labour.[47]

In a society which has achieved maturity, the Spirit no longer needs to surround itself with an aura of 'shamanistic portentousness'.[48] With the end of the domination of man over man, and the joint direction of the processes of production and the administration of things which replaces it, there comes to an end the social necessity which made it appear as if the Spirit were something ontologically ultimate and absolute. Enlightened men do not need to hoodwink themselves or others. They realize that the domination of nature seen in their history is at the same time a subjection to nature.[49] They thus recognize the role that the Spirit has played in their history, the fact that the Spirit is inconceivable as something which maintains itself in an unchanging form *vis-à-vis* the diversity of nature without dominating it, and that they will not be able to dispense with this domination in the future. The Spirit remains bound to blind nature precisely because it has not become internal to itself. 'Through the decision, in which the Spirit declares itself as domination and returns itself to nature, there vanishes the claim to domination, which previously enslaved the Spirit to nature.'[50] If the life-process, which has become petrified as nature, is dissolved into the conscious and planned acts of socialized men, the modes of false consciousness should disappear.

Marx distinguished two basic forms of false consciousness, mythology and ideology. Mythology is negatively conditioned by economic forces. An uncomprehended external nature corresponded to archaic society's undeveloped stage of production:

All mythology overcomes, and masters, and shapes, the forces of nature in and through the imagination: it disappears therefore when real mastery over those forces begins.[51]

While mythology expresses the compulsion of uncontrolled physical nature, the ideological forms of consciousness reflect the alienation of human relations, their reification into an opaque, fateful power ruling over men:

As, in religion, man is governed by the concoctions of his own brain, so, in capitalist production, he is governed by the concoctions of his own hand.[52]

Marx looked forward to the disappearance of all ideologies under a socialist organization of society, and in particular, to the disappearance of religion:

The *religious reflex* of the real world can, in any case, only vanish when the practical relations of everyday life offer to man none but perfectly intelligible and reasonable relations with regard to his fellow men and to nature. The life-process of society, i.e. the process of material production, does not strip off its mystical veil until it is treated as production by freely associated men, and is consciously regulated by them in accordance with a settled plan.[53]

When men's social being becomes rational in itself, the ideological reflections of that being lose their distorting character. Where ideology disappears entirely, social practice fulfils its basic intentions. The desires which lay hidden in religion in reified form are then satisfied.

Marx was too hasty in drawing this conclusion. Only the realized utopia can decide, in its *practice*, whether the intellectual constructions he denounced as ideological are mere appearances which will vanish along with the false society, or whether religion is absolutely posited by the being of man, as Christian apologetics would have us believe. As long as a truly human order has not been established, Christianity, especially in the shape of negative theology in which it refers to the fact that the last word has not yet been pronounced on man's destiny, will preserve, in whatever mystificatory form, the memory that the essence of man has not been exhausted by its modes of appearance in history so far.[54]

In view of the existing misunderstandings of the content of Marx's utopia, it appeared necessary to point out first the aspect of Marx's materialism which could not be transcended, to indicate the characteristics which bind the socialist society negatively with its historical predecessors. While strongly emphasizing this negative side, Marx only rarely, and then very cautiously, mentioned the positive distinctions.[55] There were two reasons for this. He did not want to fall into the abstract musings for which he had criticized all the early socialists, and he did not want to falsify the picture of the new society by transferring to it categories taken without examination from the old.

Despite the rarity of Marx's utterances on future society in his extensive works, one theme runs through all the stages of his development in identical form: the emancipation of *all sides* of human nature. The economically more well-versed Marx of the middle and later years knew that the most essential condition for such an emancipation of man was the shortening of the working day. However, even in the year 1847, he stated in *Wage Labour and Capital*:

Time is space for human development. A man who has no free time at his disposal, whose whole life, leaving aside merely physical interruptions by sleep, meals, etc., is occupied in working for the capitalists, is lower than a beast of burden.[56]

The problem of human freedom is reduced by Marx to the problem of *free time*. It is true that in the more rational society, as we have already shown, the distinction between the economic and the extra-economic sphere of life does not entirely disappear. But since (assuming a high level of development of the forces of production) men only need to devote a relatively small part of their whole time to maintaining themselves, this distinction loses something of the absoluteness and rigidity characteristic of class history.[57]

With the ending of the division of life still experienced by the majority of men, between a main content of 'alienated labour' and a subsidiary one of 'non-labour',[58] and with the beginning of man's activity in all areas of life 'for himself' in the Hegelian sense, culture is no longer the complete antithesis of material labour. The phrase 'in all areas of life' has to be introduced here because what Marx said about the continued existence of the realm of necessity, determined by nature, did not refer exclusively to practical labour. He did not mean to limit truly human labour to the 'development of human powers'[59] as an end in itself over and above practical labour. In all labour which is no longer alienated,[60] man succeeds in really returning into himself out of the estrangement of his own essential powers, and in making himself at home in the external world transformed by those powers.

It appears clearly from the *Grundrisse* that the surviving, humanized realm of necessity can just as well become a sphere of man's self-realization as the realm of freedom which depends on it. In the *Grundrisse*, Marx opposed Adam Smith's view that labour in general is a curse, and that leisure is identical with freedom:

Adam Smith seems to have no idea that the individual, 'in his normal state of health, strength, activity, skill, and agility' also has need of a normal portion of labour, and cessation of rest. Of course, the measure of labour itself appears externally given, through the aim to be accomplished and the obstacles to be overcome by labour on the way to its accomplishment. This surmounting of obstacles is in itself a manifestation of freedom. Furthermore, the external aims have shed the appearance of a merely external and naturally imposed necessity, and are posited as aims set up by the individual himself. It is therefore self-realization, objectification of the Subject, and hence the activity of real freedom, whose action is labour. Of all this, Adam Smith has no conception. He is of course right to say that in its historical forms (slave-labour, serf-labour, wage-labour) labour always appears as repulsive, and as *labour under external compulsion*, and that, as against this, the absence of labour appears as 'freedom and happiness'.[61]

The *practice* of a more rational society would have to show that, in essence, labour is richer than its alienated forms allow us to suppose. Marx went on to enumerate the real conditions under which in his view labour could become *travail attractif*, or 'the self-realization of the individual',[62] in short, free labour:

The labour of material production can only take on this character given that, first, its social character is determined and, second, it is of a scientific nature, as well as being general labour, not the exertion of a specifically trained force of nature, but of a Subject which, instead of appearing in the process of production in a merely natural, original form, appears as the activity which directs all the forces of nature.[63]

When Marx rejected, not labour as such, but its previous historical forms, he had in mind a view which stems from Hegel, that labour signifies man's fulfilment as well as his suffering.[64] However, this in no way makes him a proponent of that vulgar metaphysic of labour repeatedly promulgated for the purposes of domination and already present in the old Social Democratic movement, which consists in celebrating labour as the bringer of redemption, with no questions asked about the particular effects it has on the labourer.[65]

The Marxist view of labour in the future 'association of free men'[66] can be formulated roughly as follows: men should not be oppressed in their labour, as before; however, labour cannot altogether be abolished and replaced with what is now called leisure-time activity, in the course of which men senselessly waste their time and yet simultaneously remain bound to the rhythms and ideology of the world of labour. The free time of the future will not be merely a quantitative extension of what today is understood as free time; culture is not a fixed physical stock of things which will come into the possession of the 'whole people' in more numerous and improved editions.[67] Only when 'immediate labour-time' ceases to stand 'in abstract opposition to free time'[68] can human qualities be universally unfolded and, in their turn, again work to further the growth of the forces of production:

The saving of labour-time is the same as the increase of free time, i.e. time for the full development of the individual, which itself again works back as the greatest force of production upon the productive power of labour.[69]

The development of the forces of production was never an end in itself for Marx. The saving of labour-time, he said, should in the last analysis result in a restructuring of man:

> The free time – which is both leisure time and time for higher activity – has naturally changed its owner into another Subject, and as this other Subject he then enters directly into the process of production.[70]

Thilo Ramm points out correctly that this theory of the origin of a new man constitutes the innermost kernel of Marx's teaching.[71] According to Marx, the process of production would lose its 'makeshift and contradictory form'[72] after its socialist transformation. Equally, this transformation is not an end in itself and, at an appropriately high level of the forces of production, it results in the genuine emancipation of individuals rather than a collectivist system of compulsion:

> The free development of individualities is needed, and therefore not the reduction of necessary labour-time in order to replace it with surplus labour, but the reduction altogether of the necessary labour of society to a minimum which would suffice to create the means for the artistic, scientific, etc., education of the individuals in the time which had become free for them all.[73]

Marx made extraordinarily sharp attacks on the current assertion of the economists, that the abolition of free competition (which in any case capital itself necessarily brings about or prepares in the course of its development) means the abolition of freedom in general:

> Hence . . . the absurdity of viewing free competition as the ultimate development of human freedom; and the negation of free competition = the negation of individual freedom and social production founded on individual freedom. It is in fact only free development on a narrow and limited foundation – the foundation of the rule of capital. This kind of individual freedom is hence at the same time the most complete destruction of all individual freedom and the complete subjugation of individuality under social conditions, which assume the form of objective powers, indeed of over-powering objects – objects themselves independent of the individuals who relate to them.[74]

Thus Marx turned the tables on the ideologists of capitalism. The free individual, who apparently was to have been protected from socialism, has never in fact existed in the sense proclaimed by the ideologists, and is the result only of a correctly understood socialism:

The social relation of individuals to each other, which has made itself into an autonomous power over them, whether it is presented as a power of nature, an accident, or anything else you like, is the necessary result of the fact that the starting-point is not the Free [Marx's capitalization, A.S.] social individual.[75]

The free social individual can only come into existence with the abolition of the division of labour, and the division of labour is fundamentally identical with the division of society into classes. Marx's early, romantic belief in the possibility of a complete abolition of the division of labour is illustrated in this passage from the *German Ideology*:

For as soon as the distribution of labour comes into being, each man has a particular, exclusive sphere of activity, which is forced upon him and from which he cannot escape. He is a hunter, a fisherman, a shepherd, or a critical critic, and must remain so if he does not want to lose his means of livelihood; while in communist society, where nobody has one exclusive sphere of activity, but each can become accomplished in any branch he wishes, society regulates the general production and thus makes it possible for me to do one thing today and another tomorrow, to hunt in the morning, fish in the afternoon, rear cattle in the evening, criticize after dinner, just as I have a mind, without ever becoming hunter, fisherman, shepherd or critic.[76]

In all his later, more concrete discussions of the question, Marx took as his starting-point the tendency towards a more or less comprehensive abolition of the division of labour, which is inherent in the structure of industry itself.[77] The advancing development of machinery has in Marx's view not only a directly economic usefulness, but also results in a humanization of the labour process. As he wrote in the *Poverty of Philosophy*:

What characterizes the division of labour in the automatic workshop is that labour has there completely lost its specialized character. But the moment every special development stops, the need for universality, the tendency towards an integral development of the individual, begins to be felt. The automatic workshop wipes out specialists and craft-idiocy.[78]

In *Capital*, Marx dealt exhaustively with the technologically necessitated abolition of the division of labour. In this connection it becomes clear that he admitted the existence of certain characteristics immanent in industrial technique, and relatively independent of social organization. Production by machines is always an advance on handicraft and manufacture, irrespective of whether it is carried out in bourgeois or socialist society:

As long as handicraft and manufacture form the general basis of social production, the exclusive subjection of the producer to one branch of production, the dismemberment of the original multiplicity of his employments, is a necessary stage of development. . . . A characteristic feature is that, even down to the eighteenth century, the different trades were called *mysteries*; into their secrets none but those duly initiated could penetrate. Modern industry rent the veil that concealed from men their own social process of production, and that turned the various, spontaneously divided branches of production into so many riddles, not only to outsiders, but even to the initiated. The principle which it pursued, of resolving each process into its constituent movements, without any regard to their possible execution by the hand of man, created the new modern science of technology.[79]

The various isolated forms of the process of production are broken up into systematic applications of natural science. Marx emphasized in the *Grundrisse* that the ceaseless transformation of nature in industry also proceeds under socialist conditions. The unity of knowledge and transformation of nature, realized on a large scale in industry, should in the future become a still more determining feature of processes of production. He had in mind the *total automation* (*Verwissenschaftlichung*) of industry, which would change the worker's role more and more into that of the technical '*overseer and regulator*'.[80] This however implies *a qualitatively different* relationship between the active subject and the object:

It is no longer the modified natural object which is inserted by the labourer between the object and himself as an instrument, but the natural process, transformed by him into an industrial process, which is inserted as an instrument between himself and inorganic nature, over which he has gained control. He stands beside the process of production, instead of being its main agent. In this metamorphosis, it is neither the direct labour, done by the man himself, nor the time he takes over it, but rather the appropriation of his own general productive powers, his understanding of nature, and his mastery of the latter through the agency of his existence as a member of society – in one phrase, the development of the social individual – which now appears as the great foundation-stone of production and wealth.[81]

Elsewhere in the *Grundrisse*, the scientific character of the process of production is portrayed in the following way:

It is at once discipline with regard to the man who is coming into existence, and exercise, experimental science, materially creative and self-objectifying science with regard to the man who has come into existence and in whose head exists the accumulated knowledge of society.[82]

It is quite clear to Marx that the all-round permeation of labour-processes by science, the further development of machinery, and the shortening of labour-time resulting from this, all of which he called for, are only possible when society has radically transformed its education system and, in this sphere of life as well, brought its relations into harmony with the level reached by the intellectual and material forces of production.

In *Capital* there are a number of very interesting remarks on the subject of education. The theoretical and practical instruction of children should correspond to the unity of the processes of knowing and modifying nature:

From the *factory system* budded, as Robert Owen has shown us in detail, the germ of the *education of the future*, an education that will, in the case of *every* child over a given age, combine *productive labour* with *instruction and gymnastics*, not only as one of the methods of adding to the efficiency of production, but as the only method of producing fully developed human beings.[83]

Marx had in mind here polytechnical schools, which provide some knowledge of natural science along with practical instruction in the handling of the various instruments of labour.[84] This should make it possible to achieve 'the absolute fitness of man for the changing requirements of labour'.[85] But a consequence far more essential for Marx would be the ending of 'the lifelong subjection of the whole man to a single detail-operation'.[86] The narrow specialist must become the 'totally developed individual to whom the different social functions he performs are but so many modes of giving free scope to his own natural and acquired powers'.[87]

These reflections of the mature Marx on the division of labour admittedly form a point of contact with corresponding features of the early writings. They are, however, much more cautious when compared with the above-mentioned passage from the *German Ideology*. In *Capital* it is no longer the complete abolition of the division of labour in a more rationally organized society which is in question. Marx referred instead to the '*abolition of the old division of labour*',[88] which results from the development of industry itself.

It is not only labour itself, and a particular mode of its division, which remain in existence indefinitely. If labour remains, the *time socially necessary* for the manufacture of specific goods is still decisive, despite the fact that the products of labour will not take on the character of commodities. Marx commented on this in the *Grundrisse*:

If we presuppose production in common, temporal determination naturally remains essential. The less time society needs to produce wheat, cattle, etc., the more time is gained for other kinds of production, material and intellectual. Just as in the case of the single individual, whose all-round development, enjoyment and activity depend on the amount of time saved. All economics ultimately reduces itself to economy in time.[89]

Time determines the measure of freedom available beyond the necessary material practice. Inversely, time also determines the level of humanization attainable within this practice. This is how the economic role of time as labour-time in a society free from commodity-fetishism is seen in *Capital*:

Labour-time would . . . play a double part. Its apportionment in accordance with a definite social plan maintains the proper proportion between the different kinds of work to be done and the various wants of the community. On the other hand, it also serves as a measure of the portion of the common labour borne by each individual, and of his share in the part of the total product destined for individual consumption. The social relations of the individual producers, with regard both to their labour and to its products, are in this case perfectly simple and intelligible, and that with regard not only to production but also to distribution.[90]

The statement that the quantity of the individual's labour serves as a measure for the means of consumption allotted to him, refers to the first, lower phase of communist society, which, in the words of the *Critique of the Gotha Programme*, 'still, in all respects, economically, morally, intellectually, bears the birth-marks of the old society from whose womb it emerges'.[91] Society has not advanced from the bourgeois judgment that he who does not work should not eat. The complete socialization of the means of production by no means excludes the continued existence of considerable differences in income.

Marx recognized that the unequal physical and intellectual endowments of individuals, and the resulting differences in their capacities, were the basis for unequal rights. 'Right can never be higher than the economic formation of society and the cultural development determined by it.'[92]

However, it is otherwise in the second, and higher, phase:

In a higher phase of communist society, after the enslaving subordination of the individual to the division of labour, and therewith also the antithesis between mental and physical labour, has vanished; after labour has become not only a means of life but life's prime want; after the productive forces have also increased with the all-round development of the individual, and all the springs of co-operative wealth flow more abundantly – only then can the narrow horizon of bourgeois right be crossed in its entirety and society inscribe on its banners: From each according to his ability, to each according to his needs![93]

In a true society, it would be the needs of the individual and not his physically or intellectually conditioned capacity for labour which, in the last analysis, provided the measure of his consumption. With this idea, Marx directly returned to a theme first developed in the *German Ideology*. There is the following passage in the article against Kuhlmann, which he edited, but which was probably written by Moses Hess:

But one of the most vital principles of communism, a principle which distinguishes it from all reactionary socialism, is its empirical view, based on a knowledge of man's nature, that difference of *brain* and of intellectual capacity do not imply any differences whatsoever in the nature of the *stomach* and of physical *needs*; therefore the false tenet, based upon existing circumstances, 'to each according to his abilities', must be changed, in so far as it related to enjoyment in its narrower sense, into the tenet, 'to each according to his need'; in other words, a *different form* of activity, of labour, does not justify *inequality*, confers no *privileges* in respect of possession and enjoyment.[94]

As in the *Critique of the Gotha Programme*, so here, the tenet that labour forms the measure of enjoyment, is superseded as subject to bourgeois limitations by the tenet that only the extent of needs sets a boundary to his enjoyment.

Marx's eudemonism was not based on the abstract and general principle of labour-time, whose formal equality in fact contains an inequality of content, but on the immediate physical and intellectual needs of men in all their diversity. The defects of the old society can only be removed if equal rights are replaced by unequal rights.[95] This of course pre-supposes that sufficient goods are available and, conse-quently, other men are not harmed by the change. Social equality means, not that all are treated alike, but that the richness and the diversity of the wishes of individuals come into their own.

In addition to this, Marx again and again pointed out the historical variability of human needs and drives. Thus he criticized Proudhon for failing to grasp 'that all history is nothing but a continuous transformation of human nature'.[96]

Which desires will disappear in a society free from commodity-fetishism and hence from the compulsion to consume, and which will develop, is not a question to be decided abstractly. This, among other things, explains why Marx never discussed human sexual behaviour, even when he was speaking of the *complete man* of the future. He was of course aware that modern industry, 'by assigning a decisive part in the process of production, outside the domestic sphere, to women, to young persons, and to children of both sexes, creates a new economic foundation for a higher form of the family and of the relations between the sexes'.[97] Earlier he had reproached Feuerbachian philosophy with reducing the human community to the family nexus and, in so far as it conceived this concept practically, to the sex act, whereas in fact everything primarily depended on men's relations in production. Now, in *Capital*, at the point where, for once, 'the higher form of the family and of the relations between the sexes' really emerges above political economy into the field of vision, this possible higher form is viewed exclusively under the aspect of a humanization of economic relations:

It is, of course, just as absurd to hold the Teutonic-Christian form of the family to be absolute and final as it would be to apply that charac-ter to the ancient Roman, the ancient Greek, or the Eastern forms which, moreover, taken together form a series in historical development. Moreover, it is obvious that the fact that the collective working group is composed of individuals of both sexes and all ages, must necessarily, under suitable conditions, become a source of humane development; although in its spontaneously developed, brutal, capitalist form, where the labourer exists for the process of production, and not the process of production for the labourer, that fact is a pestiferous source of corruption and slavery.[98]

Thilo Ramm is no doubt right to speak of a very strict conception of marriage on Marx's part. One must also agree, that in 'Engels's conception of freedom . . . sensuality and instinctive activity are given far greater weight than in Marx, for whom these drives are restrained by the dictates of moral self-realization'.[99] The writings of Engels, even in their presentation, are reminiscent of the French Enlightenment, whereas the Marxist attitude belongs more to German Idealism, indeed to Kantian ethics, despite his cautiousness in the matter of uttering moral judgments.

The programme, sketched out by Engels in *Anti-Dühring*, of a life which would guarantee to men 'the completely free development and activation of their physical and intellectual aptitudes',[100] hardly differs at all from Marx's programme of the complete man, as developed in *Capital*. There are, however, certain differences between Marx and Engels on this question of men's moral attitude in the new society.

In his book *The Origin of the Family, Private Property and the State*, published in 1884, Engels handled the problem of sexual relations in the future society in a manner Marx would hardly have applauded. With the abolition of private property in the means of production, the family loses its previous economic function. The slavery of the woman comes to an end. What remains, according to Engels, is a monogamy whose sole basis is the genuine affection of the partners. The marriage should only subsist while this affection continues:

If only marriages that are based on love are moral, then, also, only those are moral in which love continues. The duration of the urge of individual sex love differs very much according to the individual, particularly among men; and a definite cessation of affection, or its displacement by a new passionate love, makes separation a blessing for both parties as well as for society. People will only be spared the experience of wading through the useless mire of divorce proceedings.[101]

Engels limited himself to general reflections of this type. Here too social *practice* will determine how relations between human beings will be shaped in a situation freed from economic compulsion.

Marx derived his demand for the emancipation of all man's essential powers from an analysis of bourgeois society. This society, he said, had a twofold character because it not only mutilated men, but also brought forth the means of their final liberation:

The universally developed individuals whose social relationships are subjected to their own communal control, as their own communal relationships, are the product not of nature, but of history. The level and the universality of the development of the capacities, through which *this* individuality is made possible, presupposes that very production on the basis of exchange-values, which first produced, along with the generality, the alienation of the individual from himself and from others, but also produced the generality and universality of his relationships and capacities.[102]

It is made clear in *Capital* how much the removal of the previous mode of production means at the same time its 'supersession'. It is not its simple negation, but the negation of the negation. It reproduces individual property and the human qualities which have become possible under the conditions of capitalism, only at a higher level, 'on the basis of the acquisitions of the capitalist era: i.e. on co-operation and the common possession of the land and of the means of production'.[103]

Thus the more rational relation of men to each other and to nature contains within itself the whole of the previous, superseded development. From this conception, it clearly emerges that Marx did not believe in the possibility of a return to the naïve immediacy of natural existence, which it is not certain ever existed, as the Romantics assumed, much even to Hegel's scorn.[104] Lenin criticized it too:

That primitive man obtained all he required as a free gift of nature is a silly fable. . . . There has never existed a Golden Age, and primitive man was absolutely crushed by the burden of existence, by the difficulties of the struggle against nature.[105]

Nature is not a positive entity to which men can simply return, but something that must be wrested from the constraints of previous history.

Even when any superstitious belief in the possibility of direct access to nature has been rejected, even when it is established that nature will continue to serve as the means and the material of man's self-realization in history, there remains open one inescapable question. In a world where everything takes on the character of a commodity, and nothing counts in the determination peculiar to it, but only when it becomes a means of exchange for something else, a ban covers natural being and our relation to it. Will it not be possible in the future to raise this ban to some extent? Precisely because nature confronts men almost exclusively as an object to be exploited, the glorification of nature assumes an implicitly false and ideological character when it is, for once, not viewed from the angle of economic benefit, as for example on a coach tour. If nature ceased to serve merely as raw material, it would no longer need idolization.

Bertolt Brecht has perceived the stunted relation of men to nature in commodity society in a way hardly any other writer of the present day has matched. Just as Kant's transcendental Subject constitutes the world of phenomena, so the social life-process in the late capitalist era constitutes all consciousness of nature and nature itself.[106] The artificial arrangements entered into *vis-à-vis* nature in the course of labour become for men the natural attitude in absolute terms. What is natural assumes tense, indeed pathological traits. This is what Brecht's character, Herr Keuner, means when he says in the *Kalendergeschichten*:

We must make use of Nature sparingly. Spending your time amidst Nature without any work, you may easily fall into a diseased condition; you are seized by something like a fever.[107]

A society which still received its nourishment through its metabolic interaction with nature, but at the same time was organized in such a way that it could renounce the ruthless exploitation of the latter, would allow the realist moment of Marx's epistemology to emerge still more strongly. The

fact that nature is *also* a being-in-itself, existing independently of the manipulatory intervention of mankind, the
'truth' of materialism, which does not see things as already
aprioristically modified, but allows them to have their say,
as it were, would come into its own. Without being fully
aware of these philosophical implications, here too Brecht
gave his Herr Keuner the right lines:

Asked about his attitude to Nature, Mr K. said: 'Now and then I like
to see a few trees when coming out of the house. Particularly because
they achieve such a special degree of reality by looking so different
according to the time of day and season. Also, as time goes on, we city
dwellers get dazed by never seeing anything but use-objects, such as
houses and railways, which, if unoccupied, would be empty, if unused,
meaningless. Our peculiar social order allows us to regard even human
beings as such use-objects; and so trees, at any rate for me, since I am
not a carpenter, have something soothingly independent about them,
outside myself, and as a matter of fact I hope that for carpenters, too,
they have something about them which cannot be put to use.'[108]

The question raised here, of the extent to which a more
humane society might also enter into a new relation with
extra-human nature, has been the subject of an extraordinary amount of discussion between interpreters of
Marx. Here too, the mature Marx withdrew from the
theses expounded in his early writings. In later life he no
longer wrote of a 'resurrection' of the whole of nature. The
new society is to benefit man alone, and there is no doubt
that this is to be at the expense of external nature. Nature
is to be mastered with gigantic technological aids, and the
smallest possible expenditure of time and labour. It is to
serve all men as the material substratum for all conceivable
consumption goods.

When Marx and Engels complain about the unholy
plundering of nature, they are not concerned with nature
itself but with considerations of economic utility. The
following comment in the *Dialectics of Nature* is typical:

All previous modes of production have only aimed at the first, most
immediate benefit from labour. The further consequences, which first
set in at a later time, and take effect gradually through repetition and
accumulation, have been entirely ignored.[109]

The exploitation of nature will not cease in the future

but man's encroachments into nature will be rationalized, so that their remoter consequences will remain capable of control. In this way, nature will be robbed step by step of the possibility of revenging itself on men for their victories over it.[110]

Karl Kautsky dealt on his own account, in *Die materialistische Geschichtsauffassung*, with the boundaries placed before progress in connection with external nature's attainment-of-itself-by-itself under socialism. He spoke of the suppression and destruction of many species of animal and plant, which socialism could restrict but never fully bring to an end:

However far the protection of rare animals and plants may go under socialism, the progress of agriculture will still continue to bring many of these species to the point of extinction.[111]

Kautsky was probably too optimistic about the possibility of a future autonomous development of extra-human nature. We should rather ask, whether the future society will not be a mammoth machine, whether the prophecy of the *Dialektik der Aufklärung*, that 'human society will be a massive racket in nature',[112] will not be fulfilled rather than the young Marx's dream of a humanization of nature, which would at the same time include the naturalization of man. There remains at best the vague hope, that men, having been reconciled with each other in the sense of Schopenhauer's philosophy, will learn to a far greater degree to practise solidarity with the oppressed animal world, and that in the true society the protection of animals will no longer be regarded as a kind of private fad.[113]

In the literature on Marx, it is Bloch's philosophy of hope which is most intensively concerned with the theme, first developed by the young Marx and the early socialists in general, of a 'resurrection', precisely of extra-human nature too, under the conditions of a rational society.

Bloch's formulation of the question has two interconnected sides. On the one hand he was concerned with the epistemologico-sociological problem of a new relation between men and the Object in production; on the other with the metaphysical problem of a 'natural Subject' and the related question of the incompleteness and utopian lack of independence of objective nature.

On the former question, Bloch first portrayed the relation of socialized mankind to nature in the following way, in his essay 'Über Freiheit und objektive Gesetzlichkeit':

In relation to nature, in socialist society, there is neither a pointless exploitation (with the profit-Subject in command), a naïve paternalism towards nature, nor an idolization of the given natural sphere.[114]

Bloch criticized bourgeois technology on the ground that its mediation of nature and man had a 'relatively external' element, since it was 'predominantly mathematical and quantitative'.[115] As he explained in more detail in *Das Prinzip Hoffnung*, it is the mediation of an 'artificial-abstract being'.[116] Bloch meant in particular the cunning interweaving of human aims with the laws proper to nature in the labour-process, as it was presented by Hegel and understood by Marx in his economic analysis.[117] A passage in the *Grundrisse* shows plainly that Marx was at one with Hegel on the question of the relation between the teleology of labour and the laws of nature:

Nature becomes . . . pure Object for man, a pure thing of utility; it ceases to be recognized as a power for itself; and the theoretical knowledge of its autonomous laws itself appears only as a stratagem for subjecting it to human needs, be it as object of consumption, or means of production.[118]

It remains to be seen whether this situation can change in any essential feature under post-capitalist conditions. How, in the future, can men avoid this outsmarting and duping of nature, as Hegel and Marx describe the labour-process? Since the realm of necessity will continue to exist as long as human history, men will always be compelled to behave towards nature in an essentially appropriative, interfering, struggling manner. Not for nothing does Marx, as we have repeatedly mentioned, present the process of production almost always in its simple and abstract moments, and not in its particular historical determinations:

As the taste of the porridge does not tell you who grew the oats, no more does this simple process tell you of itself what are the social conditions under which it is taking place, whether under the slave-owner's brutal lash, or the anxious eye of the capitalist, whether Cincinnatus carries it on in tilling his modest farm, or a savage in killing wild animals with stones.[119]

If, then, the work-situation always has the same moments, through all historical changes, this must also be true above all of the modern, technically mediated relation of man to nature. Men endeavour to change the in-itself of things into a for-us, yet ultimately the forms with which they have imprinted the stuff of nature (as opposed to the forms originally proper to it) remain something external and indifferent to nature.[120] Despite its increasing mediation, nature never becomes something completely 'made' by us, as Marx wrote following Vico.[121] This point expresses the most fundamental mark of distinction between the idealist and the materialist dialectic: even in a truly human world there is no full reconciliation of Subject and Object. This is what frustrates Bloch's hope for a philosophy of identity. The great technology which arose with the bourgeoisie remains in its main aspects relatively independent of the no longer bourgeois form of social organization. It is therefore not just the interest of the capitalists which thwarts the 'broader physics'[122] considered possible by Bloch. Not only will men continue to try to outwit nature, an endeavour which Bloch criticized, but also, in view of the immense growth of the forces of production, a non-mathematical and qualitative relation to the Object, such as he had in mind, will hardly be capable of realization.

What could be salvaged from the idea of such a very naïve relation to nature, without quantification and calculation, is the hope that when men are no longer led by their form of society to regard each other primarily from the point of view of economic advantage, they will be able to restore to external things something of their independence, their 'reality' in Brecht's sense. In such a society, men's view of natural things would lose its tenseness, it would have something of the rest and composure which surrounds the word 'nature' in Spinoza.

The other side of Bloch's formulation is connected with the first to the extent that Bloch thought that the material of nature, bound up with human labour, will become the 'natural Subject' when abstract bourgeois technique is replaced by what he called 'concrete alliance-technique':[123]

As Marxism has discovered in the working man the Subject of history which really creates itself, a discovery which will first be fully revealed under socialism, so it is likely that Marxism in technique will penetrate to the unknown Subject of natural processes, which is as yet not manifested in itself: thus mediating man with it, itself with man, itself with itself.[124]

Bloch defines the explicitly metaphysical character of his 'natural Subject' more precisely as follows:

. . . The concept of a dynamic Subject in nature is in the final analysis a synonym for the as yet unmanifested That-Force (*Daβ-Antrieb*) (the most immanent material agent) in the real as a whole. . . . In this stratum, therefore, *in the materially most immanent stratum that exists*, lies the truth of what has been designated as the Subject of nature.[125]

Whatever the origin of these reflections, whether it be the philosophy of the Renaissance, Jakob Böhme, or Schelling's romantic nature-speculation, they are as a whole incompatible with a materialist position, whether founded in a narrowly natural-scientific way or, as in Marx's case, dialectically.

Without doubt, the 'new materialism'[126] referred to by Marx in the *Theses on Feuerbach* transcended the whole previous history of materialism, with its requirement that natural reality should no longer merely be viewed 'in the form of the *Object*',[127] i.e. as a dead world of mechanico-physical bodies, but just as much in the form of the Subject, from the standpoint of transforming practice. But although reality here ceases to be a merely contemplative 'given', it still remains an existing *objective world* in itself, precisely as humanly mediated. The indestructible boundary between the Subject and the Object of labour is for Marx at once the boundary between the Subject and the Object of knowledge.[128]

The disappearance of this boundary in philosophies of identity reappears in Bloch where he inclines – at least hypothetically – towards Hegel's view that the total reality is an absolute Subject which mediates itself with itself. It matters little that this Subject is supposed to be a 'natural Subject'. In fact it has only a terminological significance in face of the in principle idealist nature of the whole conception. The phrase about the 'as yet unmanifested That-Force in the real', even when this is described as 'materially the most immanent', makes it quite plain that Bloch professes the idealist belief that 'at the basis' of the world there lies an ultimate, self-reproducing principle of being. However, such a principle is foreign to Marx's whole way of thinking. The better human order is not 'a realization of the sense of the world-process', an idea which, as previously shown,[129] breaks through again and again in Bloch's work. For Marx, the only *Subject* which has arisen from nature and works teleologically in nature is man, who has to maintain himself by working on something not at all subjective – external nature made up of things.

In contradistinction to human history which, as Marx endeavoured to show, presents a series of qualitatively distinct regularities, bound up with each particular social system, basically no change has ever occurred in the totality of the laws of physical nature. This point was formulated quite correctly in the *Dialectics of Nature* by Engels, who is covertly criticized by Bloch on this account:

Matter turns in an eternal circle, . . . and in this circle nothing is eternal but the eternally changing, eternally moving matter and the laws according to which it moves and changes.[130]

This was also Marx's view, that nature in its laws is, so to speak, *present to us in its completeness*, especially since the changes brought about by its own forces are slight and take place over long periods, in comparison with the changes conditioned by society or the changes in society itself. Bloch, however, despite all the objections he occasionally raises against his own views, flirts with the idea of an objective incompleteness of the laws of nature, even a kind of cosmic complement to the Marxist transition from mankind's prehistory to its real history:

Nature as finally manifested, no less than history as finally manifested lies on the horizon of the future, and concrete technology's long awaited future mediating categories are only heading in the direction of this horizon. . . . Nature is not a thing of the past, *but the as ye uncleared building site, the as yet inadequately available building material for the as yet inadequately available human house.*[131]

It is hard to see what Bloch's intention was in introducing this utopian latency and incompleteness into his picture of extra-human nature. In particular, it is unclear how far the higher form of metabolism between man and nature aimed at by Marx 'liberates anew the creative powers of a frozen nature'.[132] We can hardly speak of a 'renewed' liberation of the forces of nature by the higher society. There is no way back to the *qualitates occultae* behind which unknown quantitative relations are concealed. A reconciliation is not possible between the concept of nature conditioned by modern material production and natural science, and the pre-scientific, qualitative, basically magical and animistic picture of nature[133] Bloch has in mind, without admitting it, when criticizing the abstractness of what modern society calls nature. Dominion over nature turns it into an object and deprives it of its qualities from the beginning.

Bloch's nature-speculation, which is meant to be an interpretation of dialectical materialism, does not simply go beyond Marx's thought, with its metaphysical and cosmological extension of the Marxist problem of nature; it also leads directly away from it.[134] Nevertheless, this speculation has the merit of bringing out a moment of the Marxist concept of nature which previously went almost entirely unnoticed. Marx did not in fact interpret the nature which works itself out in men's social relations in an exclusively quantitative, natural-scientific way, even though his language is saturated with the terminology of natural science.[135] That nature appears under the categories of human practice is not something external to its concept. In labour (for Marx in properly organized labour in particular) nature presents to men a more differentiated, as it were 'more natural' side than in the laboratory. In the latter, nature is determined by the questions man poses to it. It is the product of the dominant problematic, determined in each case by the development of science. But in the shape of the material of labour, nature *also* confronts men as something qualitatively determined, as their own body which they must appropriate. The realm of the forces of nature has something of the 'poetical sensuous lustre'[136] ascribed to it by the Renaissance and perceived by Marx, in the *Holy Family*, even in Bacon's technologically oriented materialist concept of matter. Nature is not only an immense *material*, present under all human social conditions of existence in all its modes of appearance, but also a *potential*, whose extensive or intensive actualization takes place according to the measure of the existing level of the forces of production. There is in nature a certain disposition towards formation by man, which strives to push forward and to outstrip the natural process of creation. Human activity, as Benjamin put it, delivers nature 'of the creations, which slumber in its womb as possibilities',[137] helps to give expression to what nature is in itself.

In discussions of this kind, everything is a question of nuances. False, because over-teleological, is the idea of an internal disposition in matter towards formation by man (which would make nature a 'co-producer') if what is meant is Bloch's idea that technology is grounded absolutely in an 'objective tendency of the world towards production'.[138] However suitable the composition of the material of nature may be to its appropriation by man (all human aims are achieved through its laws), Marx and Hegel (here peculiarly materialist) still hold to the thesis that nature's co-production with labour always includes the fact that what men have in mind always remains utterly foreign and external to it. Even under socialism.

Whenever Marx writes of the 'slumbering potentialities'[139] of nature, he is always referring to the objective possibility, inherent in nature, of its transfer into definite human use-values. Bloch's apocalyptic vision, on the other hand, leaves open the question of whether, under the conditions of the new society, the 'creative powers of nature', now set free and mediated by human action, will enter into use-values, or whether nature, having been induced 'finally to manifest itself' by the establishment of the true order of human things, is supposed to bring forth new forms independently of human intervention. It is extremely dubious whether higher forms of life than human beings are possible in natural history.[140]

The peculiar idea that a fundamental change in the whole universe will go hand in hand with the proper organization of human relations can already be found in the early socialist writers of the pre-1848 era. Fourier's fantasies are moving, for, as Benjamin recalls, in Fourier rationally organized labour is supposed to have the result 'that four moons light up in the terrestrial night, that the ice retreats from the Poles, that sea-water no longer tastes of salt, and that predatory animals become the servants of man.'...[141]

Benjamin was right when he wrote that in view of the crimes men daily commit against themselves and against external nature, instead of realizing the correct practice, there is good sense even in the most eccentric fantasies and extravagant utopias. Today, when men's technical possibilities have outstripped the dreams of the old Utopians many times over, it appears rather that these possibilities, negatively realized, have changed into forces of destruction, and therefore, instead of bringing about an albeit always humanly limited salvation, lead to total destruction, a grim parody of the transformation intended by Marx, in which Subject and Object are not reconciled, but annihilated.

Note on the Appendix: The essay which follows was written in 1965 as a supplement to the German translation of a discussion, between Jean-Paul Sartre and Jean Hyppolite on the one side and Roger Garaudy, Jean-Pierre Vigier and Jean Orcel on the other, which took place on 7 December 1961 in the Paris *Mutualité*. The subject of the controversy was whether the dialectic should only be viewed as a form of motion of human, historical practice, or as part of nature 'in-itself'. This question is important both for the construction and the presentation of dialectical materialism, and the author fundamentally endorses the critical objections made by Sartre and Hyppolite to the official Communist Party conception of a purely objective dialectic of nature. This position is developed here in two directions: on the one hand, I seek to show that from an epistemological point of view the main obstacle to an 'ontological' dialectic is that, in order to be really materialist, this dialectic must be demonstrable in individual sciences if it is not to remain merely a thesis within a dogmatic *Weltanschauung*; on the other hand, I attempt to go beyond Sartre and Hyppolite, and to show that a uniform dialectical structure should not be ascribed *en bloc* even to human history.

A.S.

Appendix

On the Relation between History and Nature in Dialectical Materialism

> The dialectical method (especially when it has been set on its feet again) cannot consist in treating individual phenomena as illustrations or examples of something which already exists and is provided by the movement of the concept itself; it was this which led to the degeneration of the dialectic into a state religion.
>
> (from *Philosophie der neuen Musik*, by T. W. Adorno)

The debate on the question whether the dialectic is solely a law of history, or can also be derived from nature, may well have made it evident for the first time to people not fully conversant with the present state of philosophical discussion on Marx and Marxism that this is a genuine problem and not an invented one. The extent of the problem has been concealed by Soviet Marxism, conceived within the closure of a world outlook, and also by the Western critics of that system, with their largely Thomist orientation. The latter have taken *Diamat*'s ontological claims seriously and frequently intimate with satisfaction how little these claims have in common with Marx's position.[1] The present-day *Diamat* ontology can be discussed without any reference to Marx's works, and is no longer essentially concerned with the analysis of the capitalist mode of production. Soviet philosophers are concerned with the dynamic structure of the world in general, and have increasingly lost sight of the dynamic structure of men which was Marx's original interest. For them, the concrete nature of social relations evaporates into 'matter's highest form of motion'.

In view of this retranslation of originally critical concepts into a dogmatic world outlook, nothing is more called for than reflection on the field of validity of the dialectic. The Paris controversy initiated this reflection, although the decisive point of view by which it was determined was not sufficiently articulated during it. The subject of discussion was not the 'validity' of the dialectic as such beyond the philosophical and extra-philosophical opposition between idealism and materialism, but the answers to the following two questions:

1. Can there be a *materialist* dialectic of nature, seen as being-in-itself, in the strict sense of these terms?

2. Must not (as has been repeatedly asserted)[2] materialism and dialectics become incompatible if nature is understood to mean what the exact sciences make of 'nature'?

In what follows I shall endeavour to show that the answer to the first question must be no, and to the second, yes. I am fundamentally in agreement with the position adopted by Sartre and Hyppolite against Garaudy and Vigier, and will follow Sartre's *Critique de la Raison Dialectique*[3] in taking the view that existentialism has no theoretical contribution to make to authentic Marxist thought, since it is merely one moment of Marxism which has made itself independent of the rest. Existentialism can at most play the part of a corrective to present-day Soviet orthodoxy, by restoring the credit of a subjectivity long suppressed in the latter's objectivistically curtailed conception of dialectics.[4] Moreover, Sartre's mode of argument is not exclusively based on his existentialist doctrine, but just as much on positions which had been reached within the framework of Marxism itself long ago, but could not come to the fore for purely political reasons. It is unquestionably Lukács who deserves recognition as the first to oppose Engels's fateful attempt to extend the dialectic to cover prehuman and extra-human nature, by pointing out how important it is precisely for materialism to restrict the dialectical method to the socio-historical areas of reality. As early as 1923, in *History and Class Consciousness*,[5] Lukács dared to dispute with Engels. Whatever the weaknesses of that work, and whatever criticisms Lukács himself may subsequently have made of it, it still brings out with great emphasis the essentially historical character of Marxist theory, which undermines any tendency towards fixing extra-human reality in an ontological fashion: 'Nature is a societal category. That is to say, whatever is held to be natural at any given stage of social development, however this nature is related to man and whatever form his involvement with it takes, i.e. nature's form, its content, its range and its objectivity are all socially conditioned.'[6] It is of course possible to add to this that the converse holds as well. Society is always a category of nature, in so far as society's current form and also the segment of nature appropriated by it remain within the still largely unpenetrated total reality, nature. But the concept of nature as the whole of reality also remains within the field of human history; we can only speak of this concept in relation to the particular stage of mastery over nature which has been attained. Only a thought which has assimilated this basic consideration on the relation between nature and history and presupposes it in any specific analysis, has genuinely abandoned claims to provide a dogmatic world outlook, and fulfils the contemporary requirements of a critical understanding of Marx. The dialectic is not an eternal law of the world; when men disappear, it too disappears.

DIFFERENTIATIONS WITHIN THE CONCEPT OF A HISTORICAL DIALECTIC

For Marxist materialism, the dialectic is only possible as a *historical method*.[7] This is already stated in the *German Ideology*: 'We know of only a single science, the science of history. History can be viewed from two sides, can be divided up into the history of nature and the history of mankind. The two sides must not thereby be separated; as long as men exist, the history of nature and the history of men condition each other mutually.'[8] Consequently, in opposition to the later Engels, Marx always expressed himself very cautiously on the subject of nature 'in-itself'. All statements about nature relate to the particular stage reached in its appropriation by society. Moreover, owing to changes in the constellations in which men are linked to one another and to nature, a uniform dialectical structure cannot be ascribed to human history in general. The dialectic of productive forces and relations of production is by no means *the* law of motion of history, although many of Marx's own formulations appear to support this interpretation. 'All collisions in history,' he wrote in the *German Ideology*, 'have their origin, according to our view, in the contradiction between the productive forces and the form of inter-course. . . . These various conditions, which appear first as conditions of self-activity, later as fetters upon it, form in the whole evolution of history a coherent series of forms of intercourse, the coherence of which consists in this: in the place of an earlier form of intercourse, which has become a fetter, a new one is put, corresponding to the more de-veloped productive forces and, hence, to the advanced mode of the self-activity of individuals – a form which in its turn becomes a fetter and is then replaced by another.'[9] The 'coherent series of forms of intercourse' later, in the famous preface to *A Contribution to the Critique of Political Economy*, became the necessary succession of progressive epochs of the economic social formation, from the Asiatic mode, via the classical and the feudal, and from there to the bourgeois mode of production. It is not difficult to show that here Marx was far too willing to follow the scheme of develop-ment set out in Hegel's philosophy of history, and that the real course of history is much more complicated. However, Marx himself took account of this in his particular analyses, without for that reason simply abandoning his general con-ception. The theoretical content of these analyses goes far beyond the assertions in Marx's programmatic forewords and postscripts, which previous interpreters, including Sartre, have overvalued in the belief that they could under-stand historical materialism in isolation from the content of political economy.

Confronted as he was with an immense mass of socio-historical material, Marx felt compelled to a large extent to leave aside his historico-philosophical principle of con-struction and, both in *Capital* and in the *Grundrisse*, to introduce important differentiations into the concept of a historical dialectic.

The critique of political economy first presents the labour-process only in its simple and abstract elements, namely 'purposive activity', 'the object of labour', and the 'means of labour',[10] and indeed as 'the eternal natural necessity of human life, and therefore independent of any particular form of this life, being on the contrary common to all forms of society'.[11] Marx was concerned here not only with a methodologically useful abstraction, which would oppose the labour-process as such to its concrete historical forms, but also with the distinction between the pre-bourgeois stages of production and the bourgeois mode of production. For measured against the concrete determinacy of the labour-process as a specifically capitalist phenomenon, there is something peculiarly unhistorical and nature-like about the forms which preceded it; their distinctions are blurred, and the transition from one to the other is no longer unmistakably determined by the contradiction between growing productive forces and stagnating relations of production. The dialectic has, so to speak, an 'elemental' character. It was not for nothing that Marx repeatedly used the expression 'metabolism' when he had in mind the labour-process which takes place solely between man and nature, and that he applied this characterization equally to all forms of development. It is true that each specific form of this process extends its material foundations. But the parallel 'retreat of nature's barriers'[12] remains merely quantitative, and human activity a merely natural function entangled in nature. Only with the transition to capitalism does the mastery of nature take on a new quality; only at this point does the labour-process, which Marx initially stated was identical in its general determinations for all stages of society, become a strictly *social* process. Now, as he himself said,[13] those general determinations no longer suffice, and therefore, precisely in their abstractness, turn out to be characteristic of the particular stages of pre-bourgeois production. Therefore capitalist cooperation in the labour-process does *not* appear *vis-à-vis* the peasant economy and the independent handicraft industry historically

replaced by it, 'as a particular historical form of cooperation, but cooperation itself appears as a form peculiar to
the capitalist process of production and specifically distinguishing it'.[14] As far as pre-capitalist cooperation is
concerned, we can only speak of it from the perspective of
capitalist cooperation: 'It is based, on the one hand, on
ownership in common of the means of production, and, on
the other hand, on the fact that in those cases each individual has no more torn himself off from the navel-string of
his tribe or community than each bee has freed itself from
connection with the hive.'[15] Correspondingly, what Marx
called the natural (*naturwüchsig*) division of labour within
a tribe or a family is based on differences of sex and age, i.e.
on a 'purely physiological foundation'.[16] The division of
labour gradually starts to receive a truly social basis to the
extent that individuals, the particular organs of an abstract
because 'directly interrelated whole',[17] become progressively separated from each other, i.e. first become individuals in the true sense. The introduction of the exchange of
products with communities in other places is the reason for
this disintegration of the natural connection between men,
to which the theses of certain sociologists are far more
applicable than they are to capitalism. The exchange of
products is made possible by the fact that different communities find different means of production and nourishment
in their 'natural environment': 'It is this spontaneously
developed difference which, when different communities
come into contact, calls forth the mutual exchange of products, and the consequent gradual conversion of those
products into commodities.'[18] In this way, the connection
between individuals is restored, but as a socio-historical
connection. However, as long as the greater part of production is for the needs of the community itself – for instance
in the case of the small, archaic communities of India –
there is scarcely any commodity-production. A particular
division of labour, once legally fixed, continues to operate
over great periods of time with the 'inviolability of a law of
nature', and the community leads an as it were unhistorical
existence: 'The simplicity of the productive organism in
these self-sufficing communities that constantly reproduce

themselves in the same form, and, when accidentally destroyed, spring up again on the spot and with the same name – this simplicity supplies the key to the secret of the *immutability* of Asiatic *societies*, an immutability which contrasts so strikingly with the constant dissolution and refounding of Asiatic *states*, and the never-ceasing changes of dynasty. The structure of the basic economic elements of society remains untouched by the storm-clouds of the political sky.'[19]

This nature-like and unhistorical character of pre-bourgeois history is made particularly clear in that theoretically important section of the *Grundrisse* which deals with the economic formations which precede capitalist production.[20] As this section shows, and as Hegel himself intended, the dialectic must become absorbed in the actual writing of history if it is not to decay into an empty schema.

As his point of departure Marx took the historical conditions for the formation of the capital-relation. *Capital* presupposes, on the one side, free labour and its exchange against money, which is thereby reproduced and converted into values, and, on the other, the separation of the individual, briefly discussed above, from the natural immediacy of the community.

In Marx's view, this original natural immediacy was based on the similarly natural 'unity of labour with its material prerequisites',[21] whether this unity was realized in the form of free petty landownership or of communal landed property: 'In both these forms the relationship of the worker to the objective conditions of his labour is one of ownership. . . . The individual is related to himself as a proprietor, as master of the conditions of his reality. The same relation holds between one individual and the rest . . . either in the form of joint ownership . . . or as when the others are independent owners coexisting with him. . . .'[22] The individuals are not yet 'labourers', since they are active as members of a community which is endeavouring simply to maintain itself and not to create value. Since Marx proceeded from the assumption that pastoralism was the 'first form of maintaining existence', the tribal community appeared to him to be the precondition rather than the result of the (initially of course temporary) appropriation of the soil. Once men become settled, the degree to which this original community is modified is dependent on a large range of external natural factors, as well as on the natural and anthropological characteristics of the tribe itself. Whether they are nomads, hunters, or agriculturalists, it is always 'the herd . . . the community of blood, language, and customs'[23] which forms the most important prerequisite for the appropriation of the 'objective conditions of their life'. What is decisive here, as we have said, is that men act in relation to these conditions unreflectingly, as if to an extension of their own bodies: 'The earth is the great laboratory, the arsenal which provides both the means and the materials of labour, and also the location, the *basis* of the community. Men's relation to it is naïve: they regard themselves as its *communal proprietors*, as members of the community which produces and reproduces itself by living labour. Only in so far as the individual is a member . . . of such a community does he regard himself as an *owner* or *possessor*.'[24]

This fundamental relationship remains unaffected in forms such as oriental despotism, where the small, more or less autarchic communities are the components of an 'all-embracing unity' which appears as the superior, or indeed the sole proprietor, so that the village communities are reduced to the level of hereditary possessors. The individual is thus, legally speaking, without property. In other words, property is represented to the individual as mediated 'by means of a grant from the unity of the whole – as represented by the despot in his capacity of father of the many communities – to the individual through the agency of the particular community'.[25] However, tribal or communal property remains the basis of the self-sustaining community, part of whose surplus labour must naturally be put at the disposal of the 'higher community', which ultimately exists as a person. This situation is expressed by the rendering of tribute, or as Marx put it in a manner reminiscent of Durkheim, 'by common labour for the glorification of the unity, in part of the real despot, in part of that imagined tribal entity, the god'.

Where the starting-point is free, petty landownership, and thus a more dynamic, historical life of the original tribes, the community is still the first prerequisite. In this case, however, not as 'the substance, of which the individuals are mere accidents, or of which they form the mere naturally-given parts'.[26] Here it is no longer the country but the town which appears as the seat and centre of the owners of the land. Whereas in the original form of communal property the village was a mere appendage of the country, here the fields form part of the territory of the town. As the earth itself presents no obstacle, despite the efforts men must make to cultivate it, the difficulties encountered by the community can arise only from other communities which have either already occupied the land or disputed the community's right to it. War is therefore 'the great . . . communal labour, and it is required either for the occupation of the objective conditions for living existence or for the protection and perpetuation of such occupation. The community, consisting of kinship groups, is therefore in the first instance organized on military lines, as a warlike, military force, and this is one of the conditions of its existence as a proprietor.'[27]

The prerequisites for the individual ownership of land, whereby the community is organized as a state defending this land externally and guaranteeing it internally, increase the more individual property ceases to be utilizable only through communal labour, the more the tribe loses its natural qualities because of historical development, and the more 'its communal character tends to appear, and must appear, as a negative unity'. Under tribal conditions of absolutely natural origin, the individual is related to those conditions, in the production of his life, in the very way that he is related to the materials of the earth, i.e. to his Other, since in both cases we are dealing with the natural conditions of production. In this new situation, however, his relation, both to nature and to the social union whose 'nature' is already to a greater degree something historical and temporal, takes on more dialectical animation: his relationship with his private property in the land is necessarily accompanied by a relationship with his 'existence as a member of the community',[28] and his maintenance as a member of the community is the maintenance of the community, and *vice versa*. The community, 'which is here not merely a *de facto product of history*, but is known to be such, and therefore *had an origin*', is the precondition of property, i.e. of the relation of the working Subject to the natural conditions of his labour. But this property is mediated 'through the existence of the state', just as, inversely, the state is mediated through the particular form taken by the ownership of the objective conditions of labour.

There follow two important insights on Marx's part, which are vital for the question of the dialectical structure of pre-bourgeois stages of society:

1. In all forms where landed property and agriculture form the basis of the economic order, the individual relates to the earth as to the 'inorganic nature of his subjectivity',[29] i.e. a condition of labour which does not itself appear as the product of labour, but is provided in advance.

2. This practical attitude of the individual, who (as opposed to the proletarian of a later era) never appears merely in abstraction as a labourer, but always has an 'objective mode of existence'[30] in so far as he has the land at his disposal, is mediated from the outset through his existence as a member of a whole already more or less subject to history. However, this whole is ultimately unable to step outside its entanglement in nature and to that extent is 'lacking in history'.

For Marx, therefore, the unity of the human producers with the conditions of their metabolism with nature did not require explanation; however much this unity may have undergone modification in the course of pre-bourgeois development, it was not a result of history. Its various phases remained external to its essential nature. What the critique of political economy was concerned with, and what it wished to explain, was rather that typical phenomenon of bourgeois society, 'the *separation* of these inorganic conditions of human existence from that existence, a separation which is only fully completed in the relation between wage-labour and capital'.[31]

Slavery and serfdom know of no separation of labour

from its inorganic conditions, owing to the fact that the active Subject possesses an 'objective mode of existence' at these stages of production. The two moments merge to form an undifferentiated, uniform *natural basis* for the slave-owner or the feudal lord, who conquer the slave and serf as an 'organic accessory of the land'[32] and reduce them to the level of an inorganic factor of production: 'The slave stands in no sort of relation to the objective conditions of his labour. It is rather *labour* itself, both in the form of the slave and of the serf, which is placed among the other living things as an *inorganic condition* of production, alongside the cattle or as an appendage of the earth. . . .'[33] In contrast to this, the labourer in the capitalist mode of production is literally deprived of his own nature, converted into 'a purely subjective force of labour, without objective existence',[34] which sees its negation in the alienated, objective conditions of labour 'as a value existing for itself'.[35] For capital, the labour does not constitute a condition of production but rather the support of labour, which is appropriated by means of exchange. And yet this whole, re-established through the process of exchange, which rests precisely on the complete isolation of individuals from each other, 'in the essential coherence which accompanies their lack of coherence',[36] represents an advance over the limited local totalities based on nature and on relations of personal dependence.

Marx therefore had no intention of transfiguring the natural life-process of the pre-industrial stages of society in the irrationalist manner of the neo-romantic ideologists. Nor was he concerned to hypostatize the 'elemental' interaction of the moments, i.e. 'nature's self-mediation' (which was the form necessarily taken by labour at that stage), so as to create a world outlook of a nature-monism. It is still almost impossible to reach a final decision on the undoubted speculative moment[37] of Marx's description of the labour-process in its naturally-determined form, which is occasionally reminiscent of Hegel's and indeed even of Schelling's philosophy of nature. The concept of a 'dialectic of nature', if it can be meaningfully applied at all, is valid for those pre-capitalist processes which are bound up with the history of landed property, and which are not structurally dissimilar to the processes through which the plant or animal organism has to go in its conflict with its environment. In this way nature announces human subjectivity as its higher truth. Before the advent of capitalism, although nature is split into two parts, the working Subject and the Object to be modified, it remains 'present to itself' in this division. Man appears as a mode of nature's organic existence; nature appears, from the very outset, as 'the inorganic existence of man himself'.[38] This abstract identity of man and nature, as it is constituted by the 'pure natural existence'[39] of labour, is so lacking in specifically social content that labour must be performed even by completely unsocialized man as 'the expression and maintenance of his life'. Even an 'abnormally isolated man'[40] would be dependent on the identity of man and nature, as it exists in labour. He would admittedly have no property in the land. But, like the animals, he could 'nourish himself from it as his own substance . . .'.[41]

Marx's intended meaning is this: every interaction between man and nature which goes beyond the embryonic animal stage occurs within the framework of a definite social form, but not every one of these forms is a 'society' in the sense of bourgeois society, society *par excellence*. He therefore avoided using this concept to refer to pre-bourgeois relations. When the word does occur, it is as the result of a momentary mental slip. As we have seen, he preferred to use the terms 'community of natural origin', 'kinship-group', or 'tribe'. The distinction between what is naturally given and what has historically evolved may perhaps be valid for the individual phases of pre-bourgeois history, although Marx repeatedly pointed out that all naturally-given forms are also 'the results of a historical process'.[42] However, the distinction between Asiatic despotism, the slave economy of classical antiquity, and medieval feudalism (three forms of social relationship which are all determined by landownership) fades into insignificance in face of bourgeois society, whose emergence constitutes a decisive rupture in world history. For this reason, Marx was able to make the following succinct comment in *A Contribution to the Critique of Political*

Economy: 'In all the forms of society in which landowner-ship prevails, the natural relationship is predominant. In forms where capital is predominant, the prevailing element is of socio-historical creation.'[43] In pre-bourgeois times, the relation between the natural and the historical element formed part of the vast context of nature. In the bourgeois epoch, this relation forms part of history, even as far as unappropriated nature is concerned. Marx conducted his investigations into landownership in accordance with this principle. He compared a series of geographically separated varieties of landownership, that is to say the Oriental, South American, Slavic, Germanic, and Classical types, thrusting the question of the *temporal* succession of these forms entirely into the background. Like Hegel's forms of nature, the different forms of the pre-capitalist community stand beside each other as indifferent, unconnected forms of existence. Only through the eyes of theory does the modi-fication of a form, without itself arising from that form, prove to be its higher stage of development. For Marx, therefore, the course of history is far less linear than has commonly been assumed; it does not proceed in accordance with a uniform interpretative Idea, but is composed of constantly changing individual processes.

The bourgeois social formation has a methodologically decisive role in dialectical materialism in that it provides the starting-point for disclosing both the past and the possi-bilities of the future. Marx was the very opposite of a simple evolutionist. In itself, the historically higher stage is grounded in the lower; but the qualitative distinction between the lower form and the higher form which has proceeded from it can only be comprehended when the higher form is fully developed and has already become the object of an immanent critique: 'The anatomy of man is a key to the anatomy of the ape. But the intimations of a higher animal in lower ones can only be understood if the higher animal is already known. The bourgeois economy furnishes the key to the economy of classical antiquity, etc. But not with the method of the economists, who blot out all historical differences and see bourgeois society in every social formation. . . . The so-called historical development rests on this basis, that the last form considers its predecessors as stages leading up to itself, and always conceives them one-sidedly . . . as it is seldom . . . capable of self-criticism. . . . Thus the bourgeois economy first came to understand the feudal, the classical, and the Oriental economies as soon as the self-criticism of bourgeois society had begun.'[44]

The exceptional position of capitalism as the principle of explanation for past and future history is a result of the circumstance that history itself now finally casts off its 'first' origins in nature, and passes over into the 'absolute movement of becoming'.[45] Pre-bourgeois development had a peculiarly unhistorical character because in it the material prerequisites of labour – the instrument as well as the material – were not themselves the *product* of labour, but were found already to hand in the land, in nature, from which the active Subject as well as the community to which it belonged did not essentially differentiate themselves. Under capitalism, however, these subjective and objective conditions of production became something created by the participants in history. Relationships were no longer determined by nature, but *set up* by society. Thus even agriculture was transformed into a branch of industry. The landowner, having become a capitalist, transformed 'work on the land, which appears to be a direct source of subsistence by its very nature, into an indirect source of subsistence, dependent purely upon social relations'.[46] The *social form* of the labour-process, which first becomes relevant in the bourgeois economy, has repercussions on its material content, which originally appeared to be equally inherent as such in all social formations, but now shows itself to be specifically pre-bourgeois in its abstract and natural determinacy. Inversely, the abstract materiality of the process of production, common to all forms of production, becomes identical with the self-movement of the capital which constitutes its *content*. That is to say, the appearance itself manifests itself for its part as appearance.[47]

As we have said, Marx did not glorify the subjective and objective dependence of the pre-capitalist modes of production on nature. He realized that they necessarily correspond 'only to a level of development of human productive powers which is limited and must in principle be limited'.[48] Despite all the negativity of the capitalist system (and of course Marx did not overlook this) it signifies, precisely *in* this negativity, 'a total revolution in, and development of, material production'.[49] The price to be paid for this is that nature ceases to be recognized 'as a power for itself', and that it becomes 'a mere object for men, a mere thing of utility'.[50]

If the earlier modes of human intervention in nature were fundamentally modes of nature's 'self-mediation', since the mediating Subject (individual or community) remained a part of immediately natural existence, under capitalism the mediation of nature became something strictly historical, because social. Nature is the self-determined material of human labour and is therefore still not reducible to (social) subjectivity. However, nature's *in-itself* now only concerns the productive apparatus, which transforms the process of nature into a scientifically-directed technological process and, distorting it beyond recognition, amalgamates it with the machinery, thereby bringing about an extraordinary growth of the productivity of labour.[51] Subjectively, this radical destruction of nature's qualitative characteristics corresponds to the reduction of the worker to existing as a producer of exchange-value, which involves 'the complete negation of his natural existence', i.e. the fact that he 'is entirely determined by society'.[52] Labour becomes something utterly 'lacking in objectivity', something which while coinciding with the 'immediate corporeality' of the worker, constitutes the 'objective form of the absence of objectivity'.[53] This 'absolute deficiency', this 'negativity in relation to itself', is nevertheless the precondition for the all-round development of human aptitudes and needs.

The expanded reproduction of capital takes place on the basis provided by capital itself: once it is historically developed, it is related to its prerequisites as to 'the preliminary historical stages of its becoming'.[54] These stages are then 'superseded in its being'.[55] What originally appeared as the foundation for capital's growth now appears 'as posited by capital – not as the pre-condition of its origin but as the consequence of its own reality'.[56] Since the systems which historically preceded capitalism have thus vanished in the capitalist system, and the latter therefore develops on its own basis, the classical bourgeois economists find it that much easier to regard capital as the eternal, natural form of human production. In so far as they are aware of its historically limited character, they are inclined to present the conditions of its origin as the conditions of its present-day realization, i.e. they imply that the conditions character-istic of the fully formed bourgeois economy are the same conditions as those under which the capitalist is not yet able to act as such. In this they are expressing the difficulty of reconciling capital's prevailing practice with its theoretical understanding of itself. What particularly interested Marx in this connection, however, was the methodologically vital fact, which we have already noted, that past and future history could be illuminated by performing a series of intellectual oscillations backwards and forwards from the established bourgeois system, whose emergence marked a qualitative leap. Sartre is therefore right to refer to Marx's 'progressive-regressive method',[57] a method which is of course of Hegelian origin. The same analysis both determines the given situation as relative to a past lying behind it and shows that it is equally relative to a 'movement of be-coming'[58] which transcends it: 'While the pre-bourgeois phases appear for their part as *merely historical*, i.e. super-seded prerequisites, the present conditions of production appear as *self-superseding* and hence as positing the *historical prerequisites* for a new social order.'

It should have emerged from the above analysis that there are, strictly speaking, only two truly historical dialectics for Marxist theory (whose primary task is after all not to reconstruct mankind's whole history but to track down modern society's economic law of motion): the dialectic of the transition from the classical-feudal to the bourgeois epoch, a transition more or less revolutionary according to national peculiarities, and the dialectic of the cataclysmic and liberating transition from the bourgeois epoch to that of socialism. The latter transition is of course the more heavily stressed.

In the centuries of 'primitive accumulation', already *in themselves* dominated by the transformation of money and commodities into capital, there arose within the womb of feudal society (and later of the feudal system in its absolutist reconstruction) the capital-relation characteristic of bourgeois society as a historical form of life. This capital-relation rests on the abstract separation of the worker (as a class) from the means of production, the material prerequisites of labour. Once this separation has come into effect, the basis is provided for 'the becoming and, still more, the being of capital as such',[59] since the separation is reproduced 'on a constantly increasing scale',[60] as Marx tried to show. In historico-philosophical terms: the highly abstract, 'elemental' dialectic of the pre-industrial development is concretized into the dialect of productive forces and relations of production, the dialectic which is ultimately decisive for Marxism.[61] In other words, the historical dialect as it structures capitalism more closely arises out of a long history. This process is the 'becoming' which only goes over into 'existence' when the objective antagonisms which constitute its content have reached such a pitch that there is a real possibility of their supersession, or, in the sense of the Hegelian Logic, when 'becoming' has reached its highest stage of ripeness, the stage 'in which its destruction begins'.[62] Only at that moment is a *critique of political economy* possible as a critique of alienation, commodity fetishism, and ideology: the becoming (itself already capitalist) of the capital-relation has vanished into a system which can now be contemplated in its pure immanence.[63] In a somewhat obscure passage of the *Grundrisse*, Marx added to this the idea that 'the dialectical representation is only correct when it knows its own limits'.[64] If we take as strict a view of the concept of 'representation (*Darstellung*)' as Marx did, i.e. if we do not just view this in a literary sense, his meaning here is that the concept of a dialectic of historical materialism is only valid for fully-developed bourgeois society and for pre-bourgeois society in so far as exchange relations are anticipated in it.

NATURE, KNOWLEDGE, AND HISTORICAL PRACTICE

All the attempts made, right up to the Soviet Marxism of the present day, to prove that nature is in itself dialectically structured, derive originally from Engels's reflections on the subject. It is very difficult to make an accurate judgment of Engels's thought, however, because two concepts of nature coexist in it, in part without connection, in part confusingly intertwined. One concept is that of nature concretely mediated through society, the other is that of metaphysical materialism. We must therefore emphasize at the outset that despite any criticism of Engels it cannot simply be a question of the replacement of his conception with Marx's. In any case, this is only possible to a limited degree, since any critique of Engels must always have recourse to arguments derived from the position jointly worked out by both Marx and Engels in their earlier days.

Nevertheless, their ways parted earlier than is commonly assumed. During the early forties, they both showed a lively interest in the French materialism of the eighteenth century. However, whereas Marx praised Helvetius as a materialist because he conceived materialism 'in its relation to social life',[65] Engels from the beginning laid more emphasis on the metaphysical side. In an article which appeared in 1844 he described materialism as 'the summit of the science of the eighteenth century', 'the first system of natural philosophy', and as the result of a 'perfection of the natural sciences'.[66] Later on, too, in his writings on nature, i.e. in the essay on Feuerbach, in *Anti-Dühring*, and in the *Dialectics of Nature*, Engels stuck to the idea (which was developed in detail in Holbach's *System of Nature*) that there was a watertight connection between natural phenomena, with the intention, however, of no longer defining this connection in a limited mechanical way. Romantic philosophies of nature are also important for the understanding of Engels's conception, in particular that of the young Schelling, whereas Hegel's philosophy of nature, as we shall show, was less significant in this context than his logic of being. Finally, evolutionist theories played an important part in Engels's thought. In part these theories were implicit in the Romantics' speculations about nature, but Engels was chiefly influenced by the Lamarckian and Darwinian concept of a 'history of nature', which was in its turn already heralded in the work of Buffon and other French scholars of the eighteenth century.

When, at the end of the 1850s, Marx and Engels turned to Hegel's philosophy for the second time, the impact of Hegel on Marx was very different from Engels's reception of him. Marx, whose theme was political economy, endeavoured to bring this science 'through criticism to the point where it could be dialectically presented'.[67] As we have seen, he was well aware while doing this of the objective historical limits of such a representation. In contrast to this, Engels interpreted the finished results of modern natural science by means of dialectical categories, and did not enter into the factual problematic of the sciences themselves. He could not reshape the natural sciences – as Marx reshaped political economy – and had to content himself with systematizing the materials provided by them. He gave the following programmatic formulation of his task: 'Empirical research into nature has heaped up such an immense mass of positive knowledge that the necessity of ordering it systematically and according to its internal logic in each individual area of investigation has become absolutely imperative.'[68]

The general intellectual situation, on the basis of which Engels attempted to carry out his programme, was characterized by the final emancipation of the natural sciences from philosophy. This was expressed in the dispute over materialism around the middle of the 1850s, when there was a wild profusion of simple mechanistic writings, either of the positivist or the vulgar materialist variety. Precisely because he fundamentally accepted the materialist standpoint, Engels had to draw a critical line between himself and vulgarizers of materialism such as Büchner, Vogt, and Moleschott, and he made this distinction by introducing the dialectic into the materialist conception of nature. This raises the question, which the participants in the Paris controversy correctly viewed as decisive, of whether dialectical determinations such as 'totality', 'contradiction', 'productivity', 'immanent negation', can in any sense be ascribed to nature when the latter is reduced to abstract matter. In other words, is subjective reflection (even if only as a single moment) inescapably posited by any dialectical theory?

In view of Hegel's statement, in the preface to the *Phenomenology of Mind*, that the bud disappears as the blossom bursts forth, and the fruit supplants the blossom as the truth of the plant,[69] one might be tempted to interpret the process described here as the actual dialectic of the plant. However, Hegel was really referring not to the unconscious life of the plant but to the life of the plant's *concept*. As so often, Hegel illustrated his dialectic here by referring to organic, natural processes, and since these processes took place at an inferior level he did not allow them a constitutive role in the movement of the Concept. In its immediate existence, the plant does not achieve a being-for-itself; it 'only touches the boundary of individuality'.[70] The plant only appears as dialectically structured to a 'rational' thought, which comes upon it as an object already divided into bud, blossom and fruit by the abstract understanding, and converts these merely intellectual concepts into 'elements of an organic unity',[71] i.e. translates them into the Concept. However, to comprehend nature rationally is to comprehend it *as reason submerged in materiality*: 'Since the internal essence of nature is nothing other than the general, when we have thoughts we are at home with ourselves in this internal essence of nature.'[72] Hegel's philosophy of nature is nourished by his confidence that 'in nature concept speaks to concept, and the true shape of the Concept, which lies concealed behind the fragmentation of the infinite number of separate forms, will reveal itself to nature'.[73]

As a materialist of a natural-scientific orientation, Engels had to forego precisely this confidence. It is true that like Hegel in his 'rational physics',[74] Engels was dealing with the empirically reached discoveries of the natural sciences, and therefore with a General which is to be presented as a whole in its 'own immanent necessity'.[75] But there is this essential difference between Engels and Hegel, that the former could not bring these discoveries to the level of their dialectical 'Concept' if he wished to remain strictly scientific, because this would ultimately involve their reduction to the emanations of a divine Logos. In the nature of things, then, Engels could only provide a systematic treatment of the most general results of the empirical sciences along the lines of a positivist 'unified science'. He dealt throughout with something already subjected to intellectual operations, dependent on the historical situation, and therefore totally different from the 'in-itself' of nature. Engels's use of dialectical categories had to remain ineffective and merely assertive: facts fixed by the intellect were brought into a new context of merely external reflection. Instead of undertaking a genuine dialectical reconstruction, as Marx did, and as *could be done*, Engels prefixed dialectical forms of motion with a materialist sign, and 'applied' them to natural phenomena without being at all concerned with their speculative implications. In this way, he arrived at arid definitions of the following kind: 'The cell is Hegel's "Being-in-itself" and its development undergoes exactly the Hegelian process, resulting finally in the "Idea", i.e. the particular completed organism.'[76] Or, for example, he described geology without qualification as 'a series of negated negations', which was meant to be identical with the statement that geology is 'a series of successive disintegrations of old and deposits of new rock formations'.[77] Hegel's consciously idealist philosophy of nature gained its bad reputation precisely through the many artificialities, empty constructs and curiosities contained in it. In the case of Engels, the same constructions had a still more repellent effect, if that is possible, since his materialist tendency to maintain contact with the empirical field of the individual sciences was irreducibly opposed to his dialectical aim of presenting a totality structured in itself. Hegel could blame the obvious deficiencies of his undertaking on nature itself, asserting that nature's 'impotence' consisted in its 'externality',[78] its 'unreconciled contradiction',[79] which escapes the rigour of the Concept, although the latter provides it with its 'internal construction'.[80] Engels no longer had this line of retreat.

Whilst Hegel endeavoured to supersede empirical physics in speculative physics, but always maintained the distinction between them, Engels wanted to send all philosophies of nature packing and to anchor the dialectic in nature as it existed independently of any theoretical reflection. He was therefore forced to present the pre-philosophical procedure of the natural sciences as itself dialectical. The processes and laws discovered by the natural sciences are used by Engels as 'demonstrative examples' of his theory, which tends in the direction of a dogmatic world-outlook. For him, therefore, 'the unity of all motion in nature . . . is a fact of natural science'.[81]

Let us look more closely at the way in which Engels determines this motion of nature in individual cases. Although he asserted that this motion was not 'merely change of place' but 'also a qualitative change in the supra-mechanical fields',[82] it can be shown that he had to make far-reaching concessions to precisely the kind of mechanicism he wanted to relativize dialectically. Dialectics is secretly transformed here into a mechanicism of evolution which is at best more flexibly interpreted than the old mechanicism; for it is limited to providing 'a causal nexus for the advance from the lower to the higher, which maintains itself through all zigzag movements and momentary setbacks . . .'.[83] In particular, the *Dialectics of Nature* goes beyond the purely causal relationship and towards the conception of a 'universal interaction' which Engels saw as that knowledge which it was impossible to go beyond, 'because nothing knowable lies behind it'.[85] With this remark, however, he himself conceded that his view of nature was ultimately pre-dialectical. It is true that, in comparison with mechanical causality interaction is a higher, because a richer category. Yet, as Hegel said, it still stands 'on the threshold of the Concept so to speak. . . . If a given situation is viewed merely from the standpoint of interaction, this is in fact an attitude entirely lacking in conceptual content; one is then concerned merely with a dry fact and the demand for mediation . . . remains unsatisfied.'[86] Engels consciously left out of account 'the impact of men on nature',[87] i.e. the appearance of that particular form of mutual interaction in the natural context, called social labour. However, since labour's needs are subject to historical change, the faculty of knowledge, in order to be sure of the individual natural phenomena, must destroy their total context and return again and again to the isolated causal relationship. Only in that way can nature's necessary processes be reconciled with human aims. A materialist theory requires that the concrete dialectic be brought into operation only by the activity of social production, which determines the mental and the real transition from causality to interaction and *vice versa*, as well as the transition from interaction to teleology.

Thought which sees the limits of the mechanistic mode of interpretation is not *per se* dialectical, and the dialectic cannot be identified with a 'historical conception of nature',[88] as Engels asserted. This is precisely because the evolutionist theories of the eighteenth and nineteenth centuries were in no sense dialectical, being rather an attempt to apply the quantitative, mechanical point of view which had been successfully adopted in physics long before, to the organic world and its development in time. In Lamarck's natural-historical materialism the evolution of biological species was conditioned by the mechanical intervention and alteration of environmental factors. In the series of living things, he said, there are only purely quantitative gradations, minute changes, and not sudden leaps. There appear to be qualitative differences simply because certain intermediate members of the series are not known to science. This line is also taken, in essence, by Darwin.

Even more than empirical research, romantic speculation demonstrates the impossibility of a dialectic of nature such as Engels had in mind. In his *Erster Entwurf eines Systems der Naturphilosophie* (1799), Schelling expressly taught a kind of natural history which he endeavoured to deduce as 'a dynamic series of stages'[89] from nature considered as 'absolute activity'.[90] The word 'dynamic' referred here to a philosophy which would redeem nature from its subjection to dead Mechanicism, and make it possible to embark on a free development. Nature is absolutely productive, he said, but simultaneously infinitely limited through the fact that originally opposed tendencies are operative within it. In none of nature's products do these tendencies coincide. Therefore each of nature's products is also the drive beyond itself, an infinite productivity – 'the absolute product, which is always becoming and never is'.[91] Nature is neither productivity nor product, but the constant transition from one to the other. Since Schelling (here related to the natural scientists mentioned above), despite his idealism, accepted the individual scientific findings available in his day, he too gave an external description, in the manner of a philosophy of reflection, rather than conducting an immanent dialectical elaboration of the tension between productivity and product, or fluidity and rigidity. There can be no question here of a transitional leap from one quality to another: 'One must not be misled by the apparent lack of continuity. These interruptions of the natural stage exist only in respect of the products, for reflection, not in respect of productivity, for intuition. The productivity of nature is absolute continuity. We shall therefore present that succession of stages of organization not mechanically but dynamically, i.e. not as a succession of stages of products but as a succession of stages of productivity. There is only one product, which lives in all products. The leap from the polyp to the human being appears of course immense, and this transition would be inexplicable were it not for the existence of the members of the series intermediate between the two.'[92]

A brief comparison of this aspect of Schelling's conception of nature and the corresponding conception in Hegel is of value because it brings out the 'bad' contradiction inherent in the philosophy of nature as Engels resuscitated it: either it retains the temporal emergence of natural forms from each other, in which case it loses its dialectical character, or it retains the dialectic and must therefore (as in Hegel) deny the existence of a history of nature. This is how Hegel put it: 'Nature must be regarded as a system of stages, of which one necessarily proceeds from the other . . .: not however in the sense that one is *naturally* created out of the other, but rather in the internal idea, which constitutes the ground of nature. . . . It was a crude notion of the older (and also the more recent) philosophy of nature. . . that the transition from one natural form to a higher one . . . was seen as a case of external, real production, located in the darkness of the past. Externality is precisely characteristic of nature. It allows distinctions to disintegrate . . . and to appear as indifferent existences; the dialectical concept, which brings forth the *stages*, is the internal essence of nature.'[93]

Hegel's dialectic teaches the unity of the logical and the genetic, but in nature, which ought indeed to be nothing other than the 'externalization' of logic, this genetic process is a timeless logical becoming. The metamorphosis is limited to the Concept 'whose changing is the sole development'.[94] In so far as the Concept exists in nature as a living individual, it is the individual which undergoes development and not the species. Hegel's dialectic of nature expresses an internal order, but no real history, for real history can only arise in the mental sphere: 'It must not be thought that such a dry series is made dynamic, or philosophical, or more conceptual, or what you will, by the use of the notion of emergence.'[95]

It would be very cheap to mock Hegel here for his denial of natural history in the interests of a speculative dialectic precisely at the moment when the idea of development was beginning to spread throughout biology, and even in philosophy itself. In fact, however, this was how Hegel was able to guard against the levelling of the qualitative distinction between the natural and the historical world, which inevitably went very far in the case of Engels, because his theory of development claimed to be both 'dynamic' in Schelling's sense and 'dialectical' in Hegel's. Thus at the mercy of the above-mentioned 'bad' contradiction, Engels sought a way out by turning towards Hegel's *Logic*, in particular the logic of being, rather than to his *Philosophy of Nature* which, significantly, was still dealt with in the *Propaedeutic* under the title 'ontological logic'. Engels greeted the theorem of the 'nodal line of quantitative relationships' with enthusiasm, since this appeared to allow the real process to be conceived as simultaneously continuous and discrete. The different stages, which in the *Philosophy of Nature* are part of a timeless order, are presented in the *Logic* as qualitative leaps in a quantitative series.[96]

Hegel himself had in mind, both in the *Logic* and in the *Philosophy of Nature*, structural and not primarily developmental connections. This is partially concealed by the use of numerous 'examples', of the kind he normally despised, in order to show the transformation from quality into quantity and *vice versa* with reference to the chemistry of his own time. Engels, whose interest from the outset was in evolution rather than logic, followed the examples given in the notes, rather than Hegel's text. However, if the 'nodal line of measures on a scale of the more or the less'[97] is applied directly to natural history, and the transition from quantitative to qualitative changes is understood as a 'general law of development', this must, as Habermas has rightly pointed out, lead to a 'mechanical pseudo-dialectic of quantitative increase' which 'has more in common with the quantitative differentiation in Schelling's philosophy of nature'[98] than with a genuine dialectic such as would transcend the dualisms and polarities which stand in the centre of Schelling's discussion. Since Engels conceived the material unity of the world metaphysically rather than *practically*, his later views were somewhat analogous to the 'natural-philosophical formalism' with which Hegel (himself guilty in this respect) reproached Schelling.[99]

Engels's reaction to the logic of being was the same as his reaction to Hegel's philosophy as a whole: he closed the door to the idealist meaning Hegel attached to his own categories. Therefore, when Hegel spoke of 'objective logic', Engels immediately tended towards a natural-scientific interpretation of this objectivity. In Hegel, the objectivity of being only exists in that being returns into the essence as to its ground, to emerge finally as the 'Concept', i.e. absolute subjectivity. Instead of applying the Hegelian categories in a concrete, materialist way by redefining them in social terms, Engels applied them externally to particular scientific facts, which are dependent for their existence precisely on their abstraction from that which would bring them into dialectical motion: historical practice. They are supposed to be valid for the world in general, and Engels naïvely assumed that the conclusions of research into the world referred to its pure being-in-itself.

In fact the main difficulty, as outlined by Hyppolite, was that Engels's historicization of nature (and still more Soviet Marxism's) led to a naturalization of human history. This did not occur in the manner of Social Darwinism, whose social function and origin were spotted by both Marx and Engels. Here the naturalization of history means that Engels reduced history to the special area of application of nature's general laws of motion and development. In this way he cleared the way for the institutionalized division of theory into dialectical and historical materialism, which is characteristic of Stalinist ideology but meaningless from the Marxist point of view. In Engels's view, the fact that human history is made by beings *endowed with consciousness* is nothing more than a factor which tends rather to complicate the matter. As he laconically expressed it: 'Now the whole of nature is dissolved into history, and history is distinguished from natural history only because it is the process of development of self-conscious organisms.'[100] However, when Marx wrote of the 'natural laws' of society, of the critique of political economy's conception of the development of social formations as a 'process of natural history' in which persons have become the 'personification of economic categories',[101] this had the critical meaning that men are subjected to a system of material conditions which is outside their control and triumphs over them as a 'second' nature. This is not to say that Engels lost sight of this critical impulse; indeed he put the same point particularly clearly in *Anti-Dühring*. But because he proceeded from nature's 'value-indifferent' laws of development to those of society (although, with Marx, he had followed precisely the opposite path in the 1840s) it followed that some of his formulations could be interpreted affirmatively. On the one side, Engels had a clear awareness that the objectivity of historical laws is merely apparent, that they can only be the laws of men's 'own social action';[102] on the other, the force of this critical insight was lessened by his view that under socialism these laws would be 'applied with a full understanding of their nature, and therefore controlled'. While Marx wanted these laws to *vanish* through being dissolved by the rational actions of liberated individuals, Engels naturalistically identified the laws of man within those of physical nature, which can of course only be applied and controlled.

Stalin himself and Stalinism as a whole drew from this the dogma of the absolute objectivity of historical laws, which act independently of man's will and differ in no respect from the laws of nature.[103] It is no accident that the official ideology was able for years to unite this aconceptual objectivism with the crassest subjectivism expressed in the so-called cult of personality around Stalin: the two sides of this ideology are complementary. What in Marx is the object of a critique, is in Stalinism raised to the rank of a scientific norm. Subjects are capable at most of investigating these laws and bearing them in mind in their actions. These laws would simply not exist without human action, but this fact lies entirely outside the purview of a doctrine which is only concerned to 'reflect' already in fact completely reified relations in the interests of the ruling powers.

Dialectical laws of development and categories which should have equal validity for nature, society, and thought, were at least left by Engels in the field of the formation of concepts in the natural sciences. Stalin and Mao Tse Tung in particular took a further step towards the conversion of an originally critical and radical historical theory into an ontology by separating these dialectical laws and categories from the natural-scientific problematic itself and pronouncing them to be direct assertions about the nature of being. Hence there is an axiomatic certainty, before any specific investigation of an object, that contradictions are inherent in it, as in all other things in the world. This tendency was accentuated still more in the post-Stalin era. Authors such as V. B. Tugarinov use the concept 'ontology' in a positive sense and endeavour to construct a system of categories reminiscent of the philosophy of Hartmann. The dialectic is hypostatized into a general world-outlook,[104] yet simultaneously shrinks into a catalogue of principles which change in accordance with the temporary political conjuncture, and are imposed on the content as empty husks and schemata.

Let us turn now to the way in which Marx approached

the problem of the dialectic. It is apparent first of all that
unlike Engels he did not fall into the trap of codifying it,
and assigning to its forms of motion nature and history conceived as two distinct areas of subject-matter. From the beginning, Marx had a really critical relationship to the
dialectic. Although he considered it to be 'absolutely the
last word of all philosophy' in his lifetime, he always
emphasized the necessity of 'freeing it from the mystical
appearance it possesses in Hegel'.[105] It was clear to him
that this task could not be accomplished by making the
dialectic into a medley of philosophical declarations, but
only by showing in individual cases how it inhabits human
historical processes. He therefore rejected 'the abstract
natural-scientific materialism which excludes the historical
process',[106] and which was supposed to provide for the first
time a perspective for comprehending the existing problems
and findings of research.

Nature only appears on the horizon of history, for history
can emphatically only refer to men. History is first, and
immediately, practice. The concept of practice, as attained
in the *Theses of Feuerbach*, is precisely the most important
theoretically of Marx's concepts. One must always return to
the concept of practice in order to clarify what Marx meant
by materialism, and with what justification his materialism
can be called dialectical. Authentic Marxism, unlike all its
Soviet Marxist presentations, is not a naturalized Hegelianism which simply replaces one ontological substratum,
Spirit, with another, Matter. Nor is Marxism a 'synthesis of
the Hegelian dialectic and Feuerbachian naturalism', as
Plekhanov wrote in his attempt to situate it in the history of
philosophy. It goes without saying that Marxism has
nothing in common with the mystical cosmology developed
by Bloch as a 'philosophy of identity'. The essence of
Marxist materialism is missed if it is merely interpreted as
an alternative internal philosophy, or even world outlook,
to idealism in any of its forms. It is in fact the critique, and
the supersession, of philosophy as philosophy – although
this critique itself is still philosophically motivated.
Because of his attitude to the history of society as a whole,
Marx was able to raise himself above philosophy and see

the derivative and mediate nature of philosophical questions, without for that reason denying their factual content. Thus, what Engels described in his esssay on Feuerbach as the 'highest question of the whole of philosophy',[107] i.e. 'the relation of thought to being, of the spirit to nature', loses much of its importance when it becomes clear that concepts such as 'thought' and 'being', 'spirit' and 'nature', as well as natural-scientific modes of explanation, are products of practice, and that, with their help, men seek to solve not eternal problems but historically limited ones.[108]

It is true that material being precedes every form of historical practice as extensive and intensive infinity. But in so far as it is meaningful for men, this being is not the abstractly material being presupposed in its genetic primacy by any materialist theory, but a second being, appropriated through social labour. Throughout his whole development Marx insisted on the socially mediated character of what has at different times been called nature, and he was less concerned with the changing content of the picture of nature than with the historical conditions of this change.

In one of his last works, the marginal notes to Adolph Wagner's *Lehrbuch der politischen Ökonomie*, he stated that only a 'professorial schoolmaster' could view the 'relations of men to nature as not practical relations, i.e. relations founded in action, but theoretical relations . . .'.[109] Men are not confronted first with the external means to the satisfaction of their needs as with 'things of the external world', i.e. they do not stand in an epistemological relation to them. 'Like any animal, they begin by eating, drinking etc., and therefore do not "stand" in a relationship, but take up an active attitude, asserting control through their actions over *certain* things of the external world, and thus satisfying their needs. They begin, therefore, with production. . . .'[110] These formulations are not to be understood in the sense of practicist enmity towards theory. Historical practice is in itself 'more theoretical' than theory, as indeed it was in Hegel (although in his case of course it was determined in the last analysis as a mode of knowledge). Practice has already accomplished the mediation of Subject and Object before it becomes itself the theme of reflection. At this

point we can see once more that Engels took up the problem of the dialectic too late. In his view the 'materialist
conception of nature' meant nothing more than 'a simple
conception of nature just as it exists, without alien ingredi-
ents'.[111] This marked a naïve-realist regression in comparison with the position both he and Marx had reached in
their polemic against Feuerbach in the *German Ideology*.
'Nature just as it exists' is by no means an abstractly
quantitative product of the laboratory, divested of all an-
thropomorphic elements, but a qualitatively rich world of
matter, to be appropriated through collective labour. Of
course, the progress of industrialization makes the natural-
scientific reduction of all qualities to quantity technologically decisive, and natural science itself becomes a productive
force.

Hence, it is only the process of knowing nature which
can be dialectical, not nature itself. Nature for itself is
devoid of any negativity. Negativity only emerges in nature
with the working Subject. A dialectical relation is only
possible *between* man and nature. In view of Engels's
objectivism, in itself already undialectical, the question
whether nature's laws of motion are mechanical or dialectical is distinctly scholastic. 'Even the animal,' as Hegel
wrote, 'no longer has this realistic philosophy, because it
consumes things and thereby proves that they are not
absolutely independent.'[112] Human labour is also a consumption of the immediately given of this kind, but is
something more, both for Marx and for Hegel: 'Consumption of consumption itself; in the supersession of the
material, supersession of this supersession and hence the
positing of the same.'[113] This shows the inadequacy of
the dictum particularly frequent in Thomist literature, that
Marx was an epistemological realist. He was a realist in
considering that any productive activity presupposed
natural material existing independently of men, but he was
not a realist, in that for him men did not persist in Feuerbachian contemplation of the immediate, but continuously
transformed it within the framework of nature's laws.

Labour is in one and the same act the destruction of
things as immediate, and their restoration as mediate.

Because things existing independently of consciousness have always been filtered through historical labour, they represent something which has become what it is precisely *in* this independence of consciousness, an in-itself translated into a for-us. This also removes the primitive notion of knowledge as a reflection where consciousness and its object are placed in flat opposition to each other and the ultimately constitutive role of practice for the object is left out of account. The objective world is no mere in-itself to be reflected, but largely a social product. What appears on the side of this product 'as a static property, in the form of being',[114] should not obscure the fact that it is an addition to nature as originally given, and previously appeared on the side of the labourer, 'in the form of motion', i.e. purposive activity. Therefore consciousness always enters as an active spirit into the reality reproduced by it. It is the task of knowledge not to capitulate before reality, which stands around men like a stone wall. Knowledge, by revivifying the human historical processes which have been submerged in the established facts, proves that reality is produced by men and hence can be changed by them: practice, as the most important concept of knowledge, changes into the concept of political action.

Notes

Translator's notes in square brackets

INTRODUCTION

1. *Capital*, Vol. I, p. 186. The complete bibliographical details of all works cited are to be found in the bibliography. When no other indication is given, emphases in the text are those of the authors themselves.
2. loc. cit.
3. *Critique of the Gotha Programme*, printed in *Selected Works of Marx and Engels* (cited as *MESW*), Vol. II, p. 17.
4. loc. cit.
5. *Capital*, Vol. I, p. 177.
6. loc. cit.

CHAPTER ONE

1. cf. the work by Kurt Sauerland, *Der dialektische Materialismus*, Vol. I (Berlin, 1932), which is unoriginal, but important for this question. The inadequate understanding of Marx throughout the whole period of the Second International is essentially a consequence of the failure to grasp the connection between philosophical and historical materialism. Max Adler, in his *Lehrbuch der materialistischen Geschichtsauffassung* (Berlin, 1930), took the view that Marx's own materialism was quite irrelevant to the epistemological choice between idealism and materialism. Like the Russian followers of Mach and Avenarius, he thought he could without further ado combine Marxist theory with a subjective idealism brought in from outside. Karl Kautsky in *Die materialistische Geschichtsauffassung* (Berlin, 1927), Vol. I, p. 28, showed himself similarly unworried by the problem: 'Philosophy concerns us . . . only in so far as it touches the materialist conception of history. And the latter seems to us to be compatible both with Mach and Avenarius, and with many other philosophies.' Karl Liebknecht too, in his book *Studien über die Bewegungsgesetze der gesellschaftlichen Entwicklung* (Munich, 1922), p. 107, denied that there was any connection between the materialist conception of history and philosophical materialism: 'It is not "materialist", has no thread of materialism running through it, at least not in the actual, philisophical

sense. At the most, it has an undertone of materialism in the vulgar-moralizing sense.' Cf. also op. cit., p. 186: 'The "materialist conception of history" too is in the main a psychic and intellectual conception.' Franz Mehring, whose philosophical attitude is typical of pre-war Social Democracy, asserted in accord with Plekhanov: 'Marx and Engels always retained Feuerbach's philosophical standpoint, although they broadened and deepened materialism by transferring it to the field of history. They were frankly just as much mechanical materialists in the field of natural science as they were historical materialists in social science' (*Gesammelte Schriften und Aufsätze*, Vol. VI, Berlin, 1931, p. 337). Quite apart from the fact that Feuerbach's philosophy cannot be reduced to a crude mechanistic materialism, Mehring here turns the qualitative difference between nature and history into an absolute one, in an almost neo-Kantian fashion. For Mehring, Marx's theory consisted of two parts, a philosophical part which related *only* to the natural sciences, and a historical part which had to do with society. Even the most recent research on Marx has not yet grasped that dialectical materialism both supersedes and includes naturalistic materialism. The separation of the theory of nature from that of society is still maintained, as is shown by a remark of G. H. Sabine: 'Marx, following Hegel, has regarded the dialectic as a method especially suited to the social studies, because they have to do with a subject-matter in which development and growth is an important factor. Sciences that deal with inanimate nature like physics and chemistry, Marx assumed, are sufficiently well served by a materialism of the non-dialectical type, like that of Holbach' (*A History of Political Theory*, New York, 1953, p. 815).

2. *A Contribution to the Critique of Political Economy*, p. 308.
3. loc. cit.
4. *Holy Family*, p. 177. Lenin too regarded the Marxist conception of history as a consistent continuation of French materialism. Cf. the essay 'Karl Marx', in *Selected Works*, Moscow, 1967, Vol. I, p. 13. On the question of the connection between Marxist and French materialism, see also Roger Garaudy, *Die französischen Quellen des wissenschaftlichen Sozialismus*, Leipzig, 1954. Lines of 'natural-historical' thought can be drawn from the French Enlightenment, going through Buffon and Lamarck, and culminating in Darwin and Marx.
5. *Holy Family*, p. 176.
6. *Werke von Karl Marx und Friedrich Engels* (cited as *MEW*), Vol. I, p. 205.
7. *Holy Family*, p. 152.
8. op. cit., p. 201.
9. op. cit., p. 168.
10. *Economic and Philosophical Manuscripts*, p. 64.
11. In an article entitled 'Ludwig Feuerbach und der Ausgang der klassischen deutschen Philosophie', Karl Löwith dealt exhaustively with Feuerbach's role after the collapse of speculative idealism, and

correctly pointed out that one cannot do justice to the specific character of Feuerbach's philosophy as the consciousness of this collapse in the conditions of *Vormärz* (see p. 228, note 4a), if one measures him abstractly against the intellectual achievements of the German Idealists: 'With Feuerbach begins the epoch . . . of philosophy cut off from tradition. In hindsight, this was admittedly a relapse into primitive concepts and methods, but if we look forward, it represented the productive attempt to transform the questions posed by philosophy in accordance with the actually changed conditions of existence of these later generations' (*Logos*, Vol. XVII, Tübingen, 1928, p. 327). For an evaluation of Feuerbach's part in the origins of dialectical materialism, see also Ernst Bloch, *Subjekt-Objekt*, Berlin, 1952, pp. 378–84, where those aspects of Feuerbach's naturalistic and anthropological theory are brought out which point beyond mechanical materialism. Marx's final judgment on Feuerbach is also of interest. This judgment was formed during the 1850s and 1860s, while Marx was for the second time thoroughly working out his own relation to Hegel, in the context of his economic analysis: 'Compared with Hegel, Feuerbach is extremely poor. All the same he was epoch-making *after* Hegel because he laid stress on certain points which were disagreeable to the Christian consciousness but important for the progress of criticism, and which Hegel had left in mystic semi-obscurity' (Marx to Schweitzer, 24 January 1865, *Selected Correspondence of Marx and Engels* [cited as *MESC*], p. 185).

12. cf. Thier's introduction to his edition of the Paris Manuscripts, published as *Nationalökonomie und Philosophie* (Berlin, 1950), p. 25.

13. *Enzyklopädie der philosophischen Wissenschaften im Grundrisse* (cited as *Enzyklopädie*), II, Naturphilosophie, supplement to paragraph 248, p. 58; English translation, A. V. Miller, *Hegel's Philosophy of Nature*, Oxford, 1970, p. 19.

14. *Enzyklopädie*, 1817 edition, paragraph 244, p. 201.

15. *Enzyklopädie*, III, *Die Philosophie des Geistes*, supplement to paragraph 389, p. 54.

16. op. cit., p. 58.

17. 'Vorläufige Thesen zur Reform der Philosophie', published in *Kleine Philosophische Schriften* (1842–45), ed. M. G. Lange, Leipzig, 1950, p. 74.

18. op. cit., p. 67 et seq.

19. op. cit., p. 77.

20. op. cit., p. 73.

21. op. cit., p. 72.

22. op. cit., p. 77.

23. *Grundsätze der Philosophie der Zukunft*, paragraph 54, published in *Kleine Philosophische Schriften*, p. 167.

24. *Vorläufige Thesen*, p. 58.

25. *Grundsätze*, p. 163.

26. op. cit., p. 159.

27. op. cit., p. 170.

28. *German Ideology*, p. 59. See also *The Holy Family*, p. 224, where Marx wrote: 'In Hegel's philosophy of history, as in his philosophy of nature, the son engenders the mother, the Spirit nature . . . the result the beginning.'

29. This brings the abstract naturalist Feuerbach into a peculiarly complementary relation with Kierkegaard. Feuerbach too invited his readers to think 'in existence'. Cf. *Grundsätze*, p. 164. Both thinkers charged Hegel with excessive abstractness, in the name of principles far more abstract than those met with in Hegelian idealism. The critique of idealism does not attain a more concrete medium either with the aid of a naturalistic thesis of priority in which its socio-historical preconditions are not reflected or as religious inwardness. In his book *From Hegel to Nietzsche*, London, 1965, Karl Löwith placed Marx and Kierkegaard side by side as critics of Hegel, whereas in fact Marx, as the exponent of a theory of mediation, stands far closer to Hegel than Kierkegaard does. Marx saw that Hegel's theory of mediation could not simply be replaced with the cult of an 'immediately given', no matter how this was constituted, but rather that the only way of proceeding beyond Hegel's form of the dialectic was to turn the concept of mediation against its idealist surroundings. On the ontological character of Feuerbach's materialism, see also Lucien Sebag, 'Marx, Feuerbach, et la critique de la religion', *La Nouvelle Critique*, Paris, 1955, No. 64, p. 32.

30. cf. Henri Lefebvre, *Dialectical Materialism*, London, 1968, pp. 67–8: 'Feuerbach's humanism is thus founded on a myth: pure nature. Nature and the object seem to him to have been "given from all eternity", in a mysterious harmony with man – a harmony which the philosopher alone can perceive. The object is posited as an object of intuition, not as a product of social activity or practice. Feuerbach's nature is that of the virgin forest, or of an atoll recently arisen in the Pacific Ocean.' See also p. 106: 'Nature itself exists for us only as a content, in experience and human practice.' The critique of Feuerbach's 'pure nature' could be pushed still further. Lefebvre states correctly that nature is already modified by man; in addition to this, those areas of nature not yet drawn into the sphere of human production – Lefebvre's primitive forest or atoll in the Pacific – can only be viewed and comprehended through the categories of the already appropriated part of nature. Just as in Hegel's aesthetic the perception of natural beauty presupposes the perception of artistic beauty, in opposition to the common view, Marx saw the as yet unmediated part of nature as only relevant from the point of view of its possible future modification.

31. The youthful Engels pointed this out in the fragment on Feuerbach, printed in the *German Ideology*, pp. 673–5, which refers to paragraph 27 of the *Grundsätze der Philosophie der Zukunft*, in *Kleine Philosophische Schriften*, pp. 132 et seq. This is the passage from

Feuerbach: '*My essence is my existence.* The fish is in the water, but its essence cannot be separated from this existence. Even language identifies existence and essence. Only in human life is existence divorced from essence – *but only in exceptional, unhappy cases*; it happens that a person's essence is not in the place where he exists, but just because of this division his soul is not truly in the place where his body really is. . . . But all beings – apart from abnormal cases – are glad to be in the place where they are, and are glad to be what they are, i.e. their essence is not separated from their existence, nor their existence from their essence.' To which Engels replies, in line with the general critique of ideology: 'A fine panegyric upon the existing state of things. Exceptional cases and a few abnormal cases apart, when you are seven years old you are glad to become a door-keeper in a coal-mine and to remain alone in the dark for fourteen hours a day, and because it is your existence, therefore it is also your essence. . . . It is your "essence" to be subservient to a branch of labour.' Because Hegel's rich context of mediation shrivelled up in Feuerbach into a context of positive immediacy, the latter's naïve materialism became an equally naïve idealism, which viewed the identity of appearance and essence in man as a simple natural datum, although, precisely in social reality, this identity is not present.

32. *Kleine Philosophische Schriften*, p. 99.

33. Marx to Kugelmann, 6 March 1868, *Letters to Dr Kugelmann*, p. 63.

[33a. The word 'Vermitteltheit' has been rendered throughout as 'mediacy'.]

34. cf. *A Contribution to the Critique of Political Economy*, p. 311.

35. *Dialectics of Nature*, p. 7.

36. *Economic and Philosophical Manuscripts*, p. 164.

37. loc. cit. This principle is also valid for the mature Marx. Cf. *Capital*, Vol. I, p. 372, n. 3. Sidney Hook, in his book *From Hegel to Marx*, New York, 1936, p. 28, also takes the view that Marx regarded materialism as 'the clearest expression of the methodology of science'.

38. *Capital*, Vol. I, p. 184.

39. op. cit., p. 372, n. 3.

40. Marx criticized Feuerbach in the *German Ideology* for separating the movement of history from nature: 'As far as Feuerbach is a materialist he does not deal with history, and as far as he considers history he is not a materialist' (pp. 59–60). But even when nature does enter into the purview of history, this never occurs in such a way that nature appears as an element of social production. In particular, ever since Montesquieu there have been many different 'theories of the geographical environment', where nature is seen as an external factor, operating mechanically, to which men must conform in a similarly mechanical way. Plekhanov himself was not free from such Darwinian distortions. In his *Beiträgen zur Geschichte des Materialismus*, Berlin, 1946, p. 135, he had the following declaration to make: 'The character

of the natural environment determines the character of the social environment.' Even in Hegel's *Vernunft in der Geschichte*, Hamburg, 1955, p. 187, the 'natural context' is merely found to be the 'geographical basis of world history', and not in the first place the objective precondition for social labour, however much the labour-relation is otherwise seen to reflect the natural context. Engels emphatically opposed the theory of the geographical environment in the *Dialectics of Nature* (p. 172) bringing out against it the factor of intervention by the human Subject: 'The naturalistic conception of history, as found, for instance, to a greater or lesser extent in Draper and other scientists, as if nature exclusively reacts on man, and natural conditions everywhere exclusively determined his historical development, is therefore one-sided and forgets that man also reacts on nature, changing it and creating new conditions of existence for himself. There is damned little left of "nature" as it was in Germany at the time when the Germanic peoples immigrated into it. The earth's surface, climate, vegetation, fauna, and the human beings themselves have continually changed, and all owing to human activity, while the changes of nature in Germany which have occurred in the process of time without human interference are incalculably small.' On the relation between the theory of the environment and the Marxist conception of history, see also Leo Kofler, *Zur Geschichte der bürgerlichen Gesellschaft*, Halle, 1948, p. 511. On the merely indirect impact of geographical factors on the course of history, cf. J. V. Stalin, 'On Dialectical and Historical Materialism' (1938) in *Leninism*, London, 1940, pp. 604–05.

41. *Economic and Philosophical Manuscripts*, p. 217.

42. *Grundrisse der Kritik der politischen Ökonomie (Rohentwurf)* (cited as *Grundrisse*), p. 271. On the *Grundrisse* cf. Chapter 2, section A.

43. *Holy Family*, p. 186.

44. Marx to Kugelmann, 11 July 1868, *MESC*, p. 252.

45. On the opposition of idealism and materialism in the history of philosophy, cf. in particular Max Horkheimer, 'Materialismus und Metaphysik', *Zeitschrift für Sozialforschung*, Vol. 2, Part 1, Leipzig, 1933.

46. Marx, leading article in number 179 of the *Kölnische Zeitung* (1842), published in *On Religion*, p. 30.

47. *Capital*, Vol. I, p. 372, n. 3.

48. *German Ideology*, pp. 58–9.

49. op. cit., p. 57.

50. op. cit., p. 59.

51. *Dialectics of Nature*, Appendix I, pp. 322–3.

52. op. cit., p. 328.

53. *Grundlagen der marxistischen Philosophie*, Berlin, 1959, F. V. Konstantinov, translated from the Russian, p. 131. On the question of the non-ontological character of the concept of matter in dialectical materialism, cf. the essay by Götz Redlow, 'Lenin über den marxistischen philosophischen Begriff der Materie', *Deutsche Zeitschrift für*

Philosophie, Vol. 7, Part 2, Berlin, 1959. The view that dialectical materialism cannot admit an ultimate principle of being, to which everything else could be reduced, has only recently come to the fore in the Soviet Union. The extent of Soviet philosophy's dependence in the early 1920s on Spinoza's concept of substance in its conception of matter, during the period dominated by Deborin and his pupils, is something which G. L. Kline has brought out very plainly in his book *Spinoza in Soviet Philosophy*, London, 1952. The immediate post-Stalin phase in philosophy in the Soviet Union can be characterized as a period of realistic-ontological interpretation of the materialist dialectic, reminiscent in some ways of N. Hartmann. At this time, even the (in a Marxist sense self-contradictory) term 'materialist ontology' was used, in the same way as Aristotelian and Thomist interpreters have long used it to characterize Marxism.

54. *Dialectics of Nature*, p. 158.

55. *Enzyclopädie*, II, Naturphilosophie, paragraph 245, p. 35 (Miller, p. 4).

56. Max Horkheimer, *Anfänge der bürgerlichen Geschichtsphilosophie*, Stuttgart, 1930, p. 91.

57. loc. cit., p. 92.

58. *Die Vernunft in der Geschichte*, Hamburg, 1955, p. 29.

59. *Differenzierungen im Begriff Fortschritt*, Berlin, 1957, p. 44.

60. cf. *Economic and Philosophical Manuscripts*, p. 165, where Marx argued entirely along lines of natural-scientific enlightenment: 'The idea of the *creation of the earth* has received a severe blow from the science of *geogeny*, i.e. from the science which portrays the formation and development of the earth as a process of spontaneous generation. *Generatio aequivoca* (spontaneous generation) is the only practical refutation of the theory of creation.' In the *German Ideology*, p. 59, he upheld the thesis that organic life emerged from inorganic nature. The mature Marx, who carefully followed the progress of the discoveries of the natural sciences, referred more frequently to Darwin's evolutionism as the precondition in natural history for his theory of history.

61. *Economic and Philosophical Manuscripts*, p. 165.

62. op. cit., p. 166.

63. loc. cit.

64. loc. cit.

65. op. cit., pp. 166–7.

66. cf. also the critique of Eugène Sue in the *Holy Family*, p. 230, where Marx attacked Christianity on the ground that it 'debased nature to a creation'.

67. *On Religion*, p. 15.

68. *Economic and Philosophical Manuscripts*, p. 167.

69. *German Ideology*, p. 600.

70. *On Religion*, p. 71.

71. Heinz Maus, 'Materialismus', in the collection *Zur Klärung der Begriffe*, ed. H. Burgmüller, Munich, 1947, p. 63.

72. *Ludwig Feuerbach and the End of Classical German Philosophy*, in *MESW*, Vol. II, p. 377. Brecht has very penetratingly summed up the 'German' relation to materialism: 'The Germans have no aptitude for materialism. Where they do have materialism, they immediately make an idea out of it. A materialist is then someone who believes that ideas come from material circumstances and not the reverse, and after that matter does not appear again. One might well imagine that in Germany there are only two sorts of people, priests and opponents of priests. The upholders of the Here and Now, lean and pale figures, who know all the philosophical systems; the upholders of the Beyond, corpulent gentlemen, who are connoisseurs of wine' (*Flüchtlingsgespräche*, Berlin and Frankfurt, 1961, p. 20 et seq.).

73. Ernst Bloch, *Spuren*, Berlin, 1930, p. 39. Completely mistaken, on the other hand, is Alfred Seidel's attempt to interpret Marxist materialism as a malicious exposure of all ideals. In his dissertation, *Produktivkräfte und Klassenkampf*, Heidelberg, 1922, p. 25, there is the following statement: '. . . Marx's trait of nihilistic, analytical "truth-sadism" is expressed in that description of his conception of history as materialist. With diabolical glee he tears down all ideals and ideologies, and leads us back, sober and disenchanted, to material conditions and material interests.' We have mentioned Seidel's thesis because the views it expresses are still widely held.

74. Max Horkheimer, 'Materialismus und Moral', *Zeitschrift für Sozialforschung*, Vol. 2, Part 2, Leipzig, 1933, p. 167.

75. August Thalheimer, *Einführung in den dialektischen Materialismus*, Vienna and Berlin, 1928, Marxistische Bibliothek, Vol. 14, p. 26.

76. Peter Demetz, *Marx, Engels and the Poets*, Chicago, 1967.

77. op. cit., p. 73.

78. Marx to F. A. Sorge, 19 October 1877, *MESC*, pp. 375–6.

79. *Philosophy of Right*, translated by T. M. Knox, Oxford, 1952, introduction, paragraph 4, p. 20.

80. cf. Engels to F. A. Lange, 29 March 1865, *MESC*, p. 208.

81. *Capital*, Vol. I, p. 10.

82. *Anti-Dühring*, London, 1955, p. 498.

83. Max Horkheimer and Theodor W. Adorno, *Dialektik der Aufklärung*, Amsterdam, 1947, p. 304.

84. *Capital*, Vol. I, p. 372, n. 3.

85. cf. Kurt Sauerland, *Der dialektische Materialismus*, p. 163.

86. *Enzyclopädie*, II, Naturphilosophie, supplement to paragraph 249, p. 59 (Miller, p. 20). From such a passage as this, it is evident why Hegel was correctly criticized for the abstract idealism of his view of nature. There is a palpable and highly characteristic inconsistency here. The concept of development, taken from life, is for Hegel the moving force of the Spirit, through which the Spirit in fact loses the abstractness, barrenness, and lifelessness which are characteristic of formal logic and the philosophy of reflection. Nature, through whose image Hegel attained the full concreteness of the concept, itself

becomes, highly paradoxically, an abstraction; nature does not do well out of this transaction.

87. Review for 'Der Beobachter', Stuttgart, No. 303, 27 December 1867, printed in Marx/Engels, *Kleine ökonomische Schriften*, p. 301.

88. *Capital*, Vol. I, p. 10.

89. loc. cit.

90. V. I. Lenin, 'What the "Friends of the People" are and How they Fight against the Social Democrats' (1894), printed in *Collected Works*, Vol. I, Moscow, 1960, p. 142.

91. op. cit., p. 146. Lenin was referring here to *Capital*, Vol. I, p. 372, n. 3.

92. *Capital*, Vol. I, p. 372, n. 3.

93. *Dialectics of Nature*, p. 164.

94. *Economic and Philosophical Manuscripts*, p. 164.

95. *Capital*, Vol. I, p. 179.

96. Horkheimer and Adorno, *Dialektik der Aufklärung*, p. 264.

97. Marx to Kugelmann, 27 June 1870, *MESC*, p. 290.

98. Marx to Engels, 18 June 1862, *MESC*, pp. 156–7.

99. Engels to P. L. Lavrov, 12–17 November 1875, *MESC*, p. 368. Cf., in addition, Engels to F. A. Lange, 29 March 1865, *MESC*, p. 208. In the *Dialectics of Nature*, p. 19, Engels had the following remarks to make about Darwin: 'Darwin did not know what a bitter satire he wrote on mankind, and especially on his countrymen, when he showed that free competition, the struggle for existence, which the economists celebrate as the highest historical achievement, is the normal state of the *animal kingdom*.'

100. Karl Kautsky, *Die materialistische Geschichtsauffassung*, Vol. II, Berlin, 1927, p. 630.

101. Marx to Lassalle, 16 January 1961, *MESC*, p. 151.

102. Karl Korsch, *Die materialistische Geschichtsauffassung*, Leipzig, 1929, p. 34. Cf. also the same author's excellent book, *Marxismus und Philosophie*, Leipzig, 1930, p. 135 et seq.

103. *Capital*, Vol. I, p. 169.

104. *German Ideology*, pp. 478–9.

105. On the ideological element in the division between the method of natural science and that of history, cf. also Ernst Bloch, 'Über Freiheit und objektive Gesetzlichkeit, politisch gefasst', *Deutsche Zeitschrift für Philosophie*, Vol. 2, Part 4, Berlin, 1954, p. 831 et seq.

106. *Deutsche Ideologie*, as printed in *Marx-Engels Gesamtausgabe*, Vol. V, Part 1, Berlin, 1932, p. 567. [This textual variant was not included in the final version of *The German Ideology*, as printed in the more accessible Berlin 1953 edition, and is therefore not to be found in the English translation of the same work.]

107. *German Ideology*, p. 51.

108. op. cit., p. 58.

109. loc. cit.

110. Printed in Franz Mehring's *Aus dem literarischen Nachlass von Karl Marx und Friedrich Engels*, Vol. 2, Stuttgart, 1920, p. 456.

111. *Economic and Philosophical Manuscripts*, p. 164.

112. loc. cit.

113. loc. cit.

114. cf. the untenable assertion in the essay by Iring Fetscher, 'Von der Philosophie des Proletariats zur proletarischen Weltanschauung', that Engels appeared not to have 'any eye for the socially conditioned nature of natural-scientific knowledge as well' (*Marxismusstudien*, Second Series, ed. I. Fetscher, Tübingen, 1957, p. 42, n. 1). Here we have made the attempt to bring in precisely this side of the thought of Engels in order to further the understanding of Marx's concept of nature. What is remarkable in Engels is precisely the unrelated juxta-position of a socially mediated and a dogmatic metaphysical concept of nature.

115. *Marxismusstudien*, p. 41. It is true that *Anti-Dühring* was written between 1876 and 1878 under the impact of external party-political circumstances of that sort. But Engels had already been engaged since 1858 on the attempt at a dialectical reconstruction of the natural sciences. In a letter of 14 July 1858 to Marx he asked for the dispatch of Hegel's *Naturphilosophie* and remarked: 'This much is certain: if he had a philosophy of nature to write *today* the facts would come flying to him from every side' (*MESC*, p. 131).

116. *Anti-Dühring*, p. 15.

117. The significance of this for the Marx of the middle period and later has been overlooked by most interpreters, just as in general the fact has been ignored that his turn to positive science did not exclude philosophy as an essential component of thought, and *vice versa*. Marx had a discontinuous relationship both with the concept of science and with that of philosophy. As opposed to an empiricism void of con-cepts, which consists solely in the ordering of 'everyday experience', 'which only grasps the misleading appearance of things' (*Wages, Price, and Profit*, in *MESW*, Vol. I, p. 424), Marx stressed the role of conceptual work, in the manner of Hegelian philosophy. On the other side, he did not hesitate to use the empirical discoveries of natural history against spiritualist metaphysics of all shades, including the Hegelian variety. Dialectical materialism is neither science, in the sense of a positivist collection of data, nor philosophy, in the sense of a speculative flight above the factual. Fetscher is therefore wrong to oppose Engels's 'scientific' thought in absolute terms to Marx's 'philosophical' thought. He mistakenly clings on to the programme of the 'supersession of philosophy through its realization', to be found in the young Marx, and confronts it as 'philosophy of the proletariat' with the 'proletarian world-view' (*Marxismusstudien*, pp. 26–60) as worked out by Engels in the 1870s and 1880s. He justifiably sees in the teachings of the later Engels a problematic extension of Marx's original conception into a 'Weltanschauung'. However he simultane-ously overlooks the point that the writings of the mature Marx, namely *Capital* and its first draft, the *Grundrisse*, have a far more significant

philosophical content than the occasional return to the theme of alienation, in that they contain, in part implicitly and in part explicitly, a materialist philosophy.

118. cf. Marx to Engels, 14 January 1858, in which Marx reported his preliminary work for *Capital*, and made explicit reference to Hegel: 'In the *method* of treatment the fact that by mere accident I again glanced through Hegel's *Logic* has been of great service to me – Freiligrath found some volumes of Hegel which originally belonged to Bakunin and sent them to me as a present. If there should ever be time for such work again, I would greatly like to make accessible to the ordinary human intelligence, in two or three printer's sheets, what is *rational* in the method which Hegel discovered but at the same time *mystified* . . .' (*MESC*, p. 121).

119. Marx to Engels, 1 February 1858, *MESC*, p. 123.

120. Engels to Marx, 14 July 1858, *MESC*, p. 131.

121. It cannot be established how far Marx was conscious of this difference between his concept of nature and that of Engels. What is certain is that he was familiar with the manuscript of *Anti-Dühring*. In *Capital*, Vol. I, p. 309, he appealed to the 'law of the transformation of quantity into quality', so often mentioned by Engels, as having shown its worth both in history and in natural science. On the question of the theoretical divergencies between Marx and Engels, cf. Manfred Friedrich, *Philosophie und Ökonomie beim jungen Marx* (Frankfurt dissertation), Berlin, 1960, p. 159.

122. The attempts made in the Soviet Union and Eastern Europe to cope with the most recent stage reached by physics from a philosophical point of view, as a continuation of Marx, Engels, and Lenin, are outside the field covered by this book. They are certainly of interest, because they show that Soviet philosophers, while in appearance sticking strictly to the empirical data of the natural sciences, do not shrink from speculative formulations in the style of Schelling's or Hegel's philosophies of nature. Like Hegel when dealing with the number of the planets, they have the greatest difficulty in harmonizing the empirical results with the theses of their 'all-embracing' materialism. Under Stalin, this problem led to the grotesque episode of the outlawing of Einstein's theory of relativity, an episode which has now of course come to an end. It is always the *existing results* of the natural sciences which are to be ordered with the help of the dialectical categories used in philosophical reflection. There can be no doubt that the natural sciences in the communist countries have not *directly* continued Engels's dialectics of nature in a methodological sense. When, very occasionally, such an attempt has been made, as in the book by Jacob Segal, *Die dialektische Methode in der Biologie*, Berlin, 1958, it is immediately apparent that in this interpretation the dialectic must become a collection of commonplaces, long familiar to the empirical investigator, though in a different form.

123. cf. *Marxismusstudien*, p. 27.

124. *Ludwig Feuerbach and the End of Classical German Philosophy*, *MESW*, Vol. II, p. 353. Despite what Fetscher says, Engels had much more in common with the French materialism of the eighteenth century than with the vulgarizers of his own time. This appears from the lively interest which he already showed in the French Enlightenment in the early 1840s, at which time he emphasized the metaphysical side as opposed to Marx, who praised Helvetius in the *Holy Family*, pp. 174–5, for conceiving materialism 'immediately in its application to social life'. In 1844, in the article 'Die Lage Englands, I, Das 18. Jahrhundert', printed in *Vorwärts*, Engels described materialism, despite the criticism which was already appearing at that time, as 'the summit of the science of the eighteenth century', as 'the first system of natural philosophy', and as the result of a 'perfection of the natural sciences' (*MEW*, Vol. I, p. 551).

125. On this point, see his statements in the *Anti-Dühring*, p. 16 et seq.

126. op. cit., p. 53.

127. op. cit., p. 62.

128. op. cit., p. 70.

129. op. cit., p. 158.

130. *Dialectics of Nature*, p. 26. The 'law of the negation of the negation' came into disrepute during the Stalin era as a survival of Hegelianism, and was first 'rehabilitated' after the Twentieth Congress of the CPSU.

131. *Anti-Dühring*, London, 1955, p. 458.

132. Engels, 'Die Lage Englands, I, Das 18. Jahrhundert', *MEW*, Vol. I, p. 551.

133. *Dialectics of Nature*, p. 155.

134. op. cit., p. 179.

135. *Capital*, Vol. I, p. 19.

136. 'Outlines of a Critique of Political Economy', printed in *Economic and Philosophic Manuscripts of 1844*, London, 1959, p. 177.

137. *Ludwig Feuerbach and the End of Classical German Philosophy*, *MEW*, Vol. 20, Berlin, 1962, p. 469.

138. In Engels, therefore, nature is always 'uncomprehended in the exact Hegelian sense of the word'. 'To comprehend an object,' wrote Hegel, 'means . . . nothing other than to grasp it in the form of something *limited* and *mediated*, and, with this, in so far as it is the true, the infinite, the unlimited, to transform it into the limited and the mediated and in such a way, instead of grasping the true in thought, to change it into its opposite, the untrue' (*Enzyklopädie*, 1817 edition, paragraph 62, p. 86).

139. *Capital*, Vol. I, p. 43. See also Chapter 2, section A below.

140. Engels to Schmidt, 1 November 1891, *MESC*, p. 520.

141. cf. the first thesis on Feuerbach, printed in *On Religion*, p. 69.

142. He is followed in this by Soviet philosophy of the present day, with its rigid and dogmatic distinction between dialectical and historical materialism, introduced by Stalin in 1938 with his book *On*

Dialectical and Historical Materialism, in which the former is portrayed as having to do only with nature, the latter only with society. As if, in Marx, materialism were not historical, precisely because it is dialectical, and *vice versa*! As if men's socio-historical existence did not contain within itself nature as a moment, in the same way as nature itself contains social existence! Dieter Bergner and Wolfgang Jahn, in their pamphlet *Der Kreuzzug der evangelischen Akademien gegen den Marxismus*, Berlin, 1960, also operate with two distinct 'fields of investigation' of the dialectic. The incontestable *factual* difference between the conceptions of nature held by Marx and by Engels vanishes with these authors into a mere difference in the method of approach: 'There exists . . . the possibility of directing attention to the material basis of thought, i.e. of investigating the dialectic of the forces of production and the relations of production or, alternatively, of abstracting from this problematic and dealing with the problems of the objective dialectic in nature' (p. 51 et seq.). The authors are unaware that this abstraction itself, characteristic of Engels's theory of nature as of all materialist metaphysics, marks the boundary of the possibility of any dialectic.

143. cf. also the critical remarks of Herbert Marcuse, which relate to the continuation of Engels's conception of the dialectic in present-day Soviet philosophy: 'Consequently, in trying to present dialectic "as such", Soviet Marxists can do nothing but distil from the concrete dialectical analysis of the "classics" certain principles, illustrate them, and confront them with "undialectical" thoughts' (*Soviet Marxism*, London, 1958, p. 143). It is no accident that there is in Marx no enumeration of abstract dialectical 'laws' and 'principles' – as Marcuse says, 'empty shells' – and that, unlike Engels, Marx hardly ever used the expression '*Weltanschauung*'.

144. Jakob Hommes, *Der technische Eros*, Freiburg, 1955, p. 80.

145. Horkheimer and Adorno, *Dialektik der Aufklärung*, p. 20.

146. cf. on this point Adorno, *Aspekte der Hegelschen Philosophie*, Frankfurt, 1957, p. 31: 'In so far as the world forms a system, it does so via the closed universality of social labour. . . .'

147. cf. *Capital*, Vol. I, p. 508 et seq.

148. cf. especially Chapter 3 of *Capital*.

149. *Anti-Dühring*, p. 53.

150. Horkheimer and Adorno, *Dialektik der Aufklärung*, p. 102. Heidegger, in his 'Brief über den Humanismus', endeavoured to defend Marx from 'all too cheap refutations' by pointing out that his materialism does not consist in the bare thesis that 'everything is only matter, but rather in a metaphysical determination according to which everything existent appears as the material of labour'. He failed to see that there are not here two simple alternatives. The relationship of pre-Marxist to historical materialism is more complex than that. Marxist materialism did not simply replace earlier materialism, but is rather earlier materialism's own critical reflection on itself, since it

shows what the phrase 'everything is only matter' signifies *in the last analysis*: everything is only matter for the practice which prevails at the relevant moment. The quotation is from M. Heidegger, *Platons Lehre von der Wahrheit*, Bern, 1954, p. 87 et seq.

151. This idea is discussed more fully in Chapter 3, section A.

152. cf. Merleau-Ponty, who asks in his essay 'Marxisme et philosophie', how to constitute a materialism which would count in the strict sense as dialectical: 'It has often been asked, and with reason, how a materialism could be dialectical, how matter, if one applies this word strictly, could contain the principle of productivity and novelty which is called a dialectic' (*Sens et non-sens*, Paris, 1948, p. 228). For a criticism of Engels's dialectics of nature, cf. also the shrewd analysis by J.-P. Sartre, 'Matérialisme et révolution', in *Situations*, I, Paris, 1947. Cf. in addition I. Fetscher, *Stalin über dialektischen und historischen Materialismus*, Frankfurt, 1956, p. 22 and p. 38.

153. cf. the East European collective volume written against Bloch, *Ernst Blochs Revision des Marxismus*, Berlin, 1957. The authors endeavour to play off Engels's position against that of Bloch. They completely overlook the fact that in Bloch's 'deviation' from the orthodox teaching they are merely confronted with Engels's own position in a more consistent form. Even the 'teleologism', which Bloch is particularly charged with, has its model in Engels. Thus, in the *Dialectics of Nature*, p. 228, Engels made the following attack on Haeckel, who in this case was a stricter materialist, although a more primitive one: 'That matter evolves out of itself the thinking human brain is for him a pure accident. . . . But the truth is that it is the nature of matter to advance to the evolution of thinking beings, hence, too, this always necessarily occurs wherever the conditions for it . . . are present.' Cf. also p. 158, where matter is described as 'causa finalis'. Engels was concerned, in his conception of matter, to keep at an equal distance from Mechanism and from Vitalism. This is why, in questions like that of the nature of organic life, the hidden spiritualization of matter does not emerge so plainly as it does in Bloch. However, Bloch's further development of Engels's conception of matter in the direction of a romantic nature-speculation only reveals what is, at bottom, already true of the latter.

154. cf. Herbert Marcuse's remarks on Hegel's logic and its relation to materialism (*Soviet Marxism*, p. 143).

155. Georg Lukács, *History and Class Consciousness*, London, 1971, p. 24, n. 6.

156. *Dialectics of Nature*, p. 173.

157. *Enzyclopädie*, I, Die Logik, supplement to paragraph 156, p. 346. (Wallace, p. 281.)

158. Second thesis on Feuerbach, printed in *On Religion*, p. 69.

159. *Critique of the Gotha Programme*, MESW, Vol. II, p. 18.

160. *Capital*, Vol. II, p. 144.

161. *Capital*, Vol. I, p. 177.

162. cf. in particular loc. cit. Maurice Merleau-Ponty attempts to save the concept of a dialectic of nature for Marx in a similar manner. He writes, in the essay 'Marxisme et philosophie': 'If nature is nature, that is to say external to us and to itself, one can find in it neither the relations nor the quality necessary to bear the weight of a dialectic. If nature is dialectical, it is because it is that nature perceived by man and inseparable from human action, as Marx made clear in the *Theses on Feuerbach* and in the *German Ideology*' (*Sens et non-sens*, p. 224). Konrad Bekker also interprets the Marxist dialectic as a dialectic of nature, in his dissertation, *Marx' philosophische Entwicklung, sein Verhältnis zu Hegel*, Zürich and New York, 1940, p. 103. Marx's conception of a dialectic of nature will be discussed more fully in Chapter 2, section B.

CHAPTER TWO

1. V. I. Lenin, *Materialism and Empirio-Criticism*, in *Collected Works*, Vol. 14, p. 260.
2. loc. cit.
3. *Holy Family*, p. 65. It is of course clear that both the determinations of matter are aspects of one and the same situation, namely the unity of the labour-process and the process of cognition. On Marx's strict theoretical realism with regard to the Object, see the *Grundrisse*, p. 384 and p. 388 et seq.
4. *Economic and Philosophical Manuscripts*, p. 207.
5. loc. cit.
6. *German Ideology*, p. 59.
7. Marx recognized such an identity in the emphatic Hegelian concept of 'reconciliation', in which a mediation of contradictories appears as something positively posited in the act.
8. *Economic and Philosophical Manuscripts*, p. 206 (translation adapted).
9. *Capital*, Vol. I, p. 202.
10. op. cit., p. 215, n. 1.
11. V. I. Lenin, *Philosophical Notebooks*, in *Collected Works*, Vol. 38, p. 360.
12. cf. *Capital*, Vol. I, p. 82: 'Since exchange-value is a definite social manner of expressing the amount of labour bestowed upon an object, nature has no more to do with it, than it has in fixing the *rate of exchange*.'
13. op. cit., p. 57.
14. op. cit., p. 47.
15. op. cit., p. 43. On the natural moment in labour, cf. also the *Critique of the Gotha Programme*, *MESW*, Vol. II, p. 18, where nature is described as 'the primary source of all instruments and objects of labour'. Marx rightly attacked the ideological formulation in the original draft of the programme, to the effect that labour was 'the

source of all wealth and all culture'. 'For it follows from the natural determination of labour, that the man who possesses no other property than his labour-power must be the slave, in all states of society and civilization, of other men who have made themselves the proprietors of the objective conditions of labour. He can only work with their permission, hence only live with their permission.' On the interpretation of the role of nature in the *Critique of the Gotha Programme*, cf. T. W. Adorno, *Aspekte der Hegelschen Philosophie*, p. 28, and W. Benjamin, *Schriften*, Vol. I, Frankfurt, 1955, p. 500 et seq. In *A Contribution to the Critique of Political Economy*, p. 33, there can also be found the idea that labour is by no means the sole source of material wealth: 'Being an activity intended to adapt materials to this or that purpose, it requires matter as a pre-requisite.' The notion that labour is the sole source of wealth is part of the ideological appearance which characterizes the sphere of circulation as a whole. In the sphere of circulation, there arises the illusion that all the elements of the process of production originate in the circulation of commodities: 'This one-sided conception overlooks those elements of the process of production which are independent of the commodity-elements' (*Capital*, Vol. II, p. 101). Here too, Marx had in mind the natural materials already at society's disposal.

16. cf. *German Ideology*, p. 58.
17. *Capital*, Vol. I, p. 71.
18. op. cit., p. 189.
19. op. cit., p. 181.
20. *Economic and Philosophical Manuscripts*, p. 202.
21. *Ludwig Feuerbach and the End of Classical German Philosophy*, *MESW*, Vol. II, p. 387.
22. *Capital*, Vol. I, pp. 71–83.
23. op. cit., p. 38.
24. op. cit., p. 72.
25. op. cit., p. 82.
26. op. cit., p. 83.
27. *A Contribution to the Critique of Political Economy*, p. 31.
28. op. cit., p. 273. On the social determinacy of all appropriation of nature by man, see also *Wage Labour and Capital*, *MESW*, Vol. I, pp. 89–90.
29. *Capital*, Vol. I, p. 83.
30. op. cit., p. 77.
31. loc. cit.
32. As for example in certain passages in Bloch, whose critique of bourgeois 'commodity-thought', inspired in large measure by the early Lukács, runs the risk of abandoning the materialist position.
33. *Capital*, Vol. I, p. 58.
34. op. cit., p. 79.
35. Georg Lukács, *History and Class Consciousness*, London, 1971, p. 234.

36. Siegfried Marck, *Die Dialektik in der Philosophie der Gegenwart*, Vol. I, Tübingen, 1929, p. 131, criticizes Lukács's presentation of the Marxist concept of nature, and correctly poses the question 'whether the existence of nature is to be conceived as *in toto* the product of society'.

37. *Capital*, Vol. I, p. 178.

38. op. cit., p. 43.

39. cf. Marx's critique of the Hegelian concept of absolute knowledge, in the Paris Manuscript entitled 'Critique of Hegel's Dialectic and General Philosophy' (*Economic and Philosophical Manuscripts*, pp. 195–219). On Marx's critique and interpretation of Hegel's *Phenomenology*, cf. in particular Georg Lukács, *Der junge Hegel*, Berlin, 1954.

40. A criticism which does not of course refer strictly only to the Hegel of the *Phenomenology*. In fact, when he was first developing his theory, Marx was less concerned with Hegelian idealism itself than with its Young Hegelian distortion. Bruno Bauer and his school, as well as the 'True Socialists', had a tendency to reduce Hegel's 'Spirit' to an infinite self-consciousness conceived practically in a Fichtean manner. This was true of Karl Grün, for instance, whose extreme subjectivism was criticized by Marx and Engels in the *German Ideology*, p. 524: 'We see here, moreover, what the *true socialists* understand by "free activity". Our author imprudently reveals to us that it is activity which "is not determined by things external to us", i.e. *actus purus*, pure, absolute activity, which is nothing but activity and amounts in the last instance to much the same thing as the illusion of "pure thought". It naturally sullies the purity of this activity if one imputes to it a material basis and a material result. . . .' It is obvious that the position criticized in this passage is not simply equivalent to Hegel's. Although in the course of his polemic Marx occasionally summarily lumped together the idealism of Hegel and the idealism of the Young Hegelians, he ultimately still remained aware of the essential difference between objective idealism and the various kinds of subjective idealism. For example, in the *Holy Family*, p. 255: 'Finally, it goes without saying that if Hegel's *Phenomenology*, in spite of its speculative original sin, gives in many instances the elements of a true description of human relations, Herr Bruno and Co., on the other hand, provide only an empty caricature. . . .'

41. *Economic and Philosophical Manuscripts*, p. 201, cf. also pp. 203–04.

42. *Capital*, Vol. I, pp. 42–3.

43. The preliminary studies for the first volume of *Capital* and for *A Contribution to the Critique of Political Economy*, which date from the years 1857–59, have been published under the title *Grundrisse der Kritik der politischen Ökonomie* (*Rohentwurf*). Although the *Grundrisse* contain an extraordinary amount of new material on the question of Marx's relation to Hegel and, through Hegel, to Aristotle, they have so far hardly been used in discussions of Marx's philosophy. From the

point of view of his intellectual development, they represent the connecting link between the Paris Manuscripts and the fully-formed materialist economics of the mature Marx. The *Grundrisse*, despite their partially fragmentary character, contain without a doubt Marx's most philosophically significant statements. It emerges more plainly from the *Grundrisse* than from the final version of *Capital*, that Marx's later thought was strongly determined by Hegelian philosophical positions, although he himself was loth to admit this. A study of this work can contribute in particular to the demolition of the legend, which still presses heavily on discussions of Marx, that only the thought of the 'young Marx' is of philosophical interest, and that the later, factually economic, problematic buried all the original impulse of real humanism. A typical example of the untenable thesis that there is an absolute break between the thought of the young and the mature Marx, is provided by Ralf Dahrendorf's dissertation, *Marx in Perspektive*, Hannover, 1952, p. 165 et seq. Dahrendorf divides Marx's work into 'two parts which cannot be bound together by any sensible connection of principle'. He distinguishes a 'prophetic conception of history', in the 1840s, from the 'hypotheses of social science' produced by the middle and later Marx. Dahrendorf overlooks the fact that the essential categories of the Marxist dialectic were developed precisely in his later work and that, for an objective interpretation, it is only necessary to disentangle them from their economic disguise. The official interpretation, on the other hand, while apparently taking Marx seriously insists on the 'ethical core', the 'existential preoccupation' of the early Marx but at the same time hides from view the analysis of the total process of capitalist production, which is significant precisely for its realization of the young Marx's intentions.

44. cf. *Capital*, Vol. I, p. 183. On the dialectic of consumption and production, cf. in particular *A Contribution to the Critique of Political Economy*, pp. 276–83. It is worth noticing that where Marx unfolded the identity of consumption and production, he made use of extra-human nature as a model. For example, see p. 277: 'Consumption is directly also production, just as in nature the consumption of the elements and of chemical matter constitutes production of plants.'

45. *Grundrisse*, p. 208.

46. loc. cit.

47. *Capital*, Vol. I, p. 179. Cf. p. 181, where Marx wrote: 'But in the great majority of cases, *instruments of labour* show, even to the most superficial observer, traces of the labour of past ages.'

48. op. cit., p. 183.

49. op. cit., p. 178.

50. loc. cit.

51. loc. cit.

52. op. cit., p. 181.

53. cf. *Grundrisse*, p. 267.

54. *Capital*, Vol. I, p. 183. The further processing of use-values, the

continued transformation of nature in its inorganic, plant, animal, and human form – as the result as well as the condition of changing extra-human nature – all these processes can extend over long periods of time. This point is made on p. 181: 'Animals and plants, which we are accustomed to consider as products of nature, are in their present form not only products of, say, last year's labour, but the result of a gradual transformation, continued through many generations, under man's superintendence, and by means of his labour.'

55. op. cit., p. 183.

56. op. cit., p. 182.

57. op. cit., p. 183.

58. *Grundrisse*, p. 116.

59. *Capital*, Vol. I, p. 177.

60. cf. Ernst Bloch, *Das Prinzip Hoffnung*, Vol. II, Berlin, 1955, p. 244 et seq.

61. op. cit., Vol. III, Berlin, 1959, p. 391.

62. *Grundrisse*, p. 265.

63. op. cit., p. 268.

64. op. cit., p. 265 et seq.

65. op. cit., p. 226.

66. *Economic and Philosophical Manuscripts*, p. 155.

[66a. 'Metabolism' is a rendering of 'Stoffwechsel', a term repeatedly used in *Capital*, and translated in the English edition as 'material re-action' or 'exchange of matter'.]

67. *Capital*, Vol. I, p. 43.

68. op. cit., p. 177.

69. cf. Roger Garaudy, *La théorie matérialiste de la connaissance*, Paris, 1953, p. 301. The idea of such a 'cosmic' dimension of human action can be traced back to the alchemistic doctrine of transmutation held by the philosophers of the Renaissance, an embryonic, still magical form of modern man's mastery of nature. Man forces what is present in the world to its furthest conclusions. Paracelsus put it as follows: 'For nature is so subtle and sharp in its things, that it refuses to be made use of without the application of great skill. For nature brings nothing forth which is perfect within itself; man must rather perfect it. This perfection is called alchemy' (*Paracelsus, seine Welt-schau in Worten des Werkes*, ed. E. Jaeckle, Zürich, 1942, p. 83).

70. Human practice can of course only act in the same way as nature itself, namely change the forms of its materials. However, Marx could not have suspected that the twentieth century would succeed in raising the efficacy of the energies contained in nature in such an awesome way. The artificially produced decay of radioactive elements admittedly takes place only on the basis of the decay which is naturally present, but it does represent a qualitative change in comparison with the latter.

71. Thus Engels, in his essay on Feuerbach (*MESW*, Vol. II, p. 374), found fault with the old materialism for its inability 'to comprehend

the universe as a process, as matter undergoing an uninterrupted historical development'.

72. Pietro Verri, in Custodi's edition of the Italian economists, *Parte Moderna*, Vol. XV, p. 22. Cited by Marx in *Capital*, Vol. I, p. 43, n. 1.

73. *Capital*, Vol. I, p. 177. [The words '*durch diese Bewegung*', omitted in the English translation, have been translated here as 'through this motion' to accord with Schmidt's argument.]

74. op. cit., p. 215, n. 1.

75. *Dialectics of Nature*, Appendix 1, p. 320.

76. *Capital*, Vol. I, p. 192.

77. Leo Löwenthal, 'C. F. Meyers heroische Geschichtsauffassung', *Zeitschrift für Sozialforschung*, Vol. 2, Part 1, 1933, p. 42. Löwenthal stressed the socio-historical obstacles which, before Marx, prevented the development of a theory of the social appropriation of nature which would do justice to the facts.

78. *Capital*, Vol. I, p. 179.

79. At this point, the analysis of the labour-process in *Capital*, Vol. I, p. 177, should be recalled. Here Marx said that man 'himself confronts the stuff of nature as a force of nature'. The opposition expressed here between man as the 'self-conscious thing' (op. cit., p. 202) and the stuff of nature, is *relative* to the epistemological distinction between idealism and materialism. 'The limits of the absolute necessity and absolute truth of this relative contrast', wrote Lenin in *Materialism and Empirio-Criticism*, p. 246, entirely in line with Marx, 'are precisely those limits which define the *trend* of epistemological investigations. To operate beyond these limits with the antithesis of matter and mind, physical and mental, as though they were absolute opposites, would be a great mistake.' *Within* the mediation of all material existence through consciousness, the priority of the former continues to be upheld.

80. First thesis on Feuerbach, printed in *On Religion*, p. 69.

81. On the problem of simultaneously dialectical and materialist thought, cf. T. W. Adorno, *Zur Metakritik der Erkenntnistheorie*, Stuttgart, 1956, p. 193: 'The theoretical demarcation of idealism does not lie in the determination of ontological substrata or primeval words, but first of all in the awareness of the irreducibility of what *is* to one pole, however constituted, of an insuperable divergence.'

82. *Economic and Philosophical Manuscripts*, pp. 126–7.

83. loc. cit. Cf. *Dialectics of Nature*, p. 292.

84. *Economic and Philosophical Manuscripts*, p. 127.

85. loc cit.

86. op. cit., p. 128.

87. loc. cit.

88. *Grundrisse*, p. 391. This expression for the natural process is already found in Paracelsus.

89. op. cit., p. 398.

90. op. cit., p. 392.

91. *Capital*, Vol. I, p. 179.

92. *Grundrisse*, p. 388. [The last five words here have been italicized by the author.]

93. op. cit., p. 389.

94. op. cit., p. 763.

95. op. cit., p. 389.

96. op. cit., p. 397.

97. op. cit., p. 396.

98. op. cit., p. 397.

99. This question is dealt with in Chapter 3.

100. cf. Chapter 4.

101. *Capital*, Vol. I, p. 178.

102. op. cit., pp. 42–3.

103. op. cit., p. 177.

104. loc. cit.

105. Marcel Reding, *Der politische Atheismus*, Graz, 1957, p. 92.

106. *A Contribution to the Critique of Political Economy*, p. 273.

107. op. cit., p. 274.

108. cf. op. cit., p. 269.

109. Marcel Reding, *Der politische Atheismus*, p. 92.

110. *A Contribution to the Critique of Political Economy*, p. 279.

111. *Grundrisse*, p. 157.

112. On the historical determinacy of human nature, cf. numerous passages of the *Grundrisse*, which are of the utmost importance for the understanding of Marx. Cf. also Vernon Venable, *Human Nature: the Marxian View*, New York, 1945, a dissertation which is rich in material but does not take account either of the Paris Manuscripts or of the *Grundrisse*. Ernst Bloch comments on the relation between the history of society and the structure of instinctual drives in his attempt to give a Marxist interpretation of psychoanalysis (*Das Prinzip Hoffnung*, Vol. I, Berlin, 1954, p. 80 et seq).

113. Sixth thesis on Feuerbach, printed in *On Religion*, p. 71.

114. T. W. Adorno, 'Über Statik und Dynamik als soziologische Kategorien', *Soziologica II*, in *Frankfurter Beiträge zur Soziologie*, Vol. 10, p. 237. Cf. *Capital*, Vol. I, p. 8.

115. *Capital*, Vol. I, pp. 42–3.

116. It is interesting that, at approximately the same time, Schopenhauer, who can hardly be suspected of revolutionary inclinations, perceived the moment of identity in the different forms of domination in the same way as Marx. Schopenhauer put it as follows: 'Poverty and slavery are . . . only two forms, one might almost say two names, of the same situation, whose essence consists in the fact that the powers of a man are in large part not exercised on behalf of himself but on behalf of others; whence emerges for him in part an excessive burden of work, in part a meagre satisfaction of his needs. For nature has given man only enough vital forces to allow him to preserve his existence on earth, with a moderate exertion of the same: he has not received a great surplus of forces. If now the joint burden of the

physical maintenance of the existence of the human race is removed from a not inconsiderable portion of the latter, it follows that the remainder is by that fact excessively burdened and in misery. Thus arises that evil which, either under the name of slavery or that of the proletariat, has burdened the great majority of the human race at all times' (*Sämtliche Werke*, ed. Paul Deussen, Munich, 1913, Vol. II, *Parerga und Paralipomena*, p. 268).

117. *Capital*, Vol. I, p. 511.

118. op. cit., p. 512.

119. op. cit., pp. 511–12.

120. op. cit., p. 512.

121. On the problem of a 'negative ontology' in Marx, cf. in particular Chapter 4.

122. cf. the letters to Kugelmann, which show, like the correspondence with Engels, that Marx was familiar both with the sensualist, materialist physiologists Cabanis and de Tracy, from whom the concept of ideology originated, and with the discussion of the 1850s on materialism, in part through the medium of F. A. Lange's book on the history of materialism.

123. cf. Feuerbach's review of Moleschott's book *Lehre der Nahrungsmittel* (1850) entitled 'Die Naturwissenschaft und die Revolution', printed in Karl Grün, *Ludwig Feuerbach in seinem Briefwechsel und Nachlass sowie in seiner philosophischen Charakterentwicklung*, Leipzig and Heidelberg, 1874, Vol. II, p. 81.

124. cf. Jakob Moleschott, *Der Kreislauf des Lebens*, Mainz, 1857, p. 27 et seq. Reasoning of this kind makes Moleschott an 'epigone of the philosophy of nature' in the eyes of F. A. Lange, *Geschichte des Materialismus*, Vol. 2, Iserlohn, 1875, p. 97.

125. Jakob Moleschott, *Der Kreislauf des Lebens*, p. 40 et seq.

126. op. cit., p. 42.

127. op. cit., p. 86.

128. op. cit., p. 394.

129. We shall return to this point later in another connection. The chemist J. von Liebig, whose views were not without influence on Marx (cf. *Capital*, Vol. I, p. 506, n. 1), compared the metabolism in nature with the same process in the body politic, in his book *Chemische Briefe*, Heidelberg, 1851, p. 622 et seq.

130. cf. *Capital*, Vol. I, p. 43, n. 1.

131. op. cit., pp. 42–3.

132. Marx to Feuerbach, 30 October 1843, printed in Karl Grün, op. cit., p. 360 et seq. Cf. on the relation of Marx to Schelling, G. V. Plekhanov, *Fundamental Problems of Marxism*, p. 19, where the 'honest youthful idea' of Schelling is interpreted in the sense of a materialist monism. Georg Lukács entered in more detail into the anti-romantic, indeed the unequivocally materialistic impulses of Schelling's philosophy of nature, as reflected for example in the remarkable anti-religious poem of 1799, 'Epikuräisches Glaubens-

bekenntnis von Heinz Widerporst' (G. Lukács, *Der junge Hegel*, Berlin, 1954, p. 293).

133. cf. Karl Grün, op. cit., p. 361.

134. cf. F. W. J. von Schelling, *Ideen zu einer Philosophie der Natur*, 1797–8. Published in *Sämtliche Werke*, Section I, Vol. II, Stuttgart and Augsburg, 1857, pp. 511–54. Engels too wrote of the 'eternal cycle, in which matter moves . . . ' (*Dialectics of Nature*, p. 24).

135. Schelling, op. cit., p. 518.

136. op. cit., p. 520.

137. op. cit., p. 518.

138. *Grundrisse*, p. 116. Cf. also section A of this chapter.

139. Schelling, op. cit., p. 519.

140. *Capital*, Vol. I, p. 505.

141. op. cit., p. 506.

142. cf. in addition Ernst Bloch, *Das Prinzip Hoffnung*, Vol. II, p. 239.

143. *Capital*, Vol. I. pp. 513–14.

144. op. cit., p. 513.

145. *German Ideology*, p. 31.

146. *Capital*, Vol. I, p. 71.

147. op. cit., p. 508.

148. op. cit., p. 486.

149. loc. cit.

150. cf. op. cit., p. 180.

151. Thus he described the mechanical instruments of labour as the 'bones and muscles of production', and those instruments of labour which serve only to hold the materials as the 'vascular system of production' (*Capital*, Vol. I, p. 180).

152. Hermann Diels, *Fragmente der Vorsokratiker*, I, Berlin, 1922, fragment 90.

153. *A Contribution to the Critique of Political Economy*, p. 33.

154. cf. *Capital*, Vol. I, p. 72.

155. *A Contribution to the Critique of Political Economy*, p. 55.

156. op. cit., p. 109.

CHAPTER THREE

1. *Capital*, Vol. I, p. 71.

2. This concept of 'form', absent from Engels and repeatedly used by the mature Marx to characterize the inherent determinacy of the natural materials which are to be worked on, could well be traced back to Aristotle and to Francis Bacon's theory of forms, in which the classical heritage is often mingled with modern thinking. For Marx and, in a similar way, for Bacon, the fact that the materials possess a form is identical with the fact that they are subject to general laws. For both thinkers, knowledge of the 'forms' of nature is nothing other than the means of improving man's control of nature.

3. Marx pointed out in *Capital*, Vol. I, p. 514, n. 1, that entire branches of natural science owe their beginnings to the practical requirements of society.

4. Francis Bacon, *Novum Organon*, London, 1893, p. 11.

5. On the Hegelian concept of practice, cf. Wilhelm R. Beyer, 'Der Begriff der Praxis bei Hegel', *Deutsche Zeitschrift für Philosophie*, Vol. 6, Part 5, Berlin, 1958.

6. *German Ideology*, p. 58.

7. op. cit., p. 59.

8. *Holy Family*, p. 65.

9. Lenin, *The Agrarian Question and the 'Critics of Marx'*, in *Collected Works*, Vol. 5, p. 111.

10. cf. Bloch, *Das Prinzip Hoffnung*, Vol. II, p. 240.

11. cf. *Economic and Philosophical Maniscripts*, p. 217.

12. J.-Y. Calvez, *La pensée de Karl Marx*, Paris, 1956, p. 380; cf. also p. 378.

13. op. cit., p. 396.

14. Georges M-M. Cottier, *L'Athéisme du jeune Marx: Ses origines Hégéliennes*, Paris, 1959, p. 319.

15. op. cit., p. 321.

16. *Grundrisse*, p. 265.

17. *Capital*, Vol. I, p. 177. On the relation between matter and ontology, see also the relevant discussions in Chapter 1, section A above. [17a. 'Movement' and 'motion' are alternative renderings of the German word 'Bewegung', both of which are required by the English context at different points.]

18. Despite some metaphysical exaggerations, Bloch's reflections on the concept of matter in dialectical materialism correctly stress the elements of romantic nature-speculation in Marx. These elements are present not only in the early writings but also, as we have tried to show, in the economic works of a later period. In the history of materialism, there are two main parallel tendencies, which cross in some thinkers. The one leads from the atomism of Democritus, via the physics of the Renaissance, to the one-sided natural-scientific materialism of the eighteenth and nineteenth centuries. The other tendency, of a more pantheistic nature, which Bloch calls the 'Aristotelian left', and to which in his view Marx belongs, developed from the naturalistically inclined form/matter problematic adopted by the Latin Averroist interpreters of Aristotle, via Giordano Bruno and Bacon, whose teaching according to Marx contained within itself 'the germs of all-round development' (*Holy Family*, p. 172), and finally through Jakob Böhme to the crypto-materialist elements of the romantic philosophy of nature.

19. *Holy Family*, p. 172. On the question of the motion of matter in Marx cf. Roger Garaudy, *Perspectives de l'homme*, Paris, 1959, p. 88 et seq.; also *Dialectics of Nature*, pp. 173–4.

20. cf. Chapter 1, section A.

21. Calvez, op. cit., p. 378.
22. Marx to Kugelmann, 11 July 1868, *MESC*, p. 251.
23. Lenin, *The Economic Content of Narodism and the Criticism of it in Mr Struve's Book*, in *Collected Works*, Vol. I, p. 420.
24. *Capital*, Vol. I, p. 43.
25. *Anti-Dühring*, p. 128.
26. cf. on Wolff's teleology, Engels, *Dialectics of Nature*, p. 7.
27. Marx to Lassalle, 16 January 1861, *MESC*, p. 151.
28. *Capital*, Vol. I, p. 372, n. 3.
29. loc. cit.
30. op. cit., p. 178.
31. cf. Hegel, *Enzyclopädie*, II, Naturphilosophie, p. 36 (Miller, p. 5).
32. cf. Hegel, *Die Vernunft in der Geschichte*, p. 29.
33. *Introduction to the Critique of Hegel's Philosophy of Right*, p. 43.
34. Hegel, *Enzyclopädie*, II, Naturphilosophie, paragraph 245, p. 35 (Miller, p. 4).
35. *Capital*, Vol. I, p. 178.
36. loc. cit.
37. *A Contribution to the Critique of Political Economy*, p. 279.
38. Hegel, *Phänomenologie des Geistes*, Hamburg, 1952, p. 287 (Baillie, p. 422).
39. cf. Lenin, *Philosophical Notebooks*, p. 177.
40. Paul Valéry, *Über Kunst*, Frankfurt, 1959, p. 69.
41. *Capital*, Vol. I, p. 178.
42. op. cit., p. 179.
43. Hegel, *Enzyclopädie*, III, Philosophie des Geistes, paragraph 411, supplement, p. 248.
44. *Capital*, Vol. I, p. 179.
45. op. cit., p. 35.
46. On the relation between tool and machine in Marx, cf. op. cit., pp. 371–4.
47. Bloch, *Das Prinzip Hoffnung*, Vol. II, p. 232 et seq.
48. *Capital*, Vol. I, p. 386.
49. *Grundrisse*, p. 389.
50. *Capital*, Vol. I, p. 387.
51. On the historical interpenetration of labour, language, and thought, cf. Béla Fogarasi, *Logik*, Berlin, 1955, pp. 88–111.
52. Hegel, *Jenenser Realphilosophie*, Leipzig, 1932, p. 221.
53. *Capital*, Vol. I. p. 177.
54. op. cit., p. 179. In the same paragraph there is a discussion of the historical role of the animal as an instrument of labour. Marx uses the concept of the 'instrument' in a still broader sense. The whole of material reality is a potential instrument for achieving human aims. As such it is an instrument of production. The instruments of production in their turn can be divided into the instruments of labour, made use of by men and discussed here, on the one side, and the

things which are the objects of human labour, on the other. Cf. op. cit., p. 180.

55. Hegel, *Enzyclopädie*, I, Die Logik, paragraph 206, supplement, p. 420 (Wallace, p. 350). Whereas Marx, as a materialist, restricted the 'cunning of reason' to the human work-situation, Hegel saw the action of 'reason' in the impact of God's providence on the world and its development, and it therefore also played a great part in the construction of his theory of history.

56. *Capital*, Vol. II, p. 392.

57. Hegel, *Wissenschaft der Logik*, II, Leipzig, 1951, p. 398 (Miller, p. 747).

58. *Capital*, Vol. II, p. 162.

59. Hegel, *Enzyclopädie*, I, Die Logik, paragraph 210, p. 420 (Wallace, p. 350).

60. *Capital*, Vol. I, p. 181.

61. loc. cit.

62. loc. cit.

63. Lenin, *Philosophical Notebooks*, p. 189.

64. *Capital*, Vol. I, p. 179.

65. cf. Hegel, *Wissenchaft der Logik*, II, p. 385 (Miller, p. 735).

66. Hegel, *Enzyclopädie*, I, Die Logik, paragraph 204, p. 413 (Wallace, p. 343).

67. op. cit., paragraph 202, p. 412 (Wallace, p. 342).

68. *Grundrisse*, p. 208.

69. cf. op. cit., p. 265.

70. cf. Lenin's definition, which follows Hegel's: 'Life=the individual Subject separates itself off from the Objective' (*Philosophical Notebooks*, p. 202).

71. *Capital*, Vol. I, p. 177. Hegel, as Adorno said (cf. Adorno, *Aspekte*, p. 29), does not make the Spirit a moment of labour, but labour a moment of the Spirit. He cannot therefore, in Marxist fashion, see in the relation of purpose a self-mediation of nature, but must view the realized purpose as the achievement 'of the free, self-subsistent Concept which unites itself with itself through objectivity' (Hegel, *Wissenschaft der Logik*, II, p. 390 [Miller, p. 739]). The realized purpose is therefore not only the 'unity of the subjective and the objective' (i.e., in Marxist language, the connection between labour and the material of nature), but also, as the first stage of the Idea, its identity existing-in-itself.

72. On the relationship of the categories Mechanism, Chemism, and Teleology, cf. Georg Lukács, *Der junge Hegel*, Berlin, 1954, p. 397 et seq. Cf. also Lenin, *Philosophical Notebooks*, pp. 187–8, where he makes it plain that the category of Teleology has been insufficiently appreciated as an aspect of Marx's relationship with Hegel. Lenin translated important sections of Hegel's *Logic* into the language of dialectical materialism, emphasizing the role of mechanical and chemical laws as 'the foundations of men's activity appropriate to a

given purpose'. Mechanical and chemical causality, while being external to the purpose, is at the same time the instrument of its realization. Purposive activity and natural laws interpenetrate as two sides of one objective process.

73. Hegel, *Enzyclopädie*, I, Die Logik, paragraph 206, p. 417 (Wallace, p. 347).

74. cf. Maurice Merleau-Ponty, *Marxisme et philosophie*, p. 230.

75. Hegel, *Enzyclopädie*, I, Die Logik, paragraph 211, p. 421 (Wallace, pp. 350–1).

76. loc. cit.

77. *Capital*, Vol. I, p. 182.

78. For the reasons given, such a 'foundation' cannot be read from Marx's works. Hence the Austro-Marxists, misinterpreting Marx as a 'naïve realist', endeavoured to 'improve' or 'extend' his theory along subjective idealist or alternatively neo-Kantian lines.

79. Konrad Bekker, *Marx' philosophische Entwicklung, sein Verhältnis zu Hegel*, dissertation, Zürich and New York, 1940, p. 48.

80. *Capital*, Vol. I, p. 178.

81. *Grundrisse*, p. 269.

82. On dialectical materialism's concept of the Subject, cf. G. A. Wetter, *Dialectical Materialism*, London, 1958, p. 496.

83. *Economic and Philosophical Manuscripts*, pp. 162–3.

84. op. cit., p. 161.

85. *A Contribution to the Critique of Political Economy*, p. 294.

86. *Dialectics of Nature*, p. 172.

87. 'Randglossen zu Adolph Wagners Lehrbuch der politischen Ökonomie', printed in *MEW*, Vol. 19, p. 355. As far as the controversy between Marx and Wagner is related to the concept of value, the marginal notes are printed in the appendix of *Das Kapital*, Vol. I, p. 841 et seq. This is a reference to the editions up to 1961; after 1961 this appendix was transferred to volume 19 of the collected works in the East German edition.

88. This rigid nominalism contradicts the unity of conceptual realism and nominalism which is a feature of the economic analysis. On the essential nature of concepts in Marx, see Engels to Kautsky, 20 September 1884, *MESC*, p. 454.

89. Lenin made a similar attempt in the *Philosophical Notebooks* to derive the axiomatic character of logical expressions from accumulated experience: 'Men's practical activity had to direct men's consciousness millions of times towards the repetition of the various logical expressions, in order that these expressions could attain the significance of *axioms*' (p. 190).

90. Marx first pointed to the connection between the conceptual system of the *Phenomenology* and the concept of labour in the Paris Manuscripts: 'The outstanding achievement of Hegel's *Phenomenology* – the dialectic of negativity as the moving and creating principle – is, first, that Hegel grasps the self-creation of man as a process,

objectification as loss of the Object, as alienation and supersession of this alienation, and that he, therefore, grasps the nature of *labour*, and conceives objective man (true, because real man) as the result of his *own labour*' (*Economic and Philosophical Manuscripts*, p. 202).

91. Pierre Naville, *Psychologie, marxisme, matérialisme*, Paris, 1948, p. 171. On the practico-historical mediation of knowledge in Marx, cf. Béla Fogarasi, *Logik*, p. 366. Cf. the little-known but important book by Max Raphael, *Zur Erkenntnistheorie der konkreten Dialektik*, Paris, 1934, p. 31.

92. Lenin, *Philosophical Notebooks*, p. 319, 362. The insufficient understanding of the epistemological character of the dialectic is also connected with the fact that in authors like Plekhanov it almost always appears as a mere 'collection of examples'.

93. First thesis on Feuerbach, printed in *On Religion*, p. 69.

94. *A Contribution to the Critique of Political Economy*, p. 294.

95. *Grundrisse*, p. 594.

96. *Capital*, Vol. I, p. 508.

97. J.-P. Sartre, 'Matérialisme et révolution', *Situations*, I, Paris, 1957, p. 213.

98. *Economic and Philosophical Manuscripts*, p. 162.

99. op. cit., p. 206.

100. cf. *Capital*, Vol. I, p. 179.

101. In *Materialism and Empirio-Criticism*, Lenin emphasized the moment of material existence's independence of consciousness in a one-sided manner characteristic of naïve reflective realism. Many interpreters, failing to recognize that the book was conditioned by factors in the history of the Russian Social Democratic Party, believe that they have found in it dialectical materialism's last word on epistemological questions. In fact, however, Lenin's view only represents the abstract antithesis of the subjective idealism of Mach, Avenarius, and their Russian supporters, in the same way as Feuerbach's materialism (according to the *Theses on Feuerbach*) was the abstract antithesis of Hegel's absolute idealism. It is no accident that Lenin repeatedly called on the authority of Feuerbach. We meet with Feuerbachian abstractions in Lenin's remarks that 'matter' or 'the external world' is mirrored or copied by the senses. In real history, matter and the external world are always elements of the social relations of production. If the problematic notion of the 'reflection' is to be retained, it must be said that reality reflects men's practice, as much as their consciousness reflects reality. In other writings, of course, Lenin adopted a more dialectical position than that of *Materialism and Empiriocriticism*.

102. Lenin, *Philosophical Notebooks*, p. 212.

103. Hegel, *Phänomenologie des Geistes*, Hamburg, 1952, p. 287 (Baillie, p. 422).

104. *Capital*, Vol. I, p. 178.

105. cf. Horkheimer and Adorno, *Dialektik der Aufklärung*, p. 121 et

seq. The authors refer here to the physiological aspect of perception.
J. H. Horn, in *Widerspiegelung und Begriff*, Berlin, 1958, endeavoured
to clarify the concept of 'reflection', repeatedly used in Marxist
literature to characterize the relation of knowing. He showed that the
source of the immediate sensations must be 'nature' alone. The distinction between socially appropriated and as yet unappropriated
nature is irrelevant at the level of sensation. 'But an intellectual and
conceptual element is already contained in perceptions. . . .' (op. cit.,
p. 94, and cf. p. 96 et seq).

106. S. L. Rubinstein, *Grundlagen der allgemeinen Psychologie* (in
Russian), Moscow, 1946; German translation from Russian, Berlin,
1948, p. 131.

107. *Capital*, Vol. I, p. 19.

108. *A Contribution to the Critique of Political Economy*, p. 294.

109. op. cit., p. 293.

110. op. cit., p. 294.

111. op. cit., p. 293.

112. *Grundrisse*, p. 594.

113. op. cit., p. 599.

114. *Capital*, Vol. I, p. 423.

115. *Grundrisse*, p. 594.

116. loc. cit. On the relation between natural science, the history of
technology, and the history of material production, cf. Gerhard
Kosel, *Produktivkraft Wissenschaft*, Berlin, 1957, in which the author
traces both the social determinacy of natural science, and the development of the latter into an independent productive force within the
infrastructure.

117. Second thesis on Feuerbach, printed in *On Religion*, p. 69.

118. Max Horkheimer, 'Traditionelle und kritische Theorie', *Zeitschrift für Sozialforschung*, Vol. 6, Part 2, Paris, 1937, p. 252.

119. Lenin, *Materialism and Empirio-Criticism*, pp. 142–3.

120. Lenin, *Philosophical Notebooks*, p. 211.

121. Ernst Bloch in particular made this point in his interpretation of
the *Theses on Feuerbach*. Cf. *Das Prinzip Hoffnung*, Vol. I, section 19.
The truth of an ideology does not consist, for Marx, in its practical
effectiveness in assuring the continued existence of domination. In the
Soviet Union, after Lenin's death, and also of course under the impact
of material conditions, the idea that all thought must serve 'socialist
construction', thinly rationalized by the use of Marxist terminology,
led to a practicist narrowing of theory, and a political suspicion of any
free thought.

122. *Grundrisse*, p. 594.

123. *Capital*, Vol. I, p. 180.

124. First thesis on Feuerbach, printed in *On Religion*, p. 69.

125. Max Horkheimer, 'Traditionelle und kritische Theorie', *Zeitschrift für Sozialforschung*, Vol. 6, Part 2, Paris, 1937, p. 257.

126. *Capital*, Vol. I, p. 43.

127. In the book by J.-Y.Calvez, *La pensée de Karl Marx*, Marxist materialism is presented as a theory of the constitution of reality, which leans so far towards Kant that the elaborated material of nature is deprived of any inherent structure of its own. According to Calvez, the *dialectical* character of this materialism consists in the fact that 'the totality of experience is constituted by a relation . . . between man and nature. The relation between two terms is the whole movement of the real' (op. cit., p. 378). On the Marxist interpretation of the idealist problem of the way the world is constituted, cf. the critique of Husserl by Tran Duc Thao, *Phénoménologie et matérialisme dialectique*, Editions Minh-Than, Paris, 1951, p. 228. On the reconciliation of epistemological realism and subjectivism in the Marxist dialectic, cf. Joachim Schumacher, *Die Angst vor dem Chaos*, Paris, 1937, p. 75.

128. *Capital*, Vol. I, p. 43.

129. Hegel, *Grundlinien der Philosophie des Rechts*, Berlin, 1956, paragraph 52, p. 63 (Knox, p. 45).

130. *A Contribution to the Critique of Political Economy*, p. 33.

131. *Capital*, Vol. I, p. 512.

132. *Economic and Philosophical Manuscripts*, pp. 149–50.

133. *Grundrisse*, p. 313.

134. loc. cit. It is not by chance that Marx's use of the word 'recognition' is reminiscent of Hegel's dialectic of master and slave in the *Phenomenology*, where the slave first appears as the 'recognizing consciousness'. After men have attained industrial and technical power over natural existence, the possibility grows of their raising themselves from the position of servants to that of masters of their historical fate.

135. cf. Max Horkheimer, *Anfänge der bürgerlichen Geschichtsphilosophie*, p. 97. On the historical materialist interpretation of the concept of the Subject in the modern theory of knowledge, cf. in particular Ernst Bloch, *Das Prinzip Hoffnung*, Vol. I, p. 207, and also pp. 270–312, which contain what is as yet the most thorough analysis of the *Theses on Feuerbach*.

136. Lenin, *Once Again on the Trade Unions, the Current Situation, and the Mistakes of Trotsky and Bukharin*, in *Collected Works*, Vol. 32, p. 94.

137. *Dialectics of Nature*, p. 159.

138. *Ludwig Feuerbach and the End of Classical German Philosophy*, *MESW*, Vol. II, p. 371. On the problem of the 'thing-in-itself' and practice, see also the introduction to the English edition of Engels's pamphlet *Socialism: Utopian and Scientific*. The 'alizarin analogy' from the Feuerbach pamphlet has been brought out again and again whenever it is necessary to demonstrate Engels's philosophical incompetence. Even Lukács showed his ignorance of the real position, by writing, in *History and Class Consciousness*, p. 132: 'Above all we must correct a terminological confusion that is almost incomprehensible in such a connoisseur of Hegel as was Engels. For Hegel the terms "in itself" and "for us" are by no means opposites; in fact they are *necessary*

correlatives. That something exists merely "in itself" means for Hegel that it merely exists "for us".' However, it emerges from the context that Engels was mainly critizing an agnosticism of the Kantian type. It was Kant's, not Hegel's distinction between the 'in itself' and the 'for us' which was under discussion. Engels made use of Hegel's critique of Kant correctly, though in a popularizing fashion. The phenomena are not just opposed to the essence, but are simultaneously concrete determinations of that essence. Cf., on Engels's critique of the 'thing-in-itself', K. Bekker, op. cit., p. 46 et seq.

139. *Capital*, Vol. I, p. 76.

140. cf. Marx's critique of Proudhon, *The Poverty of Philosophy*, where the historical relativity of the economic categories is emphasized.

141. *Capital*, Vol. I, p. 19.

142. Recently, endeavours have been made, in the Soviet Union and elsewhere, to reach an understanding of the logico-historical character of the dialectical categories in materialism, as a part of the construction of the dialectic as a theory of knowledge, called for by Lenin in his *Philosophical Notebooks*. It is interesting in this context that Marx's own text is brought into the discussion far more than was previously the case. These investigations proceed from the correct idea that Marx's categories are not simply Hegel's, provided with a materialist 'sign', but that it is necessary to enter in detail into the question of how the logical categories can be at once a moment and an expression of the material structure of reality. Cf. the book by M. M. Rosenthal and G. M. Schtraks, *Kategorien der materialistischen Dialektik*, Moscow, 1956 (German translation, Berlin, 1959), a typical example of post-Stalinist thought. Here the categories are defined as 'basic concepts', which 'reflect the most general and most essential connections and relations of objects' (op. cit., p. 15).

143. cf. Arnold Hauser, *The Philosophy of Art History*, London, 1959, p. 28.

144. Ernst Bloch, *Erbschaft dieser Zeit*, Zürich, 1935, p. 202. For Lenin, the objectivity and the historical relativity of the knowledge of nature do not exclude each other. In *Materialism and Empirio-Criticism*, he wrote: 'From the standpoint of modern materialism, i.e. Marxism, the *limits* of approximation of our knowledge to objective, absolute truth are historically conditional, but the existence of such truth is *unconditional*. The contours of the picture are historically conditional, but the fact that this picture depicts an objectively existing model is unconditional' (op. cit., p. 136).

145. cf. Chapter 1, section A above.

146. *Capital*, Vol. I, p. 390, n. 1.

147. loc. cit.

148. Truth is for Marx always the process of the moments, *never* an abstract standpoint. This emerges very finely from a passage in the *Grundrisse*, p. 579, which deals with the fetishistic character of the commodity: 'The crude materialism of the economists by which

men's social relations of production and the determinations that keep things going are seen as being subsumed under these relations as *natural properties* of the things, is just as much a crude idealism, even a fetishism, for it ascribes to things social relationships as determinations immanent in them, and thus mystifies them.' Just as the social characteristics of things should not be mystified into natural characteristics, so inversely, the natural facts which appear in socially determined categories are not simply dissoluble into social facts.

149. *Dialectics of Nature*, p. 171, p. 230.

CHAPTER FOUR

1. The author adheres at least formally to Bloch's interpretation of Marx on this question, without being able to follow him altogether in his view of the content of Marx's utopia.

2. Engels, *Outlines of a Critique of Political Economy*, in *Economic and Philosophic Manuscripts of 1844*, London, 1959, p. 183.

3. *Economic and Philosophical Manuscripts*, p. 155.

4. op. cit., p. 206.

[4a. *Vormärz* indicates the period immediately preceding the German Revolution of March 1848.]

5. cf. the essay by I. Fetscher, 'Von der Philosophie des Proletariats zur proletarischen Weltanschauung', *Marxismusstudien*, Second Series, pp. 1–25, already mentioned in another context, in which Marx's philosophy is basically identified with the Paris Manuscripts. Cf. also Erwin Metzke, 'Mensch und Geschichte im ursprünglichen Ansatz des Marxschen Denkens', *Marxismusstudien*, Second Series, pp. 26–60. Marx is also interpreted in the sense of a critical anthropology by E. Thier and H. Weinstock. Bloch himself interpreted Marx in a largely anthropological sense. This list of names could be extended.

6. *Communist Manifesto*, *MESW*, Vol. I, p. 58.

7. The concept of 'alienation' is still found quite frequently in *Capital* and in *Theories on Surplus Value*, and indeed Marx's general abandonment of such terms does not mean that he did not continue to follow theoretically the material conditions designated by them.

8. *German Ideology*, p. 531.

9. loc. cit.

10. loc. cit.

11. loc. cit.

12. op. cit., p. 533.

13. loc. cit.

14. loc. cit.

15. Cited in *On Religion*, p. 93 (review of Daumer, *Die Religion des neuen Weltalters*).

16. op. cit., pp. 93–5.

17. Horkheimer and Adorno, *Dialektik der Aufklärung*, p. 177. On the

compensatory ideology of an immediate extra-economic access to nature in the post-liberal era, cf. in particular the remarks of Leo Löwenthal, 'Knut Hamsun. Zur Vorgeschichte der autoritären Ideologie', *Zeitschrift für Sozialforschung*, Vol. 6, Part 2, Paris, 1937, pp. 295–9.

18. *On Religion*, p. 95.

19. First published by the Istituto Giangiacomo Feltrinelli in Milan, in their journal *Annali*, 1959, Vol. I.

20. cf. Ernst Bloch, *Spuren*, p. 38.

21. Thus, for Karl Löwith, historical materialism is reduced to 'a bible story in the language of political economy' (*Weltgeschichte und Heilsgeschehen*, Stuttgart, 1953, p. 47 et seq). Biblical occurrences, bourgeois progress, socialism, and the theoretical attitudes corresponding to them, are according to Löwith identical in structure and he places them in unmediated opposition to a cyclical view of the historical process. He is followed in this by most representatives of the anthropologizing tendency of research on Marx.

22. Appendix to a letter from Marx to Kugelmann, 7 December 1867, printed in *Letters to Dr Kugelmann*, p. 56.

23. *Anti-Dühring*, p. 347.

24. cf. T. W. Adorno, 'Theorie der Halbbildung', *Der Monat*, No. 152, September 1959, p. 31.

25. *Anti-Dühring*, p. 307.

26. op. cit., pp. 311–12.

27. *Capital*, Vol. III, pp. 799–800.

28. cf. A. Deborin, 'Die Dialektik bei Fichte', *Marx-Engels Archiv*, ed. D. Ryazanov, Vol. 2, Frankfurt, 1927, p. 51 et seq. Cf., on the impossibility of transcending work as such, Henri Lefebvre, *Dialectical Materialism*, p. 117, where labour is interpreted as the struggle of nature with itself, 'more profound than all the conflicts between individuals or biological species'.

29. *Capital*, Vol. I, pp. 183–4. Cf. also the analysis of the establishment of the independence of the various parts of surplus-value *vis-à-vis* each other, as expressed in the 'trinity formula' in *Capital*, Vol. III, p. 809. Here Marx showed how under bourgeois relations of production the relations of the material and natural elements which must be presupposed for all stages of production *appear* to coincide with the specific historical form of society: 'In capital-profit, or still better capital-interest, land-rent, labour-wages, in this economic trinity represented as the connection between the component parts of value and wealth in general and its sources, we have the complete mystification of the capitalist mode of production, the conversion of social relations into things, the direct coalescence of the material production relations with their historical and social determination. It is an enchanted, perverted, topsy-turvy world, in which Monsieur le Capital and Madame la Terre do their ghost-walking as social characters and at the same time directly as mere things.'

30. *Capital*, Vol. III, p. 795.

31. *German Ideology*, p. 41.

32. *Economic and Philosophical Manuscripts*, p. 155.

33. op. cit., p. 157.

34. Hegel, *Phänomenologie des Geistes*, p. 356 (Baillie, p. 522).

35. The thesis of Gerd Dicke that Marx saw the classless society 'as the reality of absolute identity', depending as it does one-sidedly on the Paris Manuscripts, is completely erroneous. Nothing is more foreign to the Marx of *Capital* than a reconciliation such as Dicke outlines: 'Absolute identity itself is no longer seen dialectically: the non-identity of the individual man, society, and nature, totally disappears in their identity' (Gerd Dicke, 'Der Identitätsgedanke bei Feuerbach und Marx', *Wissenschaftliche Abhandlungen der Arbeitsgemeinschaft für Forschung des Landes Nordrhein-Westfalen*, Vol. 15, Cologne and Opladen, 1960, p. 196 et seq). This form of identity is criticized sharply by Marx, even implicitly in the Paris Manuscripts themselves. It can really not be maintained, as Dicke attempts to do, that Marx accused Hegel of insufficiently developing the moment of identity. The opposite is the case.

36. Marx, *Differenz der demokritischen und epikuräischen Naturphilosophie*, *MEGA*, Vol. I, p. 31.

37. cf. a passage in Herbert Marcuse's *Eros and Civilization*, Boston, 1955, p. 35, where the inner relation between Marx and Freud is made plain: 'Behind the reality principle lies the fundamental fact of *ananke* or scarcity, which means that the struggle for existence takes place in a world too poor for the satisfaction of human needs without constant restraint, renunciation, delay. In other words, whatever satisfaction is possible necessitates *work*, more or less painful arrangements and undertakings for the procurement of the means for satisfying needs.'

38. cf. the discussion in Chapter 2, section B.

39. Marcuse, *Eros and Civilization*, p. 34.

40. Freud, *The Future of an Illusion*, London, 1962, p. 6.

41. op. cit., p. 3.

42. *German Ideology*, p. 41.

43. *Anti-Dühring*, p. 311.

44. Max Horkheimer, 'Egoismus und Freiheitsbewegung', *Zeitschrift für Sozialforschung*, Vol. 5, Part 2, Paris, 1936, p. 219.

45. *Capital*, Vol. III, p. 799.

46. op. cit., p. 800.

47. Nothing is a better indication of the complete failure of the so-called Marxists in the communist countries to understand Marx's own problematic than their naïve talk of 'socialist ideology' or 'socialist superstructure'.

48. Horkheimer, 'Egoismus und Freiheitsbewegung', op. cit., p. 219.

49. cf. Horkheimer and Adorno, *Dialektik der Aufklärung*, p. 54.

50. loc. cit.

51. *A Contribution to the Critique of Political Economy*, pp. 310–11.

52. *Capital*, Vol. I, p. 621.

53. op. cit., p. 79.

54. On the problem of the *content* of Marx's atheism, cf. in particular Ernst Bloch, *Das Prinzip Hoffnung*, Vol. III, pp. 389–404.

55. Thilo Ramm, in his essay 'Die künftige Gesellschaftsordnung nach der Theorie von Marx und Engels', pointed to the absence of any systematic investigation of the picture of the future society, which emerges at least in outline from the writings of the two authors. In this thorough essay, devoted above all to the political and legal side of the problem, which is outside the field of the present work, Ramm comes to the conclusion that recent interpretations of Marx have looked at him from a too theological, eschatological point of view, and have therefore ignored the kernel of his thought, the directly *historical* problematic (*Marxismusstudien*, Vol. 2, pp. 77–119).

56. *Arbeitslohn*, printed in *MEW*, Vol. 6, p. 554.

57. cf. Herbert Marcuse's essay, 'Trieblehre und Freiheit', printed in *Freud in der Gegenwart*, Frankfurt, 1957, p. 420.

58. op. cit., p. 409.

59. *Capital*, Vol. III, p. 800.

60. Herbert Marcuse believes that he can go as far as to say that in a rationally organized society, labour can win back its 'originally libidinous' character. Cf. 'Trieblehre und Freiheit', p. 418. In this he follows Freud and Géza Róheim. For Marx, however, labour was originally the expression of the need to live, not the free, joyous play of human forces. Even humanized, non-alienated, and free labour was no mere amusement according to Marx. In the *Grundrisse*, p. 505, he ridiculed Fourier's romantic, 'naïve, dreaming shop-girl's view' that free labour must become fun: 'Really free labour, e.g. composing, is at the same time grimly serious, the most intensive effort.' Cf. op. cit., p. 599, where he again attacked Fourier's thesis that labour could become play in a free society.

61. *Grundrisse*, p. 505.

62. loc. cit.

63. loc. cit.

64. Labour is at once cause and effect of men's transition from natural to social history. Cf. Engels's essay, 'The Part Played by Labour in the Transition from Ape to Man', printed in *Dialectics of Nature*, pp. 279–96.

65. On the vulgar Marxist concept of labour held by the pre-war Social Democrats, see also the fine remarks of Walter Benjamin in his eleventh thesis on the philosophy of history in *Schriften*, p. 500 et seq (English translation in *Illuminations*, London, 1970, p. 260).

66. *Capital*, Vol. I, p. 78.

67. cf. in particular Max Horkheimer, 'Egoismus und Freiheitsbewegung', *Zeitschrift für Sozialforschung*, Vol. 5, Part 2, p. 219.

68. *Grundrisse*, p. 599.

69. loc. cit.

70. loc. cit.

71. cf. Thilo Ramm, 'Die künftige Gesellschaftsordnung nach der Theorie von Marx und Engels', *Marxismusstudien*, Vol. 2, p. 102.

72. *Grundrisse*, p. 593.

73. loc. cit.

74. op. cit., p. 545.

75. op. cit., p. 111.

76. *German Ideology*, p. 45.

77. Thus, for example, inventions made under capitalist conditions announce in Marx's view men's future all-round development: ' "Ne sutor ultra crepidam" – this *nec plus ultra* of handicraft wisdom became sheer nonsense, from the moment the watchmaker Watt invented the steam-engine, the barber Arkwright the throstle, and the working-jeweller Fulton the steamship' (*Capital*, Vol. I, p. 488).

78. *Poverty of Philosophy*, p. 125.

79. *Capital*, Vol. I, pp. 485–6.

80. *Grundrisse*, p. 592.

81. op. cit., p. 592 et seq.

82. op. cit., p. 599 et seq.

83. *Capital*, Vol. I, pp. 483–4.

84. op. cit., p. 488. The views of Marx and Engels on questions of education are set out systematically in the dissertation by Gotthold Krapp, *Marx und Engels über die Verbindung des Unterrichts mit produktiver Arbeit und die polytechnische Bildung*, Berlin, 1958, which is thorough and rich in material.

85. *Capital*, Vol. I, p. 488.

86. op. cit., p. 484.

87. op. cit., p. 488.

88. loc. cit.

89. *Grundrisse*, p. 89.

90. *Capital*, Vol. I, p. 79. On the question of the continued operation of the law of value under socialist relations of production, see Vol. III, p. 830, and also *Critique of the Gotha Programme*, *MESW*, Vol. II, p. 22.

91. *Critique of the Gotha Programme*, *MESW*, Vol. II, p. 21.

92. op. cit., p. 23.

93. loc. cit.

94. *German Ideology*, pp. 606–07.

95. cf. *Critique of the Gotha Programme*, *MESW*, Vol. II, p. 22.

96. *Poverty of Philosophy*, p. 128. Cf. also the following sentence from the *Grundrisse*, p. 134: 'Greed is also possible without money; the desire for riches is itself the product of a definite social development, it is not *natural* as opposed to historical.'

97. *Capital*, Vol. I, pp. 489–90.

98. op. cit., p. 490. It is no accident that Marx quoted in this connection an idea from a factory inspector's report, long since realized by

modern social technology: 'Factory labour may be as pure and as excellent as domestic labour, and perhaps more so' (op. cit., p. 490, n. 1).

99. Thilo Ramm, op. cit., p. 109 et seq.

100. *Anti-Dühring*, p. 311.

101. *The Origin of the Family, Private Property and the State*, *MESW*, Vol. II, p. 218.

102. *Grundrisse*, p. 79 et seq.

103. *Capital*, Vol. I, p. 763.

104. cf. Hegel, *Enzyclopädie*, III, Philosophie des Geistes, supplement to paragraph 405, p. 162 et seq. The proof that the mythical forms of consciousness are already *in themselves* that through which they are historically dissolved, namely enlightenment, forms an important theme of Horkheimer and Adorno's *Dialektik der Aufklärung*.

105. Lenin, *The Agrarian Question and the 'Critics of Marx'*, p. 111.

106. cf. Horkheimer and Adorno, *Dialektik der Aufklärung*, Excursus II, where it is shown that the functional integration of the whole of late capitalist production has proved itself to be ironically, the 'truth' of Kantian idealism.

107. Bertolt Brecht, *Tales from the Calendar*, London, 1961, p. 110.
108. loc. cit.

109. *Dialectics of Nature*, p. 294.

110. cf. op. cit., p. 293.

111. Karl Kautsky, *Die materialistische Geschichtsauffassung*, Vol. II, p. 836.

112. Horkheimer and Adorno, *Dialektik der Aufklärung*, p. 305.

113. On the relation between man and animals in a society free of domination, cf. Horkheimer, 'Materialismus und Moral', *Zeitschrift für Sozialforschung*, Vol. 2, Part 2, Paris, 1933, p. 184.

114. Ernst Bloch, 'Über Freiheit und objektive Gesetzlichkeit, politisch gefasst', *Deutsche Zeitschrift für Philosophie*, Vol. 2, Part 4, Berlin, 1954, p. 818.

115. op. cit., p. 829. For Bloch's critique of technology up till now, see also the book *Subjekt-Objekt*, in which essentially capitalist interests are made responsible for the continued existence of a purely quantitative relation of men to nature: 'This other possibility (of a qualitative view of nature, of a "broader physics" [p. 194] which would "exclude mathematical calculation, at least of the type made so far" [p. 195, A.S.]) is equally incompatible with the interest of the capitalist in a kind of operational calculation about nature: just as in the commodity only the price is important, so in nature only quantifiability and not the qualitative content is important' (op. cit., p. 195).

116. Ernst Bloch, *Das Prinzip Hoffnung*, Vol. II, p. 228, and cf. p. 241 et seq. In his critique of the technically mediated relation of man to nature, which is bound up with the question of its still concealed essence, Bloch agreed, interestingly enough, with Heidegger, despite sharp disagreements on other points. The latter made the following

statement in his *Letter on Humanism*, after criticizing the opinion 'that the essence of nature has been settled by the discovery of atomic energy': 'It could yet be the case that nature has in fact concealed her essence by turning to men that side which can be technically mastered' (Heidegger, *Platons Lehre von der Wahrheit*, p. 68).

117. cf. Chapter 3, section A of *Capital*.

118. *Grundrisse*, p. 313.

119. *Capital*, Vol. I, p. 184.

120. cf. *Capital*, Chapter 2, section A, and the *Grundrisse*, p. 265.

121. cf. *Capital*, Vol. I, p. 372, n. 3.

122. Bloch, *Subjekt-Objekt*, p. 194.

123. Bloch, *Das Prinzip Hoffnung*, Vol. II, p. 259.

124. op. cit., p. 246.

125. op. cit., p. 245 et seq.

126. Tenth thesis on Feuerbach, printed in *On Religion*, p. 72.

127. First thesis on Feuerbach, printed in *On Religion*, p. 69.

128. cf. the dissertation by Alfred Meusel, *Untersuchungen über das Erkenntnisobjekt bei Marx*, Jena, 1925, p. 2.

129. cf. for example the discussions in Chapter 1, section A above, on the existence of teleological elements in Marx's thought.

130. *Dialectics of Nature*, p. 24.

131. Bloch, *Das Prinzip Hoffnung*, Vol. II, p. 264.

132. loc. cit.

133. Not without reason does Bloch repeatedly quote authors like Paracelsus, Jakob Böhme, Baader, and Schelling, when he comes to deal with the problem of a richer concept of nature.

134. Bloch writes of a 'communist cosmology'. It is, he says, '*the area of the problem of a dialectical mediation between man and his labour, on the one side, and the possible Subject of nature, on the other*' (Bloch, *Das Prinzip Hoffnung*, Vol. III, p. 272). The difference between this and the mature Marx is clear.

135. The *Grundrisse*, which provide some support for Bloch's view, but which, peculiarly enough, he does not use, show that this is true. Here Marx tried to grasp the relation of Subject and Object in labour by using pairs of concepts, such as 'form-matter', or 'reality-possibility', which stem from Aristotle, whom he rated highly as a philosopher. In an immediate sense, of course, Marx depended on the corresponding categories of Hegel's logic, but as they are interpreted materialistically their Aristotelian origin shines more clearly through than it does in Hegel himself. On this side of the theory, see also Chapter 2, section B above, on the hidden nature-speculation in Marx. On the relation between Marx and Aristotle, cf. the instructive inaugural lecture by Marcel Reding, *Thomas von Aquin und Karl Marx*, Graz, 1953.

136. *Holy Family*, p. 172.

137. Walter Benjamin, *Schriften*, Vol. I, p. 501.

138. Bloch, *Das Prinzip Hoffnung*, Vol. II, p. 262.

139. *Capital*, Vol. I, p. 177.
140. cf. Horkheimer and Adorno, *Dialektik der Aufklärung*, p. 266.
141. Benjamin, *Schriften*, Vol. I, p. 501.

APPENDIX

1. As early as 1952, in his seminal work on the subject, Wetter showed that there are extraordinary parallels between the Soviet version of dialectical materialism and Thomist scholasticism: 'We think it no exaggeration to maintain that dialectical materialism, in its present-day official Soviet form, bears a far greater resemblance to the "forma mentis" of Scholasticism than to that of Hegelian dialectics, notwithstanding the presence of certain Hegelian concepts and expressions which are still adhered to, though robbed by the "materialist inversion" of their idealist meaning, and accorded an interpretation which is simply that appropriate to ordinary common sense. Indeed, it was Engels's transference of the dialectic to the realm of nature, as well as the special significance attached to Stalin's categories of "possibility and actuality", which is directly responsible for the fact that in contemporary Soviet dialectical materialism we find ourselves dealing with a mode of thought that is internally far more akin to the Aristotelian and Scholastic doctrines of act and potency than to the true Hegelian dialectic' (Gustav A. Wetter, *Dialectical Materialism*, London, 1958, pp. 556–7).
2. cf. for instance M. Merleau-Ponty, *Sens et non-sens*, Paris, 1948, p. 228.
3. Paris, 1960.
4. On Sartre's present interpretation of the relation between Marxism and Existentialism, cf. the preface to the German edition of the *Critique*, Hamburg, 1964, pp. 142 et seq. Sartre's philosophy has in fact played a corrective role of this type in recent years in Poland and particularly in Czechoslovakia.
5. Berlin, 1923. Cf. p. 17, n. 1.
6. op. cit., p. 234.
7. This point is thoroughly discussed by Herbert Marcuse as the antithesis of Hegel's 'ontological' position, in *Reason and Revolution*, London, 1968, pp. 273–87.
8. *MEGA*, Vol. 5, section 1, Berlin, 1932, p. 567.
9. *German Ideology*, p. 92 and pp. 89–90.
10. *Capital*, Vol. I, p. 178.
11. op. cit., p. 184.
12. loc. cit.; cf. p. 515.
13. op. cit., p. 181; cf. p. 508.
14. op. cit., p. 334.
15. loc. cit.
16. op. cit., p. 352.

17. loc. cit.

18. loc. cit.

19. op. cit., p. 359.

20. This section of the *Grundrisse* has appeared in English under the title *Pre-Capitalist Economic Formations*, London, 1964 (cited as *PCEF*).

21. *PCEF*, p. 67.

22. loc. cit.

23. op. cit., p. 68.

24. loc. cit.

25. op. cit., p. 69.

26. op. cit., p. 71.

27. loc. cit.

28. op. cit., p. 73.

29. op. cit., p. 83.

30. op. cit., p. 84.

31. op. cit., p. 87.

32. op. cit., p. 89.

33. op. cit., p. 87.

34. op. cit., p. 96.

35. op. cit., p. 97.

36. *Grundrisse*, p. 79.

37. See above, Chapter 2, section B, on the question of the metabolism of man and nature and its speculative aspects.

38. *Grundrisse*, p. 763.

39. *Capital*, Vol. III, p. 795.

40. op. cit., p. 861.

41. *PCEF*, p. 87.

42. op. cit., p. 97. The forms of socialization which preceded capitalist production do admittedly produce and reproduce themselves over time and to that extent *have* a history, just as pre-human nature has a history which remains external to its essence. However, they *are not* history, because the subjective *and* objective conditions of their existence do not emerge from the natural whole and become the *products* of human history.

43. *A Contribution to the Critique of Political Economy*, p. 303.

44. op. cit., pp. 300–01.

45. *PCEF*, p. 86.

46. *Grundrisse*, p. 187.

47. On this dialectic of form and content, which is decisive for the construction of the critique of political economy, Cf. op. cit., pp. 211–13.

48. *PCEF*, p. 86.

49. *Grundrisse*, p. 188.

50. op. cit., p. 313.

51. cf. also *Capital*, Vol. I, p. 386.

52. *Grundrisse*, p. 159.

53. op. cit., p. 203.
54. op. cit., p. 364.
55. op. cit., p. 363.
56. op. cit., p. 364.
57. Sartre's preface to the German edition of the *Critique*, p. 142; cf. pp. 70–131.
58. *Grundrisse*, p. 365.
59. op. cit., p. 945.
60. *Capital*, Vol. I, p. 717.
61. To assert, as Robert Heiss does (*Die grossen Dialektiker des 19. Jahrhunderts*, Cologne-Berlin, 1963, p. 402), that there existed for Marx 'one constant positive factor, the forces of production, and one constant negative factor, the relations of production' would be to make this dialectic purely mechanical. No moment of the whole maintains itself throughout in its abstract identity. Marx pointed out (*A Contribution to the Critique of Political Economy*, p. 309) that the dialectic of the concepts 'productive force' and 'relation of production' was subject to limits which could be determined, without doing away with the 'real distinction' between them. The development of the capital-relation, as a relation of production, produced an extraordinary extension of markets and exchange, and furthered the introduction of science into productive processes by bringing forth a qualitatively new form of cooperation. In this way, the capital-relation acted not only as a 'form of development' within which the productive forces could unfold, but also as a productive force, and an important one. Inversely, as Marx emphasized, once capital has become established, it begins to obstruct the growth of the productive forces.
62. Hegel, *Wissenschaft der Logik*, II, Leipzig, 1951, p. 252 (Miller, p. 602).
63. The absence of any really economic critique of capitalism at the present time (leaving aside certain unsatisfactory sketches) results not least from the fact that the existence of the communist world lessens the pure immanence of the system Marx investigated. It is today no longer possible to see the system which prevails in the East as a merely modificatory, mechanically operating external factor. As Herbert Marcuse showed in his study of Soviet Marxism, a 'definition' of Western society enters into the definition of the East, and *vice versa*.
64. *Grundrisse*, p. 945.
65. *Holy Family*, p. 176.
66. *MEW*, Vol. 1, p. 551.
67. Marx to Engels, 1 February 1858, printed in *MESC*, p. 123.
68. *Anti-Dühring*, Moscow, 1962, p. 452.
69. Hegel, *Phänomenologie des Geistes*, Hamburg, 1952, p. 10 (Kaufmann, *Hegel*, translation of the preface to the *Phenomenology*, p. 370).
70. Hegel, *Phänomenologie*, p. 187 (Baillie, p. 287).

71. op. cit., p. 10 (Kaufmann, p. 370).
72. Hegel, *Enzyclopädie*, II, Naturphilosophie, p. 48 (Miller, p. 13).
73. op. cit., p. 722 (Miller, p. 445).
74. op. cit., para. 244, supplement, p. 32 (Miller, p. 2).
75. op. cit., para. 246, p. 37 (Miller, p. 6).
76. Engels to Marx, 14 July 1858, printed in *MESC*, p. 131.
77. *Anti-Dühring*, p. 188.
78. Hegel, *Enzyclopädie*, II, Naturphilosophie, para. 247, p. 49 (Miller, p. 14).
79. op. cit., para. 248, supplement, p. 54 (Miller, p. 17).
80. Hegel, *Wissenschaft der Logik*, II, p. 231 (Miller, p. 580).
81. *Anti-Dühring*, p. 452. Soviet orthodoxy follows Engels here to this day.
82. op. cit., p. 513.
83. *Ludwig Feuerbach and the End of Classical German Philosophy*, *MESW*, Vol. II, p. 387 (cited as *Feuerbach*).
84. *Dialectics of Nature*, p. 173.
85. loc. cit.
86. Hegel, *Enzyclopädie*, I, p. 346 (Wallace, *The Logic of Hegel*, p. 281).
87. *Feuerbach*, p. 390.
88. op. cit., p. 375.
89. Schelling, *Werke*, Section 1, Vol. III, Stuttgart and Augsburg, 1858, p. 6.
90. op. cit., p. 13.
91. op. cit., p. 16.
92. op. cit., pp. 53 et seq.
93. Hegel, *Enzyclopädie*, II, para. 249, p. 58 (Miller, p. 20).
94. op. cit., p. 58 (Miller, p. 20).
95. op. cit., p. 60 (Miller, p. 21).
96. On Engels's reception of this Hegelian doctrine, see above all his letter of 14 July 1858 to Marx, printed in *MESC*, p. 132.
97. Hegel, *Wissenschaft der Logik*, I, p. 380 (Miller, p. 323).
98. J. Habermas, *Theorie und Praxis*, Neuwied and Berlin, 1963, p. 272, and Cf. pp. 270–72.
99. cf. Hegel, *Phänomenologie*, p. 41 (Kaufmann, p. 384), and in particular *Enzyclopädie*, II, para. 359, p. 629 (Miller, p. 386).
100. *Dialectics of Nature*, Appendix 1, p. 329.
101. *Capital*, Vol. I, p. 10.
102. *Anti-Dühring*, p. 388.
103. cf. J. V. Stalin, *Economic Problems of Socialism in the USSR*, London, 1953, p. 4.
104. Herbert Marcuse gives a more detailed characterization of this process in *Soviet Marxism*, London, 1958.
105. Marx to Lassalle, 31 May 1858, printed in *MEW*, Vol. 29, p. 561.
106. *Capital*, Vol. I, p. 372, n. 3.
107. *Feuerbach*, p. 369.
108. Engels himself implied a similar view when he immediately

added that this philosophical question had 'no less than all religion, its roots in the narrow-minded and ignorant notions of savagery'.

109. *MEW*, Vol. 19, Berlin, 1962, p. 362.

110. loc. cit.

111. *MEW*, Vol. 20, Berlin, 1962, p. 469.

112. Hegel, *Philosophie des Rechts*, Stuttgart, 1964, para. 44. p. 98 (Knox, *Hegel's Philosophy of Right*, p. 236).

113. *Grundrisse*, p. 208.

114. *Capital*, Vol. I, p. 181.

Bibliography

ADLER, MAX, *Lehrbuch der materialistischen Geschichtsauffassung*, Berlin, 1930.

ADORNO, THEODOR W., *Aspekte der Hegelschen Philosophie*, Frankfurt, 1957.

ADORNO, THEODOR W., *Zur Metakritik der Erkenntnistheorie. Studien über Husserl und die phänomenologischen Antinomien*, Stuttgart, 1956.

ADORNO, THEODOR W., 'Theorie der Halbbildung', *Der Monat*, No. 152, Berlin, 1959.

ADORNO, THEODOR W. and DIRKS, WALTER, *Soziologische Exkurse*, in *Frankfurter Beiträge zur Soziologie*, Vol. 4, Frankfurt, 1956.

BACON, FRANCIS, *Novum Organon*, London, 1893.

BEKKER, KONRAD, *Marx' philosophische Entwicklung, sein Verhältnis zu Hegel* (dissertation), Zürich and New York, 1940.

BENJAMIN, WALTER, 'Geschichtsphilosophische Thesen', *Schriften*, Vol. I, Frankfurt, 1955; English translation in *Illuminations*, London, 1970.

BERGNER, DIETER and JAHN, WOLFGANG, *Der Kreuzzug der evangelischen Akademien gegen den Marxismus*, Berlin, 1960.

BEYER, WILHELM R., 'Der Begriff der Praxis bei Hegel', *Deutsche Zeitschrift für Philosophie*, Vol. 6, Part 5, Berlin, 1958.

BLOCH, ERNST, *Spuren*, Berlin, 1930.

BLOCH, ERNST, *Erbschaft dieser Zeit*, Zürich, 1935.

BLOCH, ERNST, *Subjekt-Objekt, Erläuterungen zu Hegel*, Berlin, 1952.

BLOCH, ERNST, *Das Prinzip Hoffnung*, Vol. I, Berlin, 1954, Vol. II, Berlin, 1955, Vol. III, Berlin, 1959.

BLOCH, ERNST, 'Über Freiheit und objektive Gesetzlichkeit, politisch gefasst', *Deutsche Zeitschrift für Philosophie*, Vol. 2, Part 4, Berlin, 1954.

BLOCH, ERNST, *Differenzierungen im Begriff Fortschritt*, Berlin, 1957. *Ernst Blochs Revision des Marxismus*, Berlin, 1957.

BRECHT, BERTOLT, *Kalendergeschichten*, Hamburg, 1957; English translation, *Tales from the Calendar*, London, 1961.

BRECHT, BERTOLT, *Flüchtlingsgespräche*, Berlin and Frankfurt, 1961.

CALVEZ, JEAN-YVES, *La pensée de Karl Marx*, Paris, 1956.

COTTIER, GEORGES M-M., *L'Athéisme du jeune Marx. Ses origines hégéliennes*, Paris, 1959.

DEBORIN, A., 'Die Dialektik bei Fichte', *Marx-Engels Archiv* (ed. D. Ryazanov), Frankfurt, 1927.

DEMETZ, PETER, *Marx, Engels and the Poets*, London, 1967.

DICKE, GERD, *Der Identitätsgedanke bei Feuerbach und Marx*, Wissenschaftliche Abhandlungen der Arbeitsgemeinschaft für Forschung des Landes Nordrhein-Westfalen, Vol. 15, Cologne and Opladen, 1960.

DIELS, HERMANN, *Fragmente der Vorsokratiker*, I, Berlin, 1922.

ENGELS, FRIEDRICH, *Die Lage Englands, I, Das 18. Jahrhundert*, printed in *MEW*, Vol. I, Berlin, 1957.

ENGELS, FRIEDRICH, *Dialectics of Nature*, London, 1940.

ENGELS, FRIEDRICH, *Herr Eugen Dühring's Revolution in Science (Anti-Dühring)*, London, 1936.

ENGELS, FRIEDRICH, *Outlines of a Critique of Political Economy*, printed in *Economic and Philosophic Manuscripts of 1844*, London, 1959.

FETSCHER, IRING, 'Von der Philosophie des Proletariats zur proletarischen Weltanschauung', in *Marxismusstudien*, Second Series (ed. I. Fetscher), Tübingen, 1957.

FETSCHER, IRING, *Stalin über dialektischen und historischen Materialismus*, Frankfurt, 1956.

FEUERBACH, LUDWIG, *Kleine philosophische Schriften, 1842–1845* (ed. M. G. Lange), Leipzig, 1950.

FREUD, SIGMUND, *The Future of an Illusion*, London, 1962.

FRIEDRICH, MANFRED, *Philosophie und Ökonomie beim jungen Marx* (dissertation), Berlin, 1960.

FOGARASI, BÉLA, *Logik*, Berlin, 1955.

GARAUDY, ROGER, *La théorie matérialiste de la connaissance*, Paris, 1953.

GARAUDY, ROGER, *Die französischen Quellen des wissenschaftlichen Sozialismus*, Leipzig, 1954.

GARAUDY, ROGER, *Perspectives de l'homme*, Paris, 1959.

GRÜN, KARL, *Ludwig Feuerbach in seinem Briefwechsel und Nachlass sowie in seiner philosophischen Charakterentwicklung* (2 vols), Leipzig and Heidelberg, 1874.

HAUSER, ARNOLD, *Philosophie der Kunstgeschichte*, Munich, 1958; English translation, *The Philosophy of Art History*, London, 1959.

HEGEL, G. W. F., *Enzyclopädie der philosophischen Wissenschaften im Grundrisse* (First edition, 1817, in one volume, reprinted in Stuttgart, 1965 as Vol. 6 of Glockner's Edition of the Collected Works).

HEGEL, G. W. F., *Enzyclopädie der philosophischen Wissenschaften im Grundrisse* (Third edition, 1830, in three volumes, reprinted in Stuttgart, 1965 as Vols. 8, 9 and 10 of Glockner's Edition); English translation of Part I in *The Logic of Hegel*, translated by W. Wallace, Oxford, 1892; English translation of Part II in *Hegel's Philosophy by Nature*, translated by A. V. Miller, Oxford, 1970; partial English translation of Part III in *The Philosophy of Spirit*, translated by W. Wallace, Oxford, 1894.

HEGEL, G. W. F., *Grundlinien der Philosophie des Rechts*, Berlin, 1956; English translation, *Hegel's Philosophy of Right*, translated by T. M. Knox, Oxford, 1952.

HEGEL, G. W. F., *Jenenser Realphilosophie*, I, Leipzig, 1932.

HEGEL, G. W. F., *Phänomenologie des Geistes*, Hamburg, 1952; English translation, *The Phenomenology of Mind*, translated by J. B. Baillie, London, 1951.

HEGEL, G. W. F., *Die Vernunft in der Geschichte*, Hamburg, 1955.

HEGEL, G. W. F., *Wissenschaft der Logik*, II, Leipzig, 1951; English translation, *Hegel's Science of Logic*, translated by A. V. Miller, London, 1969.

HEIDEGGER, MARTIN, *Platons Lehre von der Wahrheit*, Bern, 1954.

HOOK, SIDNEY, *From Hegel to Marx*, New York, 1936.

HOMMES, JAKOB, *Der technische Eros. Das Wesen der materialistischen Geschichtsauffassung*, Freiburg, 1955.

HORKHEIMER, MAX, *Anfänge der bürgerlichen Geschichtsphilosophie*, Stuttgart, 1930.

HORKHEIMER, MAX, 'Egoismus und Freiheitsbewegung', *Zeitschrift für Sozialforschung*, Vol. 5, Part 2, Paris, 1936.

HORKHEIMER, MAX, 'Materialismus und Metaphysik', *Zeitschrift für Sozialforschung*, Vol. 2, Part 1, Leipzig, 1933.

HORKHEIMER, MAX, 'Materialismus und Moral', *Zeitschrift für Sozialforschung*, Vol. 2, Part 2, Paris, 1933.

HORKHEIMER, MAX, 'Traditionelle und kritische Theorie', *Zeitschrift für Sozialforschung*, Vol. 6, Part 2, Paris, 1937.

HORKHEIMER, MAX and ADORNO, THEODOR W., *Dialektik der Aufklärung*, Amsterdam, 1947.

KAUTSKY, KARL, *Die materialistische Geschichtsauffassung*, 2 vols, Berlin, 1927.

KRAPP, GOTTHOLD, *Marx und Engels über die Verbindung des Unterrichts mit produktiver Arbeit und die polytechnische Bildung* (dissertation), Berlin, 1958.

KLINE, G. L., *Spinoza in Soviet Philosophy*, London, 1952.

KOFLER, LEO, *Zur Geschichte der bürgerlichen Gesellschaft*, Halle, 1948.

KONSTANTINOV, F. W., *Grundlagen der marxistischen Philosophie*, Berlin, 1959.

KORSCH, KARL, *Die materialistische Geschichtsauffassung*, Leipzig, 1929.

KORSCH, KARL, *Marxismus und Philosophie*, Leipzig, 1930; partial English translation in *Marxism and Philosophy*, London, 1970.

KOSEL, GERHARD, *Produktivkraft Wissenschaft*, Berlin, 1957.

LANGE, F. A., *Geschichte des Materialismus*, 2 vols, Iserlohn, 1875; English translation, *History of Materialism*, London, 1925.

LEFEBVRE, HENRI, *Dialectical Materialism*, London, 1968.

LENIN, V. I., *The Agrarian Question and the 'Critics of Marx'*, Collected *Works*, Fourth Edition, Vol. 5, Moscow, 1961.

LENIN, V. I., *The Economic Content of Narodism and the Criticism of it in Mr Struve's Book, Collected Works*, Fourth Edition, Vol. 1, Moscow, 1960.

LENIN, V. I., *Karl Marx, Selected Works*, Vol. I, Moscow, 1967.

LENIN, V. I., *Materialism and Empirio-Criticism, Collected Works*, Fourth Edition, Vol. 14, Moscow, 1962.

LENIN, V. I., *Once Again on the Trade Unions, the Current Situation, and the Mistakes of Trotsky and Bukharin, Collected Works*, Fourth Edition, Vol. 32, Moscow, 1961.

LENIN, V. I., *Philosophical Notebooks, Collected Works*, Fourth Edition, Vol. 38, Moscow, 1961.

LENIN, V. I., *What the 'Friends of the People' are and How they Fight the Social-Democrats, Collected Works*, Fourth Edition, Vol. 1, Moscow, 1960.

LIEBIG, J., *Chemische Briefe*, Heidelberg, 1851.

LIEBKNECHT, KARL, *Studien über die Bewegungsgesetze der gesellschaftlichen Entwicklung. Aus dem wissenschaftlichen Nachlass* (ed. Dr Morris), Munich, 1922.

LÖWENTHAL, LEO, 'C. F. Meyers heroische Geschichtsauffassung', *Zeitschrift für Sozialforschung*, Vol. 2, Part 1, Leipzig, 1933.

LÖWITH, KARL, 'Ludwig Feuerbach und der Ausgang der klassischen deutschen Philosophie', *Logos*, Vol. 17, Tübingen, 1928.

LÖWITH, KARL, *From Hegel to Nietzsche*, London, 1965.

LÖWITH, KARL, *Weltgeschichte und Heilsgeschehen*, Stuttgart, 1953.

LUKÁCS, GEORG, *Geschichte und Klassenbewusstsein. Studien über marxistische Dialektik*, Berlin, 1923; English translation, *History and Class Consciousness*, London, 1971.

LUKÁCS, GEORG, *Der junge Hegel*, Berlin, 1954.

MARCK, SIEGFRIED, *Die Dialektik in der Philosophie der Gegenwart*, Part 1, Tübingen, 1929.

MARCUSE, HERBERT, *Eros and Civilization*, Boston, 1955.

MARCUSE, HERBERT, *Soviet Marxism*, London, 1958.

MARCUSE, HERBERT, *Trieblehre und Freiheit*, printed in *Freud in der Gegenwart*, Frankfurt, 1957.

MARX, KARL, *Brief an seine Frau vom 21.6.1856*, in *Annali* (Istituto Giangiacomo Feltrinelli), Vol. 1, Milan, 1959.

MARX, KARL, *Differenz der demokritischen und epikuräischen Naturphilosophie*, *MEGA*, Vol. I, Part I, Berlin, 1927; partial English translation in Norman D. Livergood, *Activity in Marx's Philosophy*, The Hague, 1967.

MARX, KARL, *Grundrisse der Kritik der politischen Ökonomie*, Berlin, 1953; partial English translation in *Pre-Capitalist Economic Formations*, London, 1964.

MARX, KARL, *Kritik des Hegelschen Staatsrechts*, *MEW*, Vol. 1, Berlin, 1957; English translation, *Critique of Hegel's 'Philosophy of Right'*, Cambridge, 1970.

MARX, KARL, *Die moralisierende Kritik und die kritische Moral*, printed in Franz Mehring, *Aus dem literarischen Nachlass von Karl Marx und Friedrich Engels*, 2 vols, Stuttgart, 1920.

MARX, KARL, *Nationalökonomie und Philosophie, Sammlung der Pariser Manuskripte* (ed. E. Thier), Cologne and Berlin, 1950.

MARX, KARL, *Randglossen zu Adolf Wagners Lehrbuch der politischen Ökonomie, MEW*, Vol. 19, Berlin, 1962.

MARX, KARL, *Capital. A Critical Analysis of Capitalist Production*, 3 vols, Moscow, 1965.

MARX, KARL, *A Contribution to the Critique of Political Economy*, Chicago, 1913.

MARX, KARL, *Early Writings*, translated and edited by T. B. Bottomore, London, 1963: 1. *On the Jewish Question*; 2. *Introduction to a Contribution to the Critique of Hegel's Philosophy of Right*; 3. *Economic and Philosophical Manuscripts*.

MARX, KARL, *Letters to Dr Kugelmann*, London, 1934.

MARX, KARL, *The Poverty of Philosophy*, Moscow, 1955.

MARX, KARL and ENGELS, FRIEDRICH, *Die deutsche Ideologie* (with variant readings), *MEGA*, Vol. 5, Part 1, Berlin, 1932.

MARX, KARL and ENGELS, F., *Kleine ökonomische Schriften*, Berlin, 1955.

MARX, KARL and ENGELS, F., *Marx-Engels Gesamtausgabe* (ed. D. Ryazanov), Berlin, 1927-32 (cited throughout as *MEGA*).

MARX, KARL and ENGELS, F., *Marx-Engels Werke*, Berlin, 1957 (cited throughout as *MEW*).

MARX, KARL and ENGELS, F., *The German Ideology*, London, 1965.

MARX, KARL and ENGELS, F., *The Holy Family, or Critique of Critical Critique*, London, 1957.

MARX, KARL and ENGELS, F., *On Religion*, London, 1958.

MARX, KARL and ENGELS, F., *Selected Correspondence*, London n.d. (cited throughout as *MESC*).

MARX, KARL and ENGELS, F., *Selected Works*, 2 vols, London, 1962 (cited throughout as *MESW*).

MAUS, HEINZ, *Materialismus* in *Zur Klärung der Begriffe* (ed. H. Burgmüller), Munich, 1947.

MEHRING, FRANZ, *Gesammelte Schriften und Aufsätze, VI: zur Geschichte der Philosophie* (ed. A. Thalheimer), Berlin, 1931.

MERLEAU-PONTY, MAURICE, *Marxisme et philosophie*, in *Sens et non-sens*, Paris, 1948.

METZKE, ERWIN, 'Mensch und Geschichte im ursprünglichen Ansatz des Marxschen Denkens', *Marxismusstudien*, Second Series (ed. I. Fetscher), Tübingen, 1957.

MEUSEL, ALFRED, *Untersuchungen über das Erkenntnisobjekt bei Marx* (dissertation), Jena, 1925.

MOLESCHOTT, JAKOB, *Der Kreislauf des Lebens*, Mainz, 1857.

NAVILLE, PIERRE, *Psychologie, marxisme, matérialisme*, Paris, 1948.

PARACELSUS, *Seine Weltschau in Worten des Werkes* (ed. E. Jaeckle), Zürich, 1942.

PLEKHANOV, G. V., *Beitrag zur Geschichte des Materialismus, Helvétius-Holbach-Marx*, Berlin, 1946.

PLEKHANOV, G. V., *Fundamental Problems of Marxism*, Moscow, n.d.

RAMM, THILO, 'Die künftige Gesellschaftsordnung nach der Theorie von Marx und Engels', *Marxismusstudien*, Second Series, Tübingen, 1957.

RAPHAEL, MAX, *Zur Erkenntnistheorie der konkreten Dialektik*, Paris, 1934.

REDING, MARCEL, *Der politische Atheismus*, Graz, 1957.

REDING, MARCEL, *Thomas von Aquin und Karl Marx*, Graz, 1953.

REDLOW, GÖTZ, 'Lenin über den marxistischen philosophischen Begriff der Materie', *Deutsche Zeitschrift für Philosophie*, Vol. 7, Part 2, Berlin, 1959.

RYAZANOV, D., *Karl Marx. Man, Thinker, and Revolutionist*, London, 1927.

ROSENTHAL, M. M. and SCHTRAKS, G. M., *Kategorien der materialistischen Dialektik*, Berlin, 1959.

RUBINSTEIN, S. L., *Grundlagen der allgemeinen Psychologie*, Berlin, 1958.

SABINE, G. H., *A History of Political Theory*, New York, 1953.

SARTRE, J.-P., 'Matérialisme et révolution', *Situations*, I, Paris, 1947.

SAUERLAND, KURT, *Der dialektische Materialismus*, Vol. 1, Berlin, 1932.

SCHELLING, F. W. I. von, *Ideen zu einer Philosophie der Natur*, printed in *Sämtliche Werke*, Vol. 2, Section 1, Stuttgart and Augsburg, 1857.

SCHOPENHAUER, ARTHUR, *Parerga und Paralipomena*, in *Sämtliche Werke*, Vol. 5 (ed. Paul Deussen), Munich, 1913.

SCHUMACHER, JOACHIM, *Die Angst vor dem Chaos*, Paris, 1937.

SEBAG, LUCIEN, 'Marx, Feuerbach, et la critique de la religion', *La nouvelle critique*, No. 64, Paris, 1955.

SEGAL, JACOB, *Die dialektische Methode in der Biologie*, Berlin, 1958.

SEIDEL, ALFRED, *Produktivkräfte und Klassenkampf* (dissertation), Heidelberg, 1922.

STALIN, J. V., *Dialectical and Historical Materialism*, in *Leninism*, London, 1940.

THALHEIMER, AUGUST, *Einführung in den dialektischen Materialismus*, Marxistische Bibliothek, Vol. 14, Vienna and Berlin, 1928.

THAO, TRAN DUC, *Phénoménologie et matérialisme dialectique*, Paris, 1951.

VALÉRY, PAUL, *Über Kunst*, Frankfurt, 1959.

VENABLE, VERNON, *Human Nature: The Marxian View*, New York, 1945.

WETTER, G. A., *Dialectical Materialism*, London, 1958.

Index

Because the names of Karl Marx and Friedrich Engels
occur throughout this book
there are no entries for them in the index

Hommes, Jakob, 57, 209n
Hook, Sidney, 201n
Horkheimer, Max, 9, 41, 45, 132, 156, 202–5n, 209n, 224–5n, 227–8n, 230–1n, 233n, 235n
Horn, J. H., 225n
Hume, David, 123
Husserl, Edmund, 226n
Hyppolite, Jean, 164, 166, 190

Jahn, Wolfgang, 209n

Kautsky, Karl, 47, 156, 197n, 205n, 223n, 233n
Kierkegaard, Søren, 200n
Kline, G. L., 203n
Knox, T. M., 204n
Kofler, Leo, 202n
Konstantinov, F. V., 202n
Korsch, Karl, 10, 47, 205n
Kosel, Gerhard, 225n
Krapp, Gotthold, 232n
Kugelmann, Ludwig, 46, 98, 201–2n, 205n, 218n, 221n, 229n
Kuhlmann, Georg, 150

Lamarck, Jean-Baptiste, 183, 187, 198n
Lange, Friedrich Albert, 46, 204–5n, 218n
Lassalle, Ferdinand, 99, 205n, 221n, 238n
Lavrov, Peter, 46, 205n
Lefebvre, Henri, 11n, 200n, 229n
Lenin, Vladimir Ilych, 44, 63–4, 96, 105, 112, 118–19, 122, 153, 198n, 202n, 205n, 207n, 211n, 216n, 220–6n, 233n
Liebig, Justus von, 218n
Liebknecht, Karl, 197n
Locke, John, 20
Löwenthal, Leo, 216n, 229n
Löwith, Karl, 198–200n, 229n
Lukács, Georg, 59, 69–70, 96, 112, 166, 210n, 212–13n, 218–19n, 222n, 226n

Mach, Ernst, 197n, 224n
Machiavelli, Niccolò, 92
Mao Tse Tung, 192
Marck, Siegfried, 213n
Marcuse, Herbert, 138, 209–10n, 230–1n, 235n, 238n